Re-Visioning Our Sources

Annette Esser, Anne Hunt Overzee, Susan Roll (eds.)

Re-Visioning
Our Sources

Women's Spirituality in European Perspectives

Pharos

© 1997 Kok Pharos Publishing House

P.O. Box 5016, 8260 GA Kampen, the Netherlands

Cover disign: Geert Hermkens

ISBN 90 390 0224 x

Contents

Contents

Her Vision

Her Journal

Preface

'Re-Visioning our Sources' - this is like coming from a journey back home - the place amongst all that one knows best - and suddenly seeing one's own country with different eyes.

This book reflects our passionate concern as European women to re-view and revise the Christian traditions we have chosen to relate to as our spiritual home. Our sense of belonging and exile within these traditions affect the way we perceive ourselves and others, and how we experience our personal, cultural and political contexts. Our ability to perceive and power to vision relates directly to a commitment and need to transform what has historically been unseen and held in shadow. Speaking it 'how it is' is traditional in European women's mystical-prophetic traditions. In this sense we acknowledge our appreciation of these women as our ancestors.

Many traditions of Christian women's spirituality derive from European sources, e.g. the visions and testimonies of women saints and mystics, such as Mechthild of Magdeburg, Hildegard of Bingen or Teresa of Avila. Central in their spiritual traditions is the vision and experience of divine love and wisdom, which empowered these women to speak out and to preach in the name of "the living light", as Hildegard would have said. Re-Visioning these traditions, we also perceive the shadow in which these European traditions deeply connected with internal and external oppressions. Women needed to speak in double-voice discourse and suppress their own physical and emotional desires in order to be accepted by their Church; and outside the European context these spiritual traditions were often misused within the missionary work in order to suppress spiritual traditions of the "other" people. European women, in search for a religious practice that is meaningful and truly connected to their own experiences, have to deal with these traditions and re-vision them; in addition they search for spiritual sources in themselves and outside the European traditions.

Within the "European Society of Women in Theological Research" (ESWTR), the issue of women's spirituality and of women mystics was reflected in ongoing subject-groups during the biennial conferences since 1987; women's liturgies and rituals were also developed and celebrated since then. In the summer of 1995, during the ESWTR-conference in Sweden, the idea of this book on European women's spirituality was born. Annette Esser from Germany and Anne Hunt Overzee from Scotland, who had wanted to work together on a project for a long time, initiated the idea; Lise Tostrup Setek from Norway, suggested not only to have a book-project but also to come together for a retreat - a time in which we could meditate and work together; Eleni Kasselouri from Greece, (where our next conference of 1997 will take place in Crete with the theme 'Sources of Feminist Theology'), and other women who were spontaneously interested gave it far-reaching perspectives.

In the developmental process after the conference, 15 women theologians were found who were known from the ESWTR-context to have worked on issues of spirituality. Coming from the Netherlands, Germany, Denmark, Norway, Scotland, Wales, Hungary, Greece, Spain, Italy, and the U.S.A., they were willing to participate in a retreat and to contribute articles from the various European perspectives in English, a second language for most! Susan Roll, who had lived and worked as an American scholar in Belgium for ten years, was willing to share the editorial work with Annette Esser and Anne Hunt Overzee.

The original idea to gather for a retreat was not feasible given the great variance in women's resources and geographic distance, not to mention busy schedules. What *did* work out though was the idea of a 'long-distance-retreat' for the Holy Week of 1996. Connected together in 'spirit', though geographically distanced, each of us took time for our own way of prayer and meditation in the place where we were. For the daily reflection Annie Imbens Fransen from the Netherlands proposed to have a topic which became a focus for us all:

Introduction	*My own spiritual context and my own spiritual practice / exercise*
Monday	*Thoughts on meditation and prayer*
Tuesday	*Thoughts on spirituality*
Wednesday	*The impact of our religion on the suffering and / or healing of women all over the world*
Maundy Thursday	*Images of love, loving. powerful, and courageous women*
Good Friday	*Wisdom or love (choose one)*
Saturday	*Strength of courage (choose one)*
Easter Sunday	*What comes to my mind that last day*

The journal of thoughts and reflections that we kept was later on shared with each other in a typed and revised form. Many had followed the suggested topics, others just wrote freely from their own spiritual context. Collectively the shared journal pages, of which some are published in this book (*Her* Journal), laid the foundation for a common reflection on the basic themes expressed in the original working title: *Love, Wisdom, and Oppression.*

Thus this book is not merely pasted together from a random collection of articles but rather has emerged through a unique process of long-distance dialogue, intimate sharing (at least on paper), and mutual support and encouragement. Surmounting the major hurdles of bringing women theologians of different native languages, cultures and denominations together was the foundation stage of this process. The odd fact that the process was completed by two editors in New York and one in Scotland points very clearly to the mobility of women theologians and the potential distancing from 'our sources'. It has become a truism to say that all women's theologizing is contextual, but clearly, contexts are not necessarily static, stable situations. Many participants have to be so to speak bi-cultural, capable of living and working both in Europe and out-of-Europe. When we 're-vision our sources' today, we set and re-set them in a multiplicity of contexts; and talking about spirituality becomes like turning a diamond or a prism to catch and reflect the light from different angles.

The very different angles from which women wrote on spirituality in this book have been put together thematically only later, namely under the rubrics: *Her* Story, *Her* Context, *Her* Sources, *Her* Vision, and *Her* Journal. Who is she? She is no composite or archetypal woman conjured forth! She is none other than each of the authors placed in relation to another, in acknowledgment of a connectedness of intention, experience, or frame of reference. In naming the particularity and through the juxtaposition of texts there is a possibility of seeing differences of 'how it is' for each women. The prism of naming that developed shows the different aspects and forms in which women 'catch and reflect the light' in writing about 'spirituality'.

Her Story

Annette Esser's introductory chapter sets the context for the whole book. From a subjective 'objective' perspective, she describes her experiences "Along the Conferences," chronicling the formative stages and the successive biennial congresses of the European Society of Women in Theological Research, 1987-1995; the focus of her attention lies in the development of dialogue in the subject groups on spirituality as well as on the growth of the use of liturgy and ritual in which all women at the conferences could participate.

Her Context

Under this heading, four women from different European countries and confessional traditions, Spanish Catholic, German Protestant, Greek Orthodox, and European American Catholic, deal with issues of spirituality in relation to their own cultural and church-contexts.

Mercedes Navarro Puerto describes '*The Religious Experience of Women*', referring to the Spanish mystical tradition - Santa Teresa de Jésus, et al. - as well as the experience of Spanish women today who have become alienated from the dominating Catholic Church - build up the context of her deep psychological reflections. Herein she examines the nature of participation as a facet of religious experience; wisdom as linked both to knowledge and the body; and as further aspects of religious experience passion and compromise, communication and ritual / fiesta.

Ursula Rudnick opens up '*Lutheran Perspectives from Hanover*'. She describes the experiences of women in the Protestant 'Evangelical Church of Germany' as a 'Discipleship of (Un) Equals'. Going through an important spiritual and institutional process of transformation, women - ordained or not - gain recognition for their own (feminist theological) issues and claim to put into practice the 'Ecumenical Decade of Churches in Solidarity with Women 1988-1998'.

Eleni Kasselouri writes about '*Women and Orthodox Spirituality*' from a Greek perspective and is thus among the first women in her country to reflect upon female / feminist theological issues at all. Claiming a participation of women into the rich spiritual and theological life of the Orthodox Church, she looks beyond the devotion of icons and starts to reflect upon women in scripture and history. In a world that needs 'unity' and 'community', she envisions the rich Orthodox eucharistic and liturgical tradition to have a special meaning and significance.

Susan Roll meditates as '*A Woman Between Two Continents*' on the theme of exile. She draws upon several scriptural texts (including in Flemish and French, the majority languages of Belgium) to explore the inner spiritual terrain of women's alienation - cultural, ecclesial, liturgical - from androcentric tradition. Creating a home in exile, or safe places in an unsafe environment, mirrors women's journey of survival in uncongenial or actively hostile settings, and challenges women to continue to respond to the voice of wisdom in the face of noise which threatens to drown it out.

Her Sources

The sources which need to be re-visioned are text-traditions, such as women's mystical traditions, as well as the spiritual and material sources, envisioned as the earth-water elements, out of which we live, and as the body that we are. Artist Caroline Mackenzie and theologian and psychotherapist Anne Hunt Overzee present here a joint project of image and text. The '*Shadow - play*' between '*Fire and Water Women*,' builds the core of this book. It is based on their common source of experience of the natural elements and of lived experience of spirituality in India - Hindu and Buddhist as well as Christian. Caroline's drawings and woodcuts, which are printed only as black and white copies, serve to illustrate the process she and Anne pursued on their retreat together. They challenge the eye and embody the power and ambivalence of fundamental elements that make up who and what we are. Anne's text sets forth an account and a reflection of this experience in the British context, wherein she re-visions the presence of Christ in the natural environment.

Ulrike Wiethaus deals directly with an important source of European Medieval tradition. By looking at '*Mechthild von Magdeburg's Mystical-Poetic language*' as an 'inspiration for women's spirituality and sexuality today', she contributes a reflection of her own profound studies of the bridal imagery of this thirteenth century Beguine. In her article she explores the different levels of discourse within a particular portion of Mechthild's writings. The viability of her spiritual vision for a contemporary women's spirituality is based on self-esteem, initiative, coming-into-speech, and passionate spiritual as well as bodily love.

Another approach to body-spirituality is taken by Annie Imbens-Fransen, who in '*Digging up Women's Sources. . .*' reflects the nature of spirituality as a source of strength and vision of justice, in the context of her research on the God-image and self-image of women survivors of incest. She delineates five steps in coming to terms with God and oneself in the course of spiritual development, and points to the necessity for liberation from the suffocation inherent in 'destructive mainstream spiritualities'.

In her '*Reading of May Sarton's "A Reckoning"* ', Maaike de Haardt grapples honestly with the process and the emotions of a woman approaching death due to cancer. Some of the issues pertinent for a feminist spirituality of the body include the relevance of death as a 'liminal' moment for those whose lives are lived on the margins; the everyday context of embodied spirituality; feminist thought on immortality; and the fragility of the mortal body.

Her Vision

The visionary and prophetic tradition did not end with Medieval women Mystics but goes on as an undercurrent stream that is the source of inspiration for women today.

Marianna Király, describes her own, very personal, spiritual journey *'Toward the Within'*. In talking about her early visions of angels and spirits, her search for God in her theology studies in 'Communist' Hungary, her 'encounter' with the presence of 'a spirit' and her serious illness and healing-process, which finally led her to being a minister in the United States, she wants to share 'that this journey is a living thing, and always a process; the process of living it, experiencing it, and listening to inner voices'.

In 'Praying with My Eyes Open', Gabriella Lettini reflects on her spiritual journey as a woman who stands in the prophetic tradition of the Waldensian Church of Italy. In describing the joy of being 'whole, powerful, and alive' she also envisions the pieces that fragmented her and puts them together in an outline of a visionary theology of liberation in which she poetically re-visions the systematic-theological notions of 'Images of God', 'The Bible', 'Christology', and 'The Reign of God and Eschatology'. Flowing on *her* river, she has the 'vision of communities of simple people, women and men, that between life and death choose life'.

'In The Beginning Was this Body' is an imaginative piece of story-telling written by Lene Sjørup 'in a moment of inspiration', in which she knitted together: 'individual development: from childhood to death, of body, feeling, gender, soul, thought, and spirit; a historical development: animism, the Great Mother, hieros gamos, polytheism, God the father, and energy' and the 'personal and political distortion, corruption and exploitation', as well as 'the insufficiency of the image of the holy in the light of history'.

Her Journal

In this rubric, three articles which were written or inspired by our 'long-distance-retreat' in the Holy Week of 1996, are to be found.

Annette Esser actually publishes her journal of that week. *'Inspired by the Women Mystics'*, she meditated and reflected about the 'topics of each day' that were given in our retreat, as well as the events of the Holy Week in the Catholic liturgy, and thereby gives a deep insight into her own spirituality.

In ' *When Good Friday Seems No Good. . .* ', Lise Tostrup Setek has written a short story that grabs the reader with the telling details of everyday life. Two women in Oslo, a social worker struggling with depression, and her woman pastor friend encounter each other in the Holy week. Their story melts the Norwegian way of spending Easter together with the Christian message of passion and resurrection given meaning in a feminist theological viewpoint.

Finally, Eva Vörös in '*And She Laughs at the Time to Come*', shares her journal that reflects her struggle as a pastor and a first feminist theologian in Hungary. Her image of the withholding of manna, the bread of life, reflects upon both the spiritual and economic situation in her homeland in the post-communist-era, and reverberates in the personal particularities of her own life. In her last Christmas letter, she finds herself in the 'real wild East of Hungary" near the Romanian border, and her courageous vision may reach out to us: "Why not make a center out of the end of the world?"

Some readers might be surprised at how personal these articles are. But talking about our spirituality is talking about us. By revealing our very personal feelings, perceptions, and intuitions, we open them up, and invite others to share with us a mutual vision and theology that is born in this process.

Acknowledgments

Those, who already have shared in the process of this book need to be thanked and deserve to be mentioned, as this whole project would not have been possible without the help and support of many women and men.

We are very grateful to the women in the Swedish ESWTR-conference-committee who gave us a donation for this project.

Many thanks go to students at Union Theological Seminary, New York, whithout whose help the making of this book would not have been possible: Anna Olson, Angelica Guel, Marc Macao helped Annette Esser with translation work from the Spanish into English. Wilma Jakobsen, Kristin Klein-Cechettini, Tawnee R. Walling, John Thornhill and also freelance editor Alice Pispek helped with important proof-reading and even typing of the English texts. Very special thanks has to go to David Saul who spent hours of unpaid computer-work, setting up the camera-ready manuscript with Annette Esser.

Thanks goes also to Susan Roll's colleagues at Christ the King Seminary who supported us emotionally and practically during two editorial meetings in the midst of a snowstorm at this place in upstate New York; special thanks to Susan's former student Debbie Wright for translation work.

And thanks also goes to Claes Overzee, who gave support to Anne's editorial work in Scotland.

Finally, we are pleased that KOK Pharos, Kampen, the Netherlands, undertook to publish this book, that intends to reach out beyond the borders of academic, as well European readership.

Annette Esser

Along the Conferences
European Women Theologians Reflect Upon Spirituality and Celebrate Rituals

In the whirlpool

> *Last night, I dreamed about a huge whirlpool of water, in which energies were created and sent out, as from a never-ending source. Somebody also touched me with this energy and I flew through the air and passed this energy further to the next person. I woke up amazed.*

In this article, I would like to envision the academic discussion and reflection on feminist spirituality, but also the development of liturgies and rituals celebrated within the "European Society of Women in Theological Research" (ESWTR) as a whirlpool: a source of energy into which each of us is drawn and from which she is sent out - again and again - with new energies. As I have participated in all the conferences and subject-groups on spirituality over the last ten years, I do not intend to describe this process "objectively" from the outside, but rather as a dynamic process from a subjective perspective.[1] I do believe that "re-visioning our sources" may start from any point and will pass the energy over to the next person involved in the same process.

Sources

The "woman question" had already been strongly flourishing all over the European Churches since the 1960's [2], but a growing interest in feminist-theological studies developed in the 1970's and 1980's in several European countries, first in the Netherlands, in England, in Scandinavia and in Germany; here the American discussion had given an important impetus. In 1977 Catherina Halkes was the first woman to be appointed lecturer in "Feminisme en Christendom" at a European university - the Theological Faculty of the R.C. University of Nijmegen, The Netherlands. She and other well-known European women theologians like Elisabeth Moltmann-Wendel, Luise Schottroff, Dagny Kaul, and Fokkelien van Dijk-Hemmes, who had all worked together in the World Council of Churches in Geneva, took the initiative to found a society not only for women in the Church but especially for feminist theologians. This took place in Boldern, Switzerland, in 1985.

The inaugural conference of the then "European Society for Women's Research in Theology"[3] was held in 1986 in Magliaso, Switzerland. Since 1987 the ESWTR-conferences have been held every two years with about 100 women theologians from 20 European and also non-European countries.[4] Since then feminist theology and also feminist spirituality have become more and more an important part of academic discourse and teaching. I gave my first university lecture on "female spirituality" at Münster University in 1990.[5]

Parallel to the feminist movement, a spiritual movement spread over Europe in the eighties. Before I came to feminism, I was personally much more drawn to Yoga, Zen, Tai Chi Chuan and various kinds of therapeutic groups. I remember having first talked explicitly about "our spirituality" in 1980, in a self-experiential program of the Catholic Faculty of Münster University, where I studied. In 1985, I went to "my" first New Age conference on "Tod und Geburt - Tore des Bewußtseins"[6]. The conference took place in the wonderful environment of the German Black Forest. Tibetan Lamas, American Zen-Masters, shamanic drummers, psychedelic missionaries and supporters of Ken Wilber's transpersonal thought mixed together with bunches of German psychotherapists, anthroposophists and disciples of Bhagwan Shree Rajneesh, including all kinds of searchers as well as (feminist) theologians like myself and some of my other friends from Münster. The "Americans" were fascinated to find at this conference such an intense atmosphere - it reminded them of their early workshops in the late 1960's. We did not only listen to lectures on reincarnation, tantra, underwater birth and prenatal experiences, but also practiced all kinds of meditation and were often guided into a phantasy world through active imagination. Thus not only the connection between orgasm, death and birth became clear to me but also Bhagwan's teaching on the chakras - differently (positive/negative) poled in men and women - and the amazing insight that there is truly something that transcends male and female: "Listen to the sound of this bell: Do you hear this now as a man or as a woman?" - I near tantra-master Anand Margo ask us. Fascinating: there is a difference between male and female, but there is also a mystical / transpersonal sphere where this difference is overcome, where there is unity, "unio mystica". I never forgot those insights. There were the new teachers. But should I follow them? - Being back in Münster, I reflected my identity as a Christian theologian. In the Christian mystics, in which women played an important role, I had found an answer to the challenge of other religions and spiritual practices. Should I not therefore look more deeply into my own religious tradition rather than getting lost in a strange land!? I made a choice: My next conference was not the one of the newly founded German Transpersonal Society, but of the "European Society of Women in Theological Research" (ESWTR).

Helvoirt (1987)

In 1987, I went to my first conference of the "European Society of Women in Theological Research" which took place in Helvoirt, The Netherlands. The theme of the conference was "Self-Denial / Self-Affirmation". Courageously, I wrote in the conference-reader: "My research is on woman and mysticism." Inspired by therapeutical self-experience groups and by Eastern forms of meditation, I had found in the mysticism of Teresa of Avila a source for my own spirituality - "a way of self-experience and God-experience"[7] as I had phrased it in Rahner's words for my thesis. At the conference, I hoped to find other women who were thinking and working in the same direction. Therefore it was clear to me that I had to choose amongst all the "subject-groups" of the conference - Hebrew scriptures; New Testament; Church history; systematic and practical theology - the spirituality-group. I found it amazing that this group was installed only late in the conference-planning - due to the numerous requests of various women. For me, spirituality seemed to be the core of any *positive* formulation of a "feminist theology" - whose fundamental *critique* of patriarchy I had dealt with only randomly over the last years. Not seeing myself as a "real feminist", I felt shy about whether and how I might be welcome in this circle of European women theologians. But soon I discovered I was not alone in my search - the split between academic, university-related theology and grass-root theologians from the (spiritual) women's movement had already formed the previous history and first conflicts of the Society. The spirituality group would mirror this conflict amongst women-theologians themselves.

I came late to my subject-group which was led by Janet Morley from England, who had just published an anthology of worship material by women, entitled "Celebrating Women"[8]. When I came, a previous discussion was re-opened as to whether we should start off with a guided phantasy journey. This offer was made in the group by Maria Kassel, at that time Germany's most profound representative of a depth-psychological approach that also included a female, and more and more a feminist-theological position.[9] She had asked the questions: "How are female self-concepts to be found without patriarchal influence? Is there any psychical memory in women (and perhaps also in men) of an archaic female spirituality which can be looked upon as a female conception of humanity and universe?"[10] Of course, I was in favor of a spiritual kind of investigation of these crucial questions of female spirituality, and working with images in a meditation seemed very attractive to me. So, I was very amazed that the group in the end voted against this offer. It felt like it was personally offensive. Or was it really about, or rather against archetypes? - I remember Denise Dijk being a strong spokesperson here. Coming from Holland, she was doing her research in the field of practical theology and looked for a close reading of liturgical texts in this spirituality-group. Her background not only of the Dutch Reformed Church, but also of feminist liturgies within that context, was not very familiar for me - and maybe also for Maria Kassel, as we both were Roman Catholics coming from Münster University in Germany. Feminist liturgy - would that in the end include or exclude our search for a female spirituality? - Then, there was the contribution of the British women that was enormously helpful. Mary Grey, dealing with issues of justice; Anne Hunt as a Christian combining Eastern concepts with her therapeutical work; and Asphodel Long, coming from a Jewish background and searching for the ancient Goddess in the Biblical figure of Divine Wisdom- Chokmah.[11] All these approaches intended to assist women to reclaim their own autonomous spirituality.[12] Janet Morley, whose liturgical texts in inclusive language became so important in the "Movement for the Ordination of Women" (MOW) guided our group-discussion and presented one of her newly written psalms in 'inclusive' language:

> *As a woman in labour who longs for the birth,*
> *I long for you, O God;*
> *and as she is weary to see the face of her child,*
> *so do I seek your deliverance.* . . [13]

With this reading, Janet Morley brought the issues she was dealing with to our attention, namely to write and publish *material* that includes women and the feminine, not just to redress a balance, but in order to acknowledge areas of ourselves and God that have been rendered 'unknowable' by exclusive (sexist) language; that integrates sexuality and spirituality; and that integrates traditional form and vision with a woman-centered approach.[14] Indeed her

material helped us to focus our discussion and to bring our different interests in spirituality together in, as I felt it, deep common ground.

Personally, I was so much impressed and touched by the female, biblical and mystical language of Janet Morley's texts that I later on initiated and undertook the translation of her book "All Desires Known" into German.[15]

At the end of the conference in Helvoirt, there was also a celebration which was planned by some women during the conference. For me coming to this celebration was self-evident, and I was again surprised to find that already the question of whether or not to hold such a celebration should take place at an academic women's conference had caused very controversial reactions. The opinion that academic discussion should not intertwine with personal forms of belief and worship was very strongly present. The women who prepared the celebration tried deliberately to find a theme and a form that was not explicitly Christian, as there were not only Jewish women amongst us but also those who called themselves "post-Christian". I enjoyed the atmosphere of darkness in which then candles were lighted. I also remember the situation in which women had to get up and come in a dancing movement to the middle: there seemed to be some kind of embarrassment amongst us to actively participate in such an unusual form. It required a kind of courage to get up, and I never forgot the situation in which Anne Hunt Overzee, who had also been in the spirituality-group, and I took our hands and moved to the middle to light our candles; with that ritual began our friendship.

Arnoldshain (1989)

Our next ESWTR-Conference took place in Arnoldshain, Germany. I had been a member of the preparation committee. We chose as conference-theme "Images of God - Gottesbilder". The intention of the two main lectures was to go beyond the Christian and European perspective, and to also connect religious belief with its political impact. Thus, Judith Plaskow from New York was asked to lecture on "Feminist Anti-Judaism and the Christian God", and Ursula King from England lectured on "The Great Indian Goddess. The Significance of Female Symbolism for the Divine and its Relationship to the Image and Status of Indian Women".

In the beginning of the Conference, it was the performance of artist Barbara Heinisch, who co-worked with two other women-artists - a dancer and a musician - that drew our attention to the still necessary dialogue between women artists and theologians. The performance with a scripture-title "Und ist noch nicht erschienen, was wir sein werden" (And not yet appeared what we shall be") gave us the image of movement and of creation in process, and so expressed our *becoming* rather than our *being* who we are. I was asked to document this performance in photographs. I failed completely as when it started, there was no film in my camera - I still feel this to be an unforgivable act. So what remains from this performance is an image on canvas, some late photos, and also - hopefully - images of a process in the minds of the women who participated . . . "and not yet appeared".

We had planned 13 subject-groups; four of them dealt with topics of the former spirituality-group: There would be one group on "*Images of God in Women's Mysticism*", led by Margaret Collier-Bendelow, a British woman who lived in France and had written her doctoral thesis on Julian of Norwich already during the time of Vatican II[16]; one group on "*Images of God in the Spirituality of Women Today*", led by Lene Sjørup, a pastor from Denmark who had studied in the United States; one group on "*The Great Indian Goddess*", was led by Ursula King, a German professor who had studied and lived in France and India and now taught in England; and one group on "*Liturgy and the Image of God*". It was hoped that with this offer more justice could be done to the various interests of women in the extending field of non-classical theological disciplines. This time, it was hard for me to choose between one of the subject-groups, and I found that I was not the only one. Due to my work on Teresa of Avila, I first went to the mystic-group. Realizing that I did not just want to deal with the historical question of mysticism, but also with its experiential quality which unites it on a transpersonal level with other religions, I switched to Ursula King's inter-religious group on the Great Goddess. Ursula King had been one of the first European women to publish academic books on women's spirituality.[17] But the group-discussion that day was still unsatisfying for me, as I did not just want to deal with other - predominantly Eastern religions - but rather with our own spirituality as women today. So, I decided to go into the Spirituality-group of Lene Sjørup. The discussion in this group had an unknown quality for me. It was as if something new and exciting was happening. We were there creating, not only talking. Lene invited us to participate in an exercise which she had learned from Starhawk. Standing in an energetic circle, holding hands, we were guided to imagine a tree in our midst from which we descended into the earth. There we could encounter an old wise woman who spoke a word to us and gave us something from underneath her garment. I was given a golden ring - for me a holistic symbol of unity. I am still able to recall this exercise well as later on, I practiced it often with other women's groups and my students at school.[18] I also realize that images coming to us in a spiritual exercise like this have probably a much deeper impact on us than any purely academic discussion; yet, they are "theoria" in a profound sense - vision. What did we envision? The wise woman, the crone, was supposed to be the part of the three-fold Goddess that was mostly lacking in our tradition, where Mary was worshipped as virgin and as mother. So what about the mature and sexual woman? What about the wise woman of age? How could we reconnect to our roots? I was really very impressed by meditating for the first time seriously on what it meant for me to pray to God as mother, as She. This felt like a tender earthquake.

The worship service was planned by Renate Jost, Monika Fander, Marlies Flesch-Thebesius and myself. In order not to slip into any of the former problems (Helvoirt!), the worship followed the schedule of this Protestant academy and was simply called "Abendandacht" (evening service), and would clearly be a Christian service. Still out of regard for the Jewish women, we changed some of the very Christian texts at the last minute. In the end what happened was very different from what we had thought it would be. No Jewish woman came anyhow, and what the participating women probably mostly remember is not the wonderful psalm by Janet Morley ("I will praise God, my Beloved, for she is altogether lovely. . .), or the other prayers, but the rather therapeutic exercise in which women were asked to draw their own image of God with coloured oil-crayons. I, inspired by art therapy, had suggested this exercise and was also conducting it here. We called it "Malmeditation". Women were not all eager to do it. Some left the room. Others said later that they felt the atmosphere of a worship service interrupted by it. Nevertheless, a varied amount of "images of God" arose: a tree, a path, a river, a rainbow, a cosmic circle, a three-fold Goddess, a community of women, a spiral, a labyrinth, a well, a water, a stone. . . but no male father God.

We closed the "Abendandacht" with a blessing, and invited the participants to the spontaneously planned event of Eastern European women talking about their experiences. In fact this talk turned out to be the most striking event that night. There were women from Poland, East Germany, and Hungary . . . , and it was not only special for them to come to the West but it was also special for us to hear about the work and experience of women theologians and pastors in a "Communist country". Somehow, I remember Eva Vörös from Hungary most of all. She talked not in any academic style, but rather as a pastor who shared with us her very personal feelings. She did not just talk about politics in a world of "real-existing materialism", but she talked about her spirituality and her womb, which for her was the center of her consciousness as a woman. It was amazing to be reminded of our own spirituality most powerfully by a woman who grew up "behind the iron curtain", a wall that was still very much in our minds.

Beside the official program, there was also a "grass-roots" spirituality going on in Arnoldshain. Asphodel Long gathered women in a circle for a morning prayer, and she and Donate Pahnke from Bremen went with us "into the woods" of the nearby Taunus. The walk with candles was a small procession of women. There, we celebrated the four elements - earth, water, fire and wind. More and more women

17

participated. It could be sensed that women's need to ritualize was not satisfied enough "indoors" but it had to include nature and spontaneity. Thus, something was developing in the undercurrent stream of the conference that had "not yet appeared" in full daylight.

Bristol (1991)

Prof. Ursula King had become the new head of the "Department of Theology and Religious Studies" at the University of Bristol, and had invited us to this beautiful site in the South-East of England. Glastonbury, the place were the Arthur and Lancelot saga took place was not far away, and many of us planned to go there for an excursion - on the path of Morgaine-the-fey and the Holy Grail. Also the Bishop of Bristol, and - most importantly - his wife welcomed us in their garden. We did not know that later on - after this invasion of feminist theologians - another event would take place in Bristol: the first ordination of women in the Anglican Church of England.

The conference-theme was 'Liberating Women. New Theological Directions' - an 'umbrella-theme - safe for England', as had been said before. The first lecture was given by Prof. Mary Grey, the then President of the ESWTR, on the theme of the conference. Prof. Dorothee Sölle, talked about "Liberating our God-talk: From Spiritual Otherness to Mystical Inwardness", and gave in my eyes and ears the most thoughtful and articulated theological and feminist reflection on spiritual issues. Rosemary Radford Ruether from Chicago talked about Women Church, by this time a very challenging issue for us and in 1995 the theme of the third volume of our Yearbook.[19] Eveline Goodman-Thau lectured on women and religion in the Jewish tradition; Prof. Catherine Halkes on new directions in feminist theological anthropology; Dr. Anne Primavesi who just had written her book on Ecology, Feminism and Christianity[20], talked about "God and Gaia"; and Dr. Eleanor Jackson on Charlotte Kirschbaum.[21]

I came to Bristol via Chartres. I had spent one week in and around the Gothic cathedral. Each day, I was more impressed by the theology of the architecture and the stained glass windows. The well underneath the Crypt was dedicated to Mary. But medieval pilgrims were not the first to use it; this was already an ancient healing-cult place of the Goddess. I was amazed by the huge labyrinth in the western part of the building, where the main entrance is, and where the stained glass window shows the scenes of the Return of Christ in the Last Judgment. We were told that during the Middle Ages the pilgrims moved on their knees through this labyrinth, and, on Easter night, the Bishop and the whole congregation danced through it - two steps forward, one step backwards.

I 'brought' this labyrinth to Bristol, where I was supposed to offer one of the three morning 'rituals'. There, I found that Caroline Mackenzie, an artist who had lived and studied in India for 15 years, offered a workshop on 'mazes'. We found each other and decided to prepare the ritual together by painting a Native American maze onto the floor of the six-corner chapel. After an introduction about the meaning of the labyrinth as a female symbol of death and resurrection, of transformation and creation, we invited women to go through this labyrinth with us. Thereby we repeated this ancient step - two steps ahead, one step backwards - and prayed rhythmically Janet Morley's canticle "Benedicte Omnia Opera":

> *All you works of God, bless your Creator;*
> *praise her and glorify her for ever.*
> *Let the wide earth bless the creator;*
> *let the arching heavens bless the creator;*
> *let the whole body of God bless the creator;*
> *praise her and glorify her for ever. . .* [22]

The last verse, "praise her and glorify her forever" was always repeated in a moment when we were standing: " In the middle of the labyrinth we had laid out flowers, leaves, and other findings of the earth in the form of a mandala. We invited women also to express their appreciation of creation there in a gesture. We were not sure whether every woman would feel comfortable with this and left the kind of gesture open. I was amazed to see what deep desire for expression and what creativity there was amongst us. After all women had gone through the labyrinth, we kept silence, and out of the silence the Hebrew song "Shalom Chaverim" was sung like a birth. Later on, I heard a woman saying: "This ritual has made my day!"

All the morning rituals went well this year. As the British women seemed to have no problem to call what we did 'ritual', and as the rituals were clearly marked as optional, there was suddenly no more problem about them. Every morning was simply prepared by some other women of different traditions and faith.

The spirituality-group had moved to place five on the list of nine subject-groups (Hebrew Scriptures, New Testament, Women and History, Christology, Spirituality, Hermeneutics, Pastoral Theology, Ecofeminism, Feminist Ethics). The group was led by Margaret Collier-Bendelow. When I came to the group, I found myself in a circle of about 30 other women. Never had a spirituality-group been that big. As I remember it now, we spent nearly all the time on the introductory round, and hardly came to any profound discussion. But the women in the group with all their varied backgrounds were so interesting. And all the time there was a new kind of surprise as to what kind of interest has led this woman into this group: there were women searching for the Celtic Goddess; women practicing yoga or Za-Zen; women who worked as therapists with sexually abused women and children; women who evidently worked with Jungian archetypes; and others who definitely opposed any Jungian concept, especially the animus-concept; there were women, who talked very personally about their pastoral praxis in a specific context; and others who still had to fight with the question of ordination; there were women who were inspired by anthroposophical and esoteric thinking and others who wanted to transform the group into a research-group on mysticism. It was very interesting to listen to each individual woman but we were stuck. Was there any path we could and wanted to go all together? Was there any common ground at all? Some doubted it. Others just played around with the ideas that came up about spirituality. We were really somewhere deep in the 'whirlpool'. There was no way of getting all the different interests together, and there was no end for our discussion in sight. This was only a start - an introduction!

Hungary (1992)

Looking back, a conference in Hungary - the first most important meeting between Eastern and Western women in our society - also challenged the question of our personal spirituality. The difficult political and economic situation demanded a new kind of theological reflection, which we have only begun to see.

Eva Vörös, who first brought feminist-theological thought to Hungary, had invited not only women from the "Women Alliance of the Hungarian Reformed Church" but also members of ESWTR to this summer-school; and a friendly group of some 'Western' women, including 'our' president Prof. Riet Bons-Storm, Margaret Collier-Bendelow, Eveline Goodmann-Thau and myself came. Interested, curious, and with the wish to support women and the little plant of feminist theology in this country, we all arrived at a small train-station with one of these strange Hungarian names called "Berekfürdö". There, we were welcomed by two friendly Hungarian women who both had studied theology in Debrecen: Margit Balog, who spoke German well as she had studied in East Berlin; and Marianna Kiraly, a young attractive woman who spoke English. Other women theologians at the conference were Edit Nagy from Budapest, who later on, in 1995, became spokes-person for the 'Eastern' women theologians in the board of the ESWTR; Elzbieta Adamiak from Poland, who had studied in the Netherlands on Catherina Halke's mariology, and therefore counted in Poland as 'feminist' [23]; and Maria Eszenyei, a Romanian Professor who taught the Hebrew Bible in Kolozsvár (Klausenburg), and was appointed by the new Bishop Lászlo Tökés - the hero of the Romanian 'revolution'- as the Dean of the new theological faculty in Oradea; she was highly respected by the Hungarian speaking women at the conference. Because of her and Elzbieta Adamiak, we often had to communicate in German as this was the only common language we all shared, not English! We then found ourselves in a room with more than fifty Hungarian, Romanian, and Ukrainian women, whose languages we could neither speak nor whose nationalities we could truly recognize.

Eva had chosen as conference-theme a word of Paul: "From Mother's Milk to Solid Food" (1 Cor 3:2). This first evening we were to hear her preaching with long sentences in Hungarian and very short translations into English. Only later, there was an introductory round. We came to realize that only some of 'these women' were pastors. Most were in some other way associated with their churches, and came here in expectation of a spiritual 'retreat', and not any kind of feminist-theological training. We "Westerners" had a good will to learn about their cultural and economic situation, but there seemed to be quite a way to go, as we could only communicate through a translator. Eveline Goodmann-Thau, an orthodox Jewish theologian who grew up in Vienna and lived in Jerusalem, had a strong interest in this country in which so many Jews were once living; she gave a lecture on her interpretation of the paradise story which was in its rabbinical teaching style very lively. I myself showed slides by the Indian artist Lucy da Souza on the "Female Image of God" - I had met Lucy during my stay with Caroline Mackenzie in India - in the Christian Indian Art Ashram of Jyoti Sahi where she lived. It was amazing for me to see that women who came from rural areas in Rumania and Ukraine seemed to connect very much with these pictures from India, at least this was my impression. Eva Vörös guided us through these hot days, including an excursion to Debrecen, where we visited the old Reformed Theological Seminary in Debrecen, were invited for a meal to talk with the people in the old people's home where she worked, and spent an evening with her women's group to whom she had introduced a 'feminist reading' of 'women in the Bible'. The fact that women were doing this meant already a lot here for in the Hungarian context our "Western" use of the word "feminism" was not very welcome. It was seen as too much connected with the politics of the Communist states that forced women to work when they would rather stay at home and be with their children. We learned that we Westerners were very much suspected of acting as feminists out of a life of affluence, not knowing any deprivation, and therefore not needing to work as hard and to care for all the basic needs like these women here. It felt in the end necessary for us to show ourselves as "real women", being married, having children, working hard too. . . But the real reaction came when Margit Balog gave her - rather classical - lecture on Paul. Unfortunately I had given myself free this afternoon, as I did not expect too much new from this lecture. So, I can only talk about what happened from what I heard afterwards: When Eveline Goodmann-Thau started to give a commentary on Paul, and one Hungarian pastor remarked that Eveline could not speak about Paul, because she was Jewish, our Dutch President exploded. All the underlying tension between us Western and Eastern women came to the surface. Suddenly things were said that could not be named openly before, and somehow this confrontation cleared the air between us. Afterwards, we had the most funny and playful evening. Laughing together on the pantomimic gesturing and singing of "My hat has got three corners" ended this Babel-language muddle and broke the ice between us. So by now we all have the best memories of this 'summer-school' in Hungary.

Some of us deepened our friendship during our excursion to Rumania, which really reminded me of India and the situation, I imagine for Europe in the last century. The economic situation in this - probably poorest European country -seemed devastating. Still people served us food and welcomed us with music. We saw the university of Kolosvar, in which Maria Eszenyei, lived as a professor in a very poor economic situation. For all these years she was subordinated to a professor of Old Testament who knew no Hebrew but was a party-member. We saw the most beautiful houses, churches and country-side with people singing in traditional folk costumes. And we saw the most devastating environmental destruction due to the most brutal operations of the chemical industry.

What impulse will come from these countries and these women in the future? Will we take up their ideas and respond to their needs? Will we be able to understand their language better? Will we be able to build up and to keep friendships? There is really a lot to do. At some point, our spirituality needs to turn into action.

Leuven (1993)

At the conference in the old University of Louvain, we got 'solid' feminist food, even though the first evening started off with female "Clowns", giving us the idea of clowning-ministry.[24] The Conference theme was "Voicing Identity: Women and Religious Traditions in Europe." In the first very important lecture Prof. Rosi Braidotti, Utrecht, who had written her dissertation at the Sorbonne on Foucault and feminism, and had since then published extensively on feminist theory and philosophy, [25] led us into the subject of "Sexual Difference as a Nomadic Political Project." She presented the various theories of 'gender' in the English-speaking tradition, which she juxtaposed with the theories of sexual difference in a more Continental tradition. In three schemata, she illustrated which differences she was talking about:

Level One: Differences between men and women
Level Two: Differences among women
Level Three: Differences within each women

Her postmodern language was new to me and well appreciated by many women because of its clarity. Here is a taste of the last words of her lecture:

> The reason why I want to continue working through the very term women - as the female feminist subject of sexual difference - that needs to be deconstructed, follows from the emphasis on the politics of desire. I think with Irigaray and Deleuze that there cannot be social change without the construction of new kinds of desiring subjects as molecular, nomadic and multiple. One must start by leaving open spaces of experimentation, of search, of transition: becoming-nomads.
>
> This is no call for easy pluralism, either - but rather a passionate plea for the recognition of the need to respect the complexities, and to find forms of action that reflect the complexity, without drowning it.
>
> I also think that a great deal of conflicts and polemics among feminists could be avoided, if we could start making more rigorous distinctions about the categories of thought that are in question, and the forms of political practice that is at stake in them. Making ourselves accountable for both these categories and the practices is the first step in the process of developing a nomadic type of feminist theory, where the discontinuities, transformations, shifts of levels and locations, can be accounted, for exchanged and talked about. So that our differences can engender embodied, situated forms of accountability, of story-telling, of map-reading. So that we can position ourselves as feminist intellectuals - as travelers through hostile landscapes, armed with maps of our own making, following paths that

are often evident only to our own eyes, but which we can narrate, account for and exchange.

Nomadism, or: sexual difference as providing shifting locations for multiple female embodied voices in quest of epistemological and political legitimation."[26]

Becoming nomads, finding open spaces for experimentation, of search, of transition - being travelers through hostile landscapes: in my understanding this language talks in images about the spiritual journey that we are going on as feminist academics. And the new postmodern language is like a chord telling us of how we might speak with each other in the future as female subjects with our differences. This may help us to find the way out of the 'spiritual' whirlpool.

The spirituality group was well structured this year. Three lectures were given which dealt with mysticism and process-thinking. Ulrike Wiethaus, who had written her dissertation on Mechthild of Magdeburg and transpersonal psychology[27], compared the 'oceanic feeling' in medieval mysticism and in sexual experiences of women today, and she criticized the patriarchal abuse of erotic language. She gave us some poetic examples which we had difficulty identifying when they were written - in the Middle Ages or today. Harriëtte Blankers was dealing with the question of corporeality in mystical texts of Teresa of Avila. She was looking for a possible dualism in Teresa's description of 'contentos' (contentments, satisfactions) and 'gustos' (enjoyment, pleasures) - the first starting in nature and ending in God, the second starting in God - the Divine source - and ending in nature. She concluded by emphasizing the importance of a mystical hermeneutic which takes into account mystical transformation by God, and a feminist hermeneutic which takes into account female corporeality. [28]
Mia Verheyen introduced us to the study of cosmology, that in her perspective had the most important impact for the ending of war, intolerance, hate, racism, and fanaticism.

Human beings, educated in a different religion, can keep their identity and in the same moment even become friends, in respect for each other, when they try to understand the reasons for their strange behavior. Some of those basics are the mystical traces. But also each worldview (scientific and philosophical) is very important. We reach the hand of the other in learning about cosmology. [29]

For her, it was surprising to find that large parts of process-thinking (A.N. Whitehead and C. Hartshorne) are absorbed in Jain philosophy, in Hinduism-Veda (Sri Aurobindo), in Chinese philosophy, long before Jesus Christ. Emphasizing the study of cosmology, she stressed the need to find out which image people are making of God or Goddess. As the world has become a village, inter-religious dialogue has to deal with this knowledge of each other's worldview. [30]

The presentations were inspiring, but unfortunately, again we found no time to really discuss them in depth. Margaret Collier-Bendelow, who again was leading the spirituality-group, had a strong wish to go into more depth and suggested having two (or more) groups at the next conference, one on mysticism, and one on women's spirituality today, possibly one on the world religions. Many women were rather against this, as the one thing we wanted to try was to connect-up these different traditions. I also saw that by splitting up we would repeat the same thing that we already had done before in Arnoldshain, and which did not really work out. Still the question remained as how we could deepen our discussion instead of always just starting it.

Leuven did not just cause a 'headache'. It also let us walk and celebrate. Susan Roll went with us in a hot midday break to visit to the nearby Beguine court - something that was not really planned in the program. We walked through this little village with beautiful stone-houses and little rivers; we saw the Church with a fresco of the five wise and the five foolish virgins, and imagined how these medieval women who were neither married nor real nuns had lived here in a community of work and of faith. Some of the most important women mystics - Mechthild von Magdeburg, Hadewijch von Brabant - had been Beguines, and some of us started having phantasies about a new kind of Beguine-life for today. . .

There were two rituals, one on the morning of the first conference day, one on the evening of the second day. [31] The first one was already planned by three women from the Faculty of theology at Leuven - Marta Sañudo from Mexico, Agnes Brazal from the Philippines, and Susan Roll from the United States. Meeting in a conference room, where two big baskets with rich red apples came to the middle, we celebrated wisdom, not only in prayer, but in sharing the apples with each other. The second ritual was planned during the conference by Susan Roll, and once again Caroline Mackenzie and myself. As a theme, we thought about how women were denied their own voice throughout history. As the ritual would take place in the evening, we thought about candlelight and got the idea of a 'litany of lamentation', in which we could mourn all the women in history that had been silenced, oppressed, and abused. Susan Roll described this ritual:

The Wednesday evening ritual took place following the last lecture of the day when it was already quite dark and a bit cool out in the courtyard, and the grass was damp. We gathered in a circle three or four deep around a yellow pillar candle. . . . We began in a circle dance to a Taizé melody, which could be used again at the end of the liturgy. Then participants, who were all holding individual candles with paper lanterns, were invited to give voice, and identity, to women who as individuals or groups, throughout history, had been denied their voice, silenced, or oppressed. Whoever wished could come forward, name a special person or group of persons, and light her candle from the tall candle in the center, as the assembly responded with the Hebrew "Schelachnû chokmah werûach" (Let wisdom inspire us). As it happened, we were interrupted at that point by young students from the men's residence hall adjacent to the courtyard who set their stereo speaker in the open window and blasted rock music; quick action on the part of the residence assistant cut off the harassment after a few minutes. Ironically the opposition encountered down through the ages by women who "voiced their identity", the way we had thought of expressing the theme of voicing identity" in this litany of naming women throughout history who had been silenced, was perfectly illustrated by the boys' actions. Ritual aligned with the lived moment, and we knew and felt that this was no fluffy poetic play-action but an immediate symbolic expression of a drama linking us to generations of women.

And the women came forward, continuously, each one naming women in history in their own language, not just English, German, and French - the three official languages of the society, but also Dutch, Spanish, Portuguese, Italian, Swedish, Hungarian, Polish, . . . We then invited anyone who had not yet come forward, to come and light their candle, and we moved in a procession out of the courtyard, through the dark hallways and up the stairs to the conference room, where the celebration was completed with a reading of Luke 15:8-10 (on the woman who lost one coin, searched the house, and called her neighbours when she had found it), a silent meditation, and an exchange of thoughts with our neighbours. All this was an extension of the idea of seeking and finding precious wisdom and knowledge. The Taizé-song and a brief benediction closed our celebration.

On the edges of the conference, there were two other important meetings, in which I participated. In regard to spirituality, some German women met on the grass, and planned to work together in a project - I was one of them. After the conference, Ursula Rudnick invited us for a meeting in Burgdorf; I organized a round-table discussion on the critical questions about spirituality, which took place at the center of the Catholic German Women's League in my hometown Cologne; and Donate Pahnke, together with Regina Sommer-Gerlach finally published the book under the title "Göttinnen und Priesterinnen. Facetten feministischer Spiritualität". This was the first result of the spirituality-discussion in the context of the ESWTR.[32]

At the last evening, there was also a spontaneous meeting by all the women from 'Eastern' countries, who gathered in order to formulate their interests better - at least at the next conference. Even though this theme had been taken up in some dialogues [33], they had found themselves alienated and partly silenced through the Western feminist academic discourse, which was not their own.

In a theater piece at the last evening of the conference, Peri Aston gave us the last "Triple Image" of this conference: "A woman looks in a mirror and sees three aspects of herself - maiden, mother, crone. The archetypal image of the ancient Goddess, 'three-in-one' represents the whole nature of woman. . . . Cut off the past, stuck in the present; the future looks bleak. The way out is. . . in search of the lost child."

Höör, Sweden (1995)

Sweden gave us the most wonderful warm summer, and the most exquisite food.

The conference-theme in Sweden was "One Household of Life". A dialogue was planned between the 'North' and the 'South' of the globe, which also had already started within our society.[34] Now, we were aware that with the break-up of the Eastern bloc, the global balance of power had shifted significantly. The Conference-reader reflects:

> Ideological bases for conflict are increasingly being replaced by fundamentalist reactions within Christianity, Judaism, Hinduism and Islam. The former East / West political confrontation has given way to an economic one between North and South, with some of the most acrimonious debates focused on the glaring divisions of wealth and poverty between the two.

The fact that feminist theology after 1989 had also changed, was also reflected here:

> Not only did feminist theologians from the South and from the margins of Northern societies tell us that our theology is a white project, they also pointed out that they were *not*

being treated as our sisters, but in the contrary were being exploited by us. Our theology in fact was often part of their problem.

Therefore, aims were formulated, and the conference-theme was reasoned:

> We will try to engage in the North/South debates, acknowledging that we in the North need consciousness-raising. We also need to understand and re-evaluate theologically how to practice justice in the global context of spiritual, social, and cultural differences.
>
> We have chosen the concept "one household of life" as the conference theme so that we may acknowledge and explore theologically the oneness we see in nature and in the global society. The concept affirms the interdependence of all life-forms in and through fragile life support systems. It affirms the interdependence of human communities, of rich and poor, of our consumerist culture n the North and poverty and degradation of the environment in the South.
>
> Theologically, the concept of one household affirms the interdependence of human beings and of all creation with God. Its is a new ecumenical symbol, primarily in the women's movement but increasingly among men also.[35]

The conference started off with a discussion on the Balkans, where we had war. Three main lectures were given. The first morning, a dialogue-lecture between Luise Schottroff, Germany, and Joyce Nonhlanhla Tsabeze from Africa was planned on "Spirituality in a Household of Deprivation and Affluence". To our great regret - and Luise Schottroff expressed that strongly - the African woman could not come. Luise Schottroff related in her research in feminist social history of the Early Church to the economical and political situation today. In talking about her own childhood experiences in Nazi-Germany, she contextualized her theology, which she consequently described as "theology after Auschwitz". She ended her lecture with the question for the possibilities of change.[36]

The second morning had the theme: "Spirituality in a multi-cultural and multi-religious Household". In view of a Europe that becomes increasingly multi-cultural, including not only Christians but also Jews, Muslims, Hindus, and Buddhists, Ursula King envisioned that concepts and ideas of feminist theologians who are not coming from a (North-) American context will gain increasing importance. She defined spirituality as the struggle for life, or survival. Her dialogue-partner was then Chung Hyun Kyung, well-known through her ritual at the WCC-meeting in Canberra, and awaited with high expectations. Chung put an enormous wall-chart at the front where we could "read" and "see" her lecture in images, symbols, words - painting not only the Tao, but also CNN, and CIA. "Who has the key to this common house?", she asked quite seriously. She reminded us to the millions of women on the Southern hemisphere and also in Europe. For her, spirituality always needs to be a spirituality of justice and of caring. Such, she introduced her spirituality of "Shalim", which unites the oppositions of the different cultures:

non-touch with erotic
emptiness with fullness
humility with the strength to affirm one's own power
the inner with the outer
the psychological with the political and economic

Even though the lecture was criticized for not being "academic", many of us liked Chung's imaginative lecture-style very much. But there was also a regret that Chung had to leave early and therefore the issues brought up could not really be discussed; the dialogue had only begun.

The third morning had the theme: "Spirituality in view of the whole Household". Excellent lectures were given by Kwok Pui-lan and Anne Primavesi. Kwok Pui-lan started with Christology in order to describe spirituality. Following her, new christological models should be 'organic', regarding the connection between women and nature. They should look at Jesus as the figure of Wisdom, and should stress the epiphanic Christ. Just as for Buddhists there were many Buddhas, the various forms of the appearance of Christ should be envisioned. Anne Primavesi, who was by now holding the chair of 'Theology and Environment" in Bristol, looked then upon the function of our concepts of God in the present economical and ecological situation. At least then a more intense exchange of ideas took place.

In the spirituality group, we had solid discussion. To me it seemed that issues we had been talking about in the conferences before came up again, and I am not able to recall very many details of it. I was pleased to meet Lise Tostrup Setek, who like me was interested in the practical application of the mystical tradition in the spirituality of women today. Participants included also Marianne Witting from the Swedish conference-committee, Brigitte Enzner-Probst[37], Maggie Hamilton, and others. Maggie Hamilton, a British musician, who worked in South

Africa, also invited us every morning to sing her whole composition of "Celebrating Life":

> *The time is ripe for changing, the moment is now.*
> *Let's walk together, no one's alone, so come and join.*
> *Get in a circle with all the people, come!*
> *Your hands and hearts are important so come and join!*
> *I'm all alone in the dance,*
> *my open arms ache for you;*
> *I want people to know what sadness surrounds me.*
> *I dance but you never come,*
> *your steps do not match with mine;*
> *I long to touch your hand.*
> *I need to dance out your love.*
> *"Oh where has my falcon flown?"*. . . [38]

The integration of 'spirituality' as theme and as celebration into the conference-room had taken place. The celebration at the last evening put together what all women had come to share with each other: Story-telling from Sami-women in Lapland, Flamenco-dance by a Spanish sister, Jazz-song by a Swedish pastor, and singing and meditation by all of us.

Then one afternoon, Anne Hunt Overzee and I sat together and thought about the realization of a common book- and retreat project on spirituality by European women in the English language. Everything was suddenly very easy. Women from all different European countries wanted to participate in such a project; amongst them was Eleni Kasselouri from Greece, where the next conference would take place in an orthodox academy in Crete in 1997; and as a publisher Kristin de Troyer from KOK-Pharos, with whom I had also worked together on the first volume of the ESWTR-Yearbook showed her interest.

Conclusion

Along the conferences. . . this is where we have come far in our discussions on spirituality and our celebrations together. But, there are still important things to do. We have talked a lot about spirituality only to understand that we have to realize it in our lives and the world, not just in ourselves but in our relationships and also especially in the 'East' of Europe, and in the 'South' of the globe. We still have to work on the introduction and the use of inclusive language in all Church-services, and engage ourselves in the "Ordination of Women Worldwide" (WOW). Also, the research work on our own religious and cultural traditions in connection with the other religions, and with modern psychology and psychotherapy, needs to be continued. Being busy in the future, I hope that our academic work remains connected with the practical needs of women, men, and children, and that we are also connected with a true 'source' - the wisdom of God. Using my initial image, I would like to say: We have been in the whirlpool together, now it is time to take the energy we have received, and work for a better world of justice and love.

Notes

1 This article does not intend to be a full account of all that has happened during the ESWTR-conferences. Also not all women who are mentioned could be asked beforehand for their viewpoints. It was my intention to positively stress the contributions of many women in the described process, not to dismiss anyone. In case, any woman feels herself to be missing or to be put into the wrong picture, I want to apologize; this was not my intention.

2 Catherina Halkes, Towards a History of Feminist Theology in Europe, in: Annette Esser / Luise Schottroff (eds.), Feminist Theology in a European Context. Yearbook of the European Society of Women in Theological Research, Vol. 1 (1993), p. 11-37

3 The official German and French names of the society are: "Europäische Gesellschaft für theologische Forschung von Frauen" and "Association Européenne des femmes pour la recherché théologique"

4 The History of the ESWTR has been recently recounted by Helen Schüngel-Straumann, in "Herderkorrespondenz" 3/96, p. 142-145; and by Renate Jost in "Schlangenbrut" 1996.

5 The German title of this course was "Dimensionen weiblicher Spiritualität".

6 Conference-theme: "Death and Birth. Gates of Consciousness"

7 Annette Esser, Die Mystik Teresas von Avila als Weg der Selbsterfahrung und der Gotteserfahrung. Münster 1985 (unpublished)

8 Janet Morley & Hannah Ward (eds.), Celebrating Women. Women in Theology and Movement for the Ordination of Women. 1986

9 Maria Kassel, Biblische Urbilder. Tiefenpsychologische Auslegung nach C.G. Jung (München 1980); Sei der du werden sollst. Tiefenpsychologische Impulse aus der Bibel (München 1982); Das Auge im Bauch. Erfahrungen mit tiefenpsychischer Spiritualität (Olten 1986); Traum, Symbol, Religion. Tiefenpsychologie und feministische Analyse (Freiburg 1991); cf. also book-review by Annette Esser in ESWTR Yearbook, Vol 1 (1993), p.185-87.

10 Cf. Helvoirt conference-reader, p. 195

11 Cf. Wisdom of Solomon, 6-9

12 Asphodel Long has later formulated the result of her research in her book: In a Chariot drawn by Lions: the Search for the Female in Deity. Exploding the great myth that God is male, London: The Women's Press, 1992; cf. also book-review by Mary Phil Korsak in: Elizabeth Green / Mary Grey (eds), Ecofeminsm and Theology. Yearbook of the ESWTR, Vol 2: (1994), p.125-26.

13 Janet Morley, All Desires Known, London: MOW, 1988, p.53

14 Cf. Helvoirt Conference-reader, p. 203

15 Janet Morley, All Desires Known. London: SPCK, 2nd. ed. 1992 (German translation by Cornelia Amecke-Mönnighoff and Annette Esser: Janet Morley, Preisen will ich Gott meine Geliebte. Psalmen und Gebete, Freiburg: Herder 1989); cf. also book-review in ESWTR Yearbook, Vol 1 (1993), p.239.

16 Reprint in German translation: Margaret Collier-Bendelow, Gott ist unsere Mutter. Die Offenbarung der Juliana von Norwich, Freiburg: Herder 1989

17 Ursula King, Voices of Protest - Voices of Promise: Exploring Spirituality for a New Age, London 1984; Ursula King (ed.), Women in the World's Religions. Past and Present, New York 1987; Ursula King, Women and Spirituality: Voices of Protest and Promise, Basingstoke 1989.

18 Cf. Annette Esser, Macht, Weisheit und Kontemplation. Weibliche Spiritualität im Religionsunterricht. In: RU 2/95, p. 47-51.

19 Angela Berlis / Julie Hopkins / Hedwig Meyer-Wilmes (eds.), Women Churches: Networking and Reflection in the European Context. Yearbook of the European Society of Women in Theological Research, Vol. 3 (1995), Kampen: KOK Pharos / Mainz: Grünewald

20 Anne Primavesi, From Apocalypse to Genesis. Ecology, Feminism and Christianity, Turnbridge Wells: Burns & Oats, 1991

21 Cf. Ursula King (ed.), Liberating Women. New Theological Directions. Conference Reader, Bristol 1991

22 Janet Morley, All Desires Known, London: MOW, 1988, p. 46-47

23 Elzbieta Adamiak, Feministische Theologie in Polen? Ein beinahe unmögliches Thema. In ESWTR-Yearbook, Vol. 3, p. 106-112

24 Cf. Gisela Matthiae, Die Clownin in mir. Über eine heilige Figur, der nichts heilig ist. In: Donate Pahnke / Regina Sommer (ed.), Göttinnen und Priesterinnen. Gütersloh 1995.

25 Rosi Braidotti, Patterns of Dissonance: an essay on women in contemporary French Philosophy. Polity Press, UK 1991; Rosi Braidotti, The Subject in Feminism. Text of inaugural lecture, Women's Studies Dept. , Univ. of Utrecht, reprinted in Hypathia vol. 6, No. 2, 1992; Rosi Braidotti, The Politics of Ontological Difference", in: T. Brennan (ed.), Between Feminism and Psychoanalysis, Routledge: London 1989

26 Rosi Braidotti, Sexual Difference as a Nomadic Political Project", in: ESWTR Conference Records. Louvain 1993, p.20-21

27 Ulrike Wiethaus, Ecstatic Transformation. Transpersonal Psychology in the Work of Mechthild of Magdeburg. Syracuse University Press, 1995.

28 Cf. Henriëtte Blankers, Dilemmas in corporeality: the interpretation of mystical pleasure in Theresa of Avila, in: Tijdschrift voor Theologie 32 (1992) 4, p. 367-387

29 Mary Phil Korsak (ed.), Voicing Identity. Women and Religious Traditions in Europe. Conference Reader, Louvain 1993, p. 41

30 Mia Verheyen, "Ongehoord anders", eigentijdse Spiritualiteit, Acco Leuven / Amersfort 1992

31 Cf. Susan Roll, Liturgy in the Company of Women: The ESWTR Conference. In: Questions Liturgiques. Studies in Liturgy. Vol. 74 - 1993/3-4, p. 231-234

32 Donate Pahnke / Regina Sommer-Gerlach, Göttinnen und Priesterinnen. Facetten feministischer Spiritualität. Gütersloh 1995.

33 Mary Grey and Jana Opocenska, Upheavals and Changes in Eastern Europe and its Reflection in Feminist Theology: a Dialogue, in: Annette Esser / Luise Schottroff (eds.), Feminist Theology in a European Context . Yearbook of the European Society of Women in Theological Research, Vol. 1 (1993), p. 68-83

34 Teresa Martinho Pereira, 500 Ans de colonisation en Amérique Latine vus d'une perspective européenne. Rosa Adela Osorio Sierra, Kunaite - A Dream filled with Hope: A latin American Perspective, in: in: Annette Esser / Luise Schottroff (eds.), Feminist Theology in a European Context . Yearbook of the European Society of Women in Theological Research, Vol. 1 (1993), p. 84-110

35 One Household of Life, ESWTR-Conference-reader, Åkersberg - Höör, 1995

36 The summaries of the lectures are also based on the text of Renate Jost in the German ESWTR-Newsletter (Rundbrief 2/96): Auf dem Weg zu einer erneuerten Theologie. 10 Jahre Geschichte der Europäischen Gesellschaft für theologische Forschung von Frauen - (EGTFF/ESWTR)

37 Brigitte Enzner Probst, Pfarrerin. Als Frau in einem Männerberuf, Stuttgart 1995; Wenn Himmel und Erde sich berühren. Texte und Anregungen für Frauenliturgien, Gütersloh 1993

38 Maggie Hamilton, Celebrating Life. Full Score. Christian Aid (unpublished document)

Mercedes Navarro Puerto

The Religious Experience of Women
Psychological Reflections in a Spanish Context

Introduction: Information within its context

My reflections take place within a context. Some of their particular features have to do with the way in which Spanish women situate themselves in relation to the Religious (clerics, nuns, monks). While women in the Western world already rise up against the wave of secularization and join ancient and new religious movements, Spanish women have not yet socially assimilated, the transition which permits a free personal to take on a religious commitment.

It is said that in Spain one goes backwards - that everything eventually arrives, but late. I am not so sure about this, but it is certainly true that we have a history that we cannot deny and with which one has to reckon. The changes are there. Certain (ambivalent) facts which we have in common with other countries combine with factors of our own which make them particularly characteristic. For this reason they need to be interpreted. I will cite some of them, although to give them a sociological and historical interpretation is not my goal nor that of this study.

As is occurring in other places, the number of clairvoyants has recently increased in Spain. The vast majority of them are women. It is also women who comprise the majority of those who join sects which have a religious character.

The Catholic church (the largest in Spain) is slowly becoming empty of its women. The conservative wave which invades the episcopate, the seminaries and the clergy in general, can be felt in this progressive abandonment of women of which, what I observe, the same Church is scarcely aware. The majority of women who abandon religious practice do so because of moral rigidity, discriminatory ecclesial sexism and because of the death of liturgical symbols which end up saying nothing. The experience of the body and the relational experience (of couples) have in their ethical dimension a strong influence upon the flight of women from religion. Their gains do not seem to be compatible with those of institutional religion. The awareness many women have leads them inevitably to leave the Church in order to escape its multiple contradictions. For this reason the Spanish Catholic Church fears and fights against feminism so much. Its women are increasingly less submissive.

The new Christian movements, of a conservative and fundamentalist nature, have in their ranks a majority of women. I have observed that as the years go by these women are becoming more and more critical. Their attitude, their experience, and even their thoughts are changing. This gradual change can provide us with some interesting surprises.

The majority of enlightened women, being well-educated or being in the process of religious and theological education, who do not want to abandon the Church but feel that they can no longer live with it as it is now, find themselves associated with the various religious groups of women which have arisen mostly in the past ten years.[1] This shapes a type of women's religious experience which tests out the search and the pleasure of personal discoveries.

Catholic women's religious communities have very few young people in their novitiates. This is usually interpreted as a serious vocational crisis. But the fact that the most conservative communities continue to have many young women is often used against a possibly more open and liberal form of religious life, against the experiences of living amongst the poor in the *barrios*, and against a more liberal and responsible form of living institutional compromises and a greater flexibility of norms. From my point of view, we are not dealing with a vocational crisis. I think what is in crisis here is the model of the religious life which needs to be re-thought in all of its aspects.

Many young and middle-age women take on firm social commitments from a religious perspective and motivation. I have met a significant number of married women, with children, who feel an overwhelming enthusiasm and passion for their religious commitments which they do not feel about anything or anyone else. This fact, which greatly surprises me, has given me much to think about.

My reflections look at these facts within the present Spanish context. This is not an empirical work but it is based on my observations and the facts I deal with everyday. In this work, I assume the principle of the exclusion of transcendence (Th. Flournoy), which belongs to the Psychology of Religion, and because of that I do not ever present myself as a believer, theologian or bible scholar. This would require both a different method and different presuppositions.[2]

At a descriptive level, I will look at the particular characteristics that I encounter in the religious experience of women.[3] If psychologists generally have difficulties in introducing the category of gender[4] into the method of observation and interpretation in order to say what occurs in this field of applied psychology, then women spare with this category, and we can hardly encounter established gender explanations. With these limits and from this gender perspective, I put forward this work.[5]

I start from a concept of experience that has found a considerable consensus within the present psychodynamic theory, among professionals in the field of psychology of religion: *it is the way of knowing by intuitive and affective comprehension the significance and the values that are perceived as coming from a world full of qualitatively differentiated signs and signals. It is the spontaneous involuntary movement by virtue of which a person finds him/herself appealed by the world, by one object or the other.*[6] From this definition, I am particularly interested in emphasizing the form of intuitive or affective knowledge and the implication of perception. This is only one point of departure. However, I will not define the religious experience of women from a psychological point of view. I prefer to describe it.

1. Religious experience as participation

Phenomenologically, a particular characteristic emanates from the religious psychology of women which, in general, usually centers around the manifestations and experiences of those whom we call *mystics*. Yet, this feature is feminine, when one uses the stereotype. I am referring to *participation*, a form of entering into contact with reality and, as we will see, with wisdom. It is also a form of entering into contact with ourselves and others.

We can better see this in the world of relationships and of daily contact with practical issues. For many women it is a common experience to enter into contact with reality through participation. We contact directly and only later on, we can *think* about the experience, or detain ourselves to reflect upon the nature of reality with which we had contact. Therefore, one has often the impression from the outside that women *know* in another way. But when one finally asks them how they define or make abstractions, it seems that they do not know how to answer. In some cases, they are able to *describe* the experience.

What is this so? In my thinking, this is about a phenomenon which is related to the influence empathy has in sensual perception. Women perceive reality with a high level of empathy. They participate in this reality. This gives them a knowledge that, at first, does not pass as reason but nevertheless can compete with typical knowledge of rational thought. Firstly, one captures and perceives. Afterwards, the questions may come. At other times, instead of asking questions, we are explicitly left with the existence of a *sensation*. It is particular for this form of participation that the senses enter together, even if in turn one of them focuses and organizes the perception (for example, the eye centers on an object, but the other senses perceive it together).

This occurs explicitly in many daily events, but whenever it has a direct affect on interpersonal relationships, it usually creates a certain discomfort, especially in men. Women, as a rule, *know* when a relationship works and when not. But in many cases they cannot explain why and respond vaguely to questions about the reasons for which they are so sure. I have frequently seen how one woman would ask another person whether she or he had a problem, and when that other person asked *how did she notice this*, the woman would respond vaguely, without knowing how to explain the signs by which she had known that something was not going well. Men, in many cases, become nervous because they feel that they cannot control what they are expressing and they fear being at the mercy of the observation of women.[7]

Something similar happens in religious experience. There is a level that resists entering into the channels of rationality, because it involves an experience of participation. This happens frequently and is most easily analyzed in religious rites and celebrations. Women come into contact with their own interior reality or with interpersonal and symbolic reality. When they are requested to narrate these experiences, they find them impossible to define. Sometimes they describe these experiences, but at other times they do not even try because doing this seems to be poor and reductive. Here we are truly dealing with something that happens in mystical phenomenology, but, I repeat, this can be extended to frequent experiences and is not particular to the world of the Religious.

Participation, as a way of entering into relation with concrete, daily reality and with the religious dimension, has to do with psychological mechanisms that are typical for empathetic processes: *identification*, which is a perceptive shortening of the distance between a determined reality and the person; the following *splitting* which claims to establish the necessary distance in order not to confuse delight with reality; and finally the *integration* which results from the two previous movements. In all this, emotionality and sensory awareness are present.

1.1 Empathic identification

Religious experience is always mediated. Even when the participation is very intense and prolonged and privileges the moment of identification that shortens distances, it continues to be mediated by the intensity of the affective level of the emotion. This intensity blocks the discerning character of the sensory perception. The empathetic identification causes the whole person to center on internal or external stimulus, away from sensory perception.

We can describe this in the following way: it is a question of paying attention to the stimulus (the other one, the Other, an object, a phenomenon, . . .) and permitting oneself to stay absorbed in the contemplation of that stimulus. It is a phase of *instinctive*[8] imitation and of a relaxation of the conscious controls, after having been absorbed by the object of empathy.

Rationality suffers a blockade because of this saturation. The stimulus takes a position at the first level of consciousness and the person seems to be alienated by this stimulus. It is the same psychological mechanism that underlies fascination or that experience which we call *love at first sight*. The impression of being within that perceived reality in which the person feels 'taken' away can vary in intensity and produce the illusion that there is no distance. When these stimuli are supported by external senses, then this illusion passes by rapidly. When, on the other hand, the stimuli appeal to a reality of non-external senses, one has the sensation of having been in a different dimension that is detached from oneself.

1.2. Splitting

Many women talk about religious experiences in which they are at the same time protagonists of their own lives as well as observers of it. This is not (at least not at first) a schizophrenic experience. But indeed, it is the schizoid mechanism of the psychic function, common to the majority of sane people[9], that makes this splitting possible. In religious experience, inasmuch as it is a reality that is not perceptible empirically, the mechanism of splitting usually follows the moment of participation. With splitting women overcome various obstacles:

- they do not alienate themselves in the participation and, thus, recapture the experience of the Ego at the same time as maintaining it in the Id.10

- they have a strong experience of change within themselves that provides them with a psychological channel for the experience of change of the one we call God.

- they live an internal situation of frontier, of limit that is characteristic of determinate religious experiences.

Within this phase, there is a moment which the empathic process calls *reverberation*. It happens when the mediation in the participation is a person. Then the woman feels the experience of the other person when, simultaneously, she can observe the cognitive and affective associations of herself which resemble this experience. This is a moment of resonance between the internalized feelings of the other one and the evocation of our own experience and phantasy.

This moment is connected to religious experiences mediated through love, friendship, group-relationships, and in many cases, appears attached to stories. This is very important in the experience of reading, as much when this is private as when the person is a listener to a story that someone else reads out loud. A religious experience can be given that arises from the reading of a biblical narrative, and in which the mechanisms of identification, splitting and reverberation are functioning.

The moment of distancing that is characteristic of this splitting is resolved when the relation of interior confluence returns to a position of separate identity, which allows a responsiveness that reflects as much the understanding of the stimulus as the distancing from it. This return is necessary in order to effect a clear differentiation between the Self and the stimulus.

The last phases of reverberation and of distancing increase in amplitude and complexity with age. The phase of reverberation is necessary in order to explain the religious experience of women as a motivation of social actions and communications. When we deal with a personal mediation, it is possible that a change of affects is produced which shared or vicarious *with the other (empathy)* becomes an affect *for the other (sympathy).* [11]

The religious experience of *participation* does not always resolve itself in this mode. This participation is conditioned by factors like personality, environment, learning, and the cultivation of the cognitive dimension[12] . . . and, although to a lesser degree, by one's own culture. Therefore participation as an element of religious experience can take on positive connotations of self-expansion and of motivation to compromise in the reality of daily life. But it also can take on immature and regressive connotations, or even negative and self-destructive ones.

1.3. The multivalence of women's religious experience of participation

The religious experience of women, with regards to knowledge of and familiarity with the reality called God/dess, is a multivalent capacity and ability. Knowing one's own psychological mechanisms may help in understanding the different results of very similar experiences, even on the descriptive level. The psychological mechanisms of knowledge through empathetic participation involve risks. The risks increase when they are less controlled by rational processes and more exposed to affective and emotional mechanisms. Therefore, they depend greatly on the maturity of women.

Within the many possibilities of one symbol or another, it is worth pointing out the factor of *need / superabundance*. There are women who enter the world of religious experience based on their personal needs, especially affective needs. The resulting religious experience, if it is through participation, produces a higher level of emotional satisfaction which *compensates* for these needs. Generally, this type of religious experience does not make women more active in the sphere of daily life and rarely contributes effectively to truly liberating work, although in moments of intense participation, the illusion may occur that this is the case. We are going to briefly look at each one.

. . . religious experience as participation through need

When the affective needs are profound and the wounds are grave, the religious experience through participation may have a regressive character which, in its extreme, can lead to self-harm or *possession*, can result in a schizophrenic crisis, genuine pathological hallucinations, and so on. In addition, the context can be very influential, favoring and extending the experiences in benefit of third parties. [13]

. . . religious experience of participation through superabundance

Superabundance is related to the affective maturity of the girl-child in respect to the process of separation from her mother. But it also has to do with a special vitality of many women which, on the one side, leads them to relate to reality at a highly contemplative level, and, on the other side, lets them be strongly committed.

The religious experience through participation which is based on superabundance is characterized by both aspects. *Contemplation* converts into a mode of perceiving reality and to relate oneself to it, which is closely connected with the experience of the world of the Religious. The experience of the divine, the sacred. . . imprints a stamp of admiration and respect on what one sees and senses in the environment of this person, whether inanimate or animate stimuli (nature, people). In this way, contemplation ends up being a means of knowledge and of understanding reality. For many women this experience leads to a behaviour that - though mature like knowledge - remains merely in one pole of reality, the one of beauty and harmony. Surely this behaviour *transforms* reality. It can result in selection and defense in front of the most disagreeable and ugly face on earth. This religious experience turns many women into people who are isolated from reality. We may encounter this type of woman in all social layers and contexts because her limited space is usually the celebration of ritual. The religious experience of celebrations and rites can be lived in proper superabundance but in isolation from the other face of reality, which appears again as something separate after the person has left the group or the moment of experience (prayer, meditation. . .). In this way, religious experience through participation neither changes women nor does it enable them to become more active or committed. The world will not be changed by them. This serves only as a refuge, a break and a way to stay alive in decent shape. This should not be depreciated, but from my point of view, this is very incomplete.[14]

On a smaller scale, there are experiences of participation based on superabundance that motivate social actions and communications. In this case women know in which way to expand themselves and how the superabundance that they live allows them to become creative and constructive. Contemplative experiences result in different modes of exercise and artistic expression, and social behaviour becomes concrete in the form of compromise and social struggles in the hardest and most difficult aspect of our world. In this way, the internal and the external stimulus build up an alliance and the participatory and religious contemplation of reality does not reduce itself to the pole of beauty but expands itself in empathic sensitivity, very rich in emotional nuances, that sets off cognitive recourses and initiates decisions and behaviour. From this form, the religious experience of women turns gradually into a *religious attitude* - the most mature, most human and most humanizing level that one can achieve. [15]

We are, one must suspect, in front of a paradoxical religious experience in which one pole (the empathy of participation) stimulates the other (the sympathy and the distance that facilitate behaviour), and in which the latter pole stimulates the first.[16]

In my context, I find this is in minority groups and amongst isolated women, who are in general highly aware of solitude and have also taken a serious path of personal maturation and gender-consciousness.

The strong experience of solitude that carries this experience is in most cases an unnecessary form of suffering. If women who live the religious experience of participation in this positive superabundance can communicate with each other, then this type of solitude and the suffering it bears will disappear.

2. Religious experience as wisdom

I have already spoken explicitly about the religious experience of participation as a form of knowledge. The psychological mechanisms of empathy that activate this experience result in an expansion of knowledge and in the end are converted into true wisdom. I want to deal with both aspects.

2.1. Knowledge

I must clarify the type of knowledge to which I refer. I would also like to indicate where this knowledge is situated. The religious experience of participation bears a different dimension of knowledge than the knowledge gained from information. The latter occurs principally through cognitive-rational means. The experience to which I refer binds (*religio*) reality to the Other, perceived as distant and inaccessible while at once close and comprehensible (paradoxical perception, experience and knowledge). This *bond* (*religio*) is the source of knowledge. Here, one does not know the *properties* of the object, nor its functioning, nor its internal rules or its logic; one knows *that what is* in an unfragmented, integrated perception - as I try to describe it. One knows about this in oneself but bound, related to an instance that does not belong to the order of reality. And this causes the object/subject to be become more fully whole. In this sense, the process of binding is a fundamental element of this perception which allows this form of knowledge to take place.

In this way, a woman knows the external reality as well as she knows herself, each time to a greater degree (self-expansion).If in a certain sense this can be said of any human being, it is important to recognize that there are gender differences which favor women. As I have already indicated, women are able to acquire knowledge through participation without as much resistance as men. In addition, women's knowledge is profoundly tied to relationships. Knowledge already implies a relational mechanism, and women have - for better or for worse - such a socialization in their relationships that it develops *almost* naturally.

. . . body- knowledge in the religious experience

Another element distinguishes religious experience as a source of knowledge: the gender-relation. I refer to the role of the body as a factor and as a recipient of knowledge. Religious experience in women takes place with the body and in the body. This is clearly evident in mystical phenomenology[17], but in daily (non-extraordinary) phenomenology it occurs with more or less consciousness. The experience of *bonding (religio)* with the Other, that which is called God/dess, alters a woman's corporeality, from respiratory, circulatory and gastrointestinal functioning, to reactions of the skin and other senses. This is true whether this experience is a solitary one or one which occurs in a group or multitude; whether it takes place in the context of rites, storytelling or in an explicitly religious context (community-based, social activity. . .).It is important to point out that in its infinite hues, it embraces the pain-pleasure polarity. Therefore, masochistic phenomena, in which the polarities come together (union of opposites), appear to be tied to the religious experience of women throughout the ages (especially in Christianity).[18] By the same token, phenomena involving intense bodily pleasure with strong erotic-sexual connotations also appear, causing great suspicion among ecclesiastical authorities who observe them from afar and are afraid to know too much about what really goes on.

The body is both a factor and a recipient of knowledge. The bodily resonances of religious experiences bring a unique and integral form of physical knowledge to women. And women, for their part, use their bodies to understand the religious reality and, from there, to understand their environment and other people. One way or another, the body cannot be left out of the process.

The results are also polyvalent due to the wide range of shown behaviours. On the one hand, the result may be to initiate a maturation of bodily perception and an increase in positive body consciousness; we could call this a fulfilled body. On the other hand, diminution of positive consciousness may be initiated; and by allowing oneself to be invaded by unconscious processes whose support is the body, the body may become degraded, subjected to self-torture, self-mutilation and, as I said before, open to mild or severe levels of sadomasochistic behaviour.

2.2. Wisdom

Knowledge, however, is no more than a step to wisdom. The great religious masters are used to modify their bodily functioning in the quest for religious wisdom. They generally employ asceticism as their method. Many women throughout the ages and in a variety of religious traditions have shown that this is not the only path. Asceticism is about practices that are fundamentally tied to masculinity and to men. Mastering the body out of religious motivation, overcoming bodily passions, subjugating the impulses. . . reflect an orientation toward religious experience which belongs to men and is promoted by men. The experience of women is frequently situated on the margins, and even when it becomes acquiescent and appears to be a common experience, many cases demonstrate that the differences are in fact substantial. A man, in general, does not concern himself with his body. When he notices it, it is a source of bother. But, at the same time, he cannot detach himself from his body, particularly when it comes to his genitalia, for here he is fixated on his sexuality. Woman also endures her body in a culture that forces her to adjust to predetermined standards. But it is equally true that even its symptoms cause her to relate to her body in a special way. Her physical functioning gives her information about her own psychic functioning, giving her command of determined wisdom about herself and other people. Relationships of love and maternal relationships, relation to things everyday life likewise give rise to a type of wisdom which, up to the present time, is unique to her gender.

Religious experience is also tied to women's bodily wisdom. Faith is not only *Something*, an ensemble of abstract truths confirmed by mere cognitive assent. It is also *Someone*, perceived as a personal being to whom something is offered, from whom something is received, with whom one can communicate, and who motivates one to live in a certain way. All of this is relational in nature and appears tied to corporeality. The body *knows* in a different way than through purely cognitive means. In the experience of many women the two modes of knowing are worlds apart and the body becomes a symptom of precarious unity, or perhaps better stated, a brutal religious schizophrenia. However, in the more recent experience of women who have cultivated the rational and reflexive dimension of faith (theology), it is common to hear about the ways in which the content of their reflection transfers to other dimensions of their person. Some resist and ask for moderate alternatives which do justice to the entire personal experience and to its way of seeing and understanding life. In these cases, frequently, convictions about faith become bodily wisdom. Faith is thus converted into a paradigm of knowledge that includes different levels of the person, and in a special way, the body.

For example, the belief in a God/dess as creator of life becomes the motivation for a vital experience of the body, with the body and from the body; for a fuller and more satisfying sexuality; for a commitment to protect endangered life and the threatened lives of others; all stemming from a vital expansion in which women taste the union with God, creator and provider.[19] Or, the belief in the incarnation and redemption of God in Jesus accompanies the perception of one's own pain and the pain of others, which is a factor of wisdom about human fragility deriving from consciousness and bodily experience of limits.[20]

3. Religious experience as passion and as surrender

3.1 Passion

The previous notes precede and prepare for another psychological characteristic of women's religious experience, passion. I use the term in its two possible meanings: passion as suffering and passion as intense and overwhelming affection. The shared empathy and the knowledge and wisdom that derive from it are rooted in the world of affections and emotions; not exclusively, but predominantly. This affective and emotional world escapes the control of the ego, most of the time; it is unconscious, and its wealth depends on its content and the use that other personal demands make of it. Passion feeds on this humus. When many women wholeheartedly enter the religious world, they often do so in a passionate way - fruit, perhaps, of the very claim to totality that religion makes - as well as the small resistance that exists in women towards the affective and relational world. I have heard frequently how certain behaviours of religious women resemble the behaviour of a passionate lover. The projective elements that exist in the former also exist in the latter. They are not simply derivatives of affectionate passion but are facilitated by seemingly similar mechanisms and physical functioning. The relational structure of religion (at least Christianity) prefers this mechanism and makes it similar to affectionate passion.

It is necessary to point out something about the relationship between passion and knowledge. In the patriarchal concept of cognitive human capacity as reasoning (predominantly of the logical and rational flow), passion is opposed to knowledge because knowledge is conceived exclusively in terms of reason. It is commonly believed that passion impedes thought. In this way, the opposition is strengthened and the cognitive capacity is reduced to rational logic. Passion is even conceived as an irrational force, whereas reason appears as a fact of the objective world, more closely bound to the empirical. And, we think that passion is hot while reason is cold. So, reality is better known with a cold mind than with the heat that passion brings. If we carry this argument to end, we have to deny all possibility of thought and comprehension of reality as art, and in our case, religiosity as capable experience to comprehend a reality that does not fit with the empirical characteristics.[21]

On the other hand, our way of dividing reality does not respond to the true experience of the human being in general because our experiences are not simple (linear, separated...) but complex, conflicting and often oppositional (paradoxes in the most important elements). If we need reason to know, it is not less certain and important that we need all our perceptive capacity. Moreover it is, whether we like it or not, tightly bound to our known and unknown - conscious, preconscious and unconscious - interests. The new epistemological paradigm imposed in some circles of knowledge, and in many cases motivating women, introduces criteria of complexity and interrelationship that displace some excessively reductive a priori notions with regard to knowledge. We should not forget that Freud in studying the unconscious and its dynamic potential classified desire as the driving force of culture.

Also influential is the *deficit of rationality*[22] , proper to religion, where rational logic is displaced by emotional logic. This deficit, inasmuch as it is typical, is present in the way men live and act religiously, but there is no doubt that they offer great resistance to the emotional ground of women - with all its objections and advantages, with its risks and possibilities. Those who are not bound by this generalization are the male mystics and it has been recognized that their way of experiencing is *feminine*, if one can use this expression.

3.2. Surrender and radicalism

Often, religious passion determines attitudes and orients behaviours. The peacock opens his fan, and we experience a lot of diversity. Unfortunately, when narcissism predominates in this spread, religious fanaticism and therefore intolerance in its varied degrees are the resulting attitudes and behaviours. Today we know it abounds. There are religions that have a higher propensity for the fanatical component than others. They are the ones that most inhibit the ego and rational elements, those who profit from vicarious respect for power and authority. There are eminently masculine religions that function in this way and there are others that, during different stages of their history (the different Christian confessions, for example), have functioned in this way, as well. But when we deal with women, we should concentrate on them. Less inhibition of the emotional components and more inhibition of the ego elements of control and rationality of the majority of religious women, let religious passion degenerate into fanaticism, intolerance and radicalism in an ample sector of the female collective.

Radicalism as the guiding indicator for inner passion is one of the characteristics of religious behaviours in women that has led men of religious institutions to be suspicious. But we have to recognize that it has been this same radicalism that has inspired the surrender which many religious women have shown throughout a large part of history. Or, to say it in another way, passion has acted as the motivating energy and as the orientation for attitudes and behaviours that involve the whole person, and that has lead to the subordination of essential aspects of human and of physical life.

Whether passion is erroneous or adequate can be deduced from the results, from the level of satisfaction and enjoyment that is gained, from the level of maturity and self-realization that follows, from the inner transformations that are obtained, etc. Sometimes the results are humanitarian, constructive, creative, and fulfilling, and in other cases, they are self-destructive or destroy others, they are degrading, or void of the satisfaction and enjoyment of life. Passion, as such, is axiologically (and morally) neutral. The results depend upon its content and orientation. It does not exist on its own, but only in making possible or in obstructing a specific life project.

Later on, I will return to the *deficit of rationality*, but here the recourse to the cultivation of ego qualities in a human being and to the satisfactory employment of women's potential for passion is necessary. One of the challenges that women have to face is perhaps in being themselves the managers of this potential. Frequently, radical and impassioned surrender in religious affairs has been used institutionally against the same women. Essentially, what is a great absence of inhibition and a potential of energy, has canceled out creative capacity. Still, more has to be said about the confusion of truly impassioned behaviour in religious affairs with the compensations of severe lack and frustration.[23]

We have already said something about the aspects of passivity and of suffering that are typical for religious passion; in any case , the larger topic is the form in which a woman suffers through religious motivation. We encounter, face-down, the pleasure-pain ambivalence and the difficult theme of religious sadomasochism for many women.

4. Religious experience as communication

Communication is, without doubt, typical for women's world. It explains an aspect that defines, at least, two ways of religious behaviour associated with them, and frequently ridiculed (by the non-psychological perspective of men). One is the form prayer *(rezo, oración)*, and particularly the prayer of intercession *(plegaria)*. And the other is direction of consciousness that touches the terrain of confession, also called spiritual direction or in more critical terms, control of conscience.

4.1. Women's prayer of recitation and the religious experience of communication

Religious women generally and particularly Spanish women is well-known for her skills in prayer that are popularly characterized by the over-pious *(beata)* and her propensity to faithfully attend church, dedicate much time to prayer *(rezo)*, and be considered to be pious due to her devotions to God, the Virgin Mary and to the Saints in heaven. This is certainly populai behaviour, but is more typical for women. Men, even those who are extremely religious, are known for not praying much. Also, primarily women practice the prayer of petition. I would like to expound this point a little more.

Women are not the only ones who pray in petition to God but, they express this more often and with a behaviour that is overwhelmingly devotional. What can psychology say of this behaviour, its basic motives, and its effects? In general terms we can note that to petition means to be a human being that is subjected to needs. If one never asked, then one would deny one's finite condition and reality. To put oneself before the one who is called God in order to ask him/her for something is to be aware of the fact that God belongs to another reality. If God were in the same order, then this behaviour would not have meaning. Therefore, true prayer of petition can never reduce or magically manipulate this Other that we call God. This is not to say that the human being does not magically try this again and again.

The human being asks God for possible and impossible things, changes, and different states of mind. She/he asks for her/himself and personal issues, and also on behalf of others, thus expanding her/his own issues beyond her/himself, and in this way affirming the Christian religion. In the event that the object of petition is not strictly personal, the prayer of petition may be expanded human memory (the needs of others, based on the perception of one's own, are perceived on some communal level), may promote human solidarity, and may extend the circle of personal needs and wishes. It allows knowledge of a part of reality. It could be a *centrifugal* prayer of petion. And, when successful prayer is in solidarity, it is possible (if it is authentic) that a consciousness of complicity takes over, which each one needs - either in the conflict or in the desire from which one asks for God. This is why the prayer of petition does not (necessarily) cover the human task with passivity.

And from a psychological point of view, to what should this greater inclination to prayer (rezo) in groups of women be attributed to? I think, in the first place this is owed to the inclination and need that women have for verbal communication; and also, as I just suggested, to women's great ease of awareness of their own needs as well as the needs of others, thanks to their empathy and self-development. Prayer (*rezo*) is a beseeching (*plegaria*) or a conversation with the One that is perceived as the Other: God/Goddess, the Virgin...somebody, always a person. If a personal reference did not exist then probably this behaviour would not be as common, and I dare to say, it would probably not exist. The same feature can be found in the content of prayer (*rezo*): the majority of women invoke God in order to ask something of God that is to say, the prayers of beseeching (*plegaria*) abound. And, in nearly all other contents, prayer (*oración*) is a conversation with God or his/her intercessors. Prayer can be spontaneous or it can be ritualized in public intercessions (*plegaria*), composed beforehand. Mostly verbal and loud-spoken prayers predominate. Women like to talk and enjoy explicit verbalization and conversation. They have more verbal fluidity than the majority of men, and, I repeat, they feel a special pleasure in this conduct. Therefore, it is not strange that women, while engaging in these religious rites, *communicate* more with the Other than they lead one to believe.

When petitioning prayers are spontaneous (and not already formulated), the content of the prayers allude to the daily preoccupations of women's lives: their daily problems with family, partnership, friends, acquaintances, groups. . . the vast world of interpersonal relationships. Included in these prayers one often finds the larger problems of humanity (hunger, war, injustice) that directly affect people and their possibilities for a viable life. This reinforces the subjective experience of nearness between this world and the supernatural in which women believe. For a woman, prayer is an action brings two separate worlds close to each other and creates contact between them.

Peculiarly, in the same way women get *together* for prayer. Especially in public places and places that are religiously more traditional (villages, neighborhoods, popular religious fiestas, many religious congregations). Women prefer to be and pray together as opposed to praying alone. Therefore communicative behaviour is reinforced.[24] But at the same time there exists an underlying element of social control amongst these women that is not so readily seen but which has efficient results: the women know who will lead the prayers and who will not, who sticks with the norms and who has overstepped them. In other moments of our history, very recently, this control has been a factor of terrible oppression. Today, this has changed in the immense majority of Spanish villages, but it still exists in the constitutional female religious groups (religious orders).[25]

The association of peititonal prayer with women is related to the assumed psychological fact that women concretize the object of their request. And I believe this is reasonable. Women ask on behalf of concrete people and they ask for concrete things. The general opinion is that this concretization is due to the fact that women are more dependent, less self-sufficient, or simply more credulous, superstitious and less mature. This is the stereotype, and in some ways this is true. But, on the other hand, it has been forgotten that women are generally more in touch with their needs, and therefore with the needs of others. Generally, women are more conscious of *interdependent* relationships (not just dependent relationships that are one-sided). Women are aware of empty pockets, limitations and incapabilities, and most of the time, this knowledge is born out of affective relationships, where human needs show up and uncover the most radical human desire. Without doing much analysis, women habitually perceive the intricate net-work of internal relationships in the same way as complex reality. Paradoxically, this allows them to pray more concretely (petition). The background of humanity and the background of reality is, in the last instance, very similar. Clearly, there might be a danger of over-simplification.

4.2. The religious experience of communication and spiritual counseling

Until most recently and still often today, spiritual direction has been the other mode of communicative expression that characterizes the religious behaviour of women. The most usual form was confession and consultation with the priest. Although the practice of confession has diminished amongst women (at least amongst Spanish this is notable), they still frequently seek a consultation with the priest. Sometimes, this has been explained on the basis of the great immaturity of women and their lack of religious education and autonomy. But even so the religious institutions have kept women in the situation of a psychological minority and have made it difficult and even denied them the recourses which are easily accessible for men, I do not believe that this is the only explanation. In the case of women's insecurity in moral issues - themes that constitute the majority of consultations - it is necessary to say that the psychological mechanism that holds women in this situation is guilt. Without doubt this is most effective. To escape guilt has liberated many women in their personal and religious dimension. But many of them have seen how their obsessions and scruples have been reinforced by the same confessors to which they came in order to resolve their doubts and insecurities.

But, as I already said, this is also a question of communication which implies for many women a type of relation with men that they cannot establish in other social forms. And, what also needs to be added here is the attraction that priests and monks often have for many women, since they escape the masculine stereotype. These are men who listen to them and with whom they can talk, while in the meantime it proves to be very difficult to establish a profound communication with their male partner. Men continue to think that women are complicated and show neither interest nor capacity to enter into their interior world. In contrast, a priest or a monk cultivates his internal life and thus, in a certain way, the capacity to be able to understand the inner religious world of women minimally, particularly the religious world in which they live. When I say minimally, I want to suggest that priests and monks are not as capable as they think of understanding the inner religious world of women and their various religious experiences, but that still the image of the woman-guide or spiritual counselor is not sufficiently available; therefore the majority of women are in the habit of going more to men (priests and monks).

5. Religious experience as ritual

Coming together for prayer is not the only religious rite that joins women. They come in and organize, increasingly often, religious rites and celebrations. They are particularly present in the religious rites in the context of the great phases of cyclical life: religious rites of initiation (Christian baptism), of passage (first communion, confirmation, wedding), and funeral rites (funerals and burials). Because of their close contact to life, they participate quasi *naturally* in the religious interpretation that these rites suppose.[26] In my point of view their cyclic nature is important. For a long time, the male interpretation of the Bible and of linear consciousness in Jewish and Christian history dominated, to a great extent induced by Hegelian philosophy. The cyclical quality of life-processes and of the same history was relegated to an inferior evolutionary scale, very close to the animal. Woman, whose cyclical experience of her own body has brought her very close to nature, was regarded to be of an inferior origin.[27] Access to superior culture had to come from this consciousness of advancement and linear progress. Thus, women received a negative message with regard to their bodies (cyclic in functions that are typical feminine), to the importance of *nature*, and to their own way of living time and history. What remained was the world of religious experiences, if it was not also affected by these implicit messages.

The religious rites are organized according to the cyclic repetition of the stages of life. We do not face the eternal return here but a process that every human being can experience in a spiral. The same philosophical and religious ideology that has interpreted history as a progressive line perceives with bias what returns since time immemorial: the repetition, again and again, of a cyclical routine. The Catholic Church celebrates each year the same fiestas, the same rites, and it attaches itself onto the routine of repetition which offers security and the control it needs over its faithful. How do women perceive and experience this posture of the same Church that is controversial in its message? We still lack empirical data for a precise analysis.[28]

It is impossible to generalize, even though we are able to make extensive reflections. There are women who live their religiosity basically immersed in the routine-cycle of rites. They have given way to the security that the same rite maintains, and they do not allow themselves to hesitate about its validity and efficiency. These women participate fully (meaning emotionally and effectively) in the religious ceremonies of the different stations of the year and they share in religious celebrations of different moments in the lives of the persons they love and with whom they live - baptisms. first communions, weddings, burials. . . Anyhow, a part of their lives and life itself recovers and maintains the meaning of these rites for them, in the same way as profane rites of the annual fiestas in the village or in the town. These women have not formed themselves. They live without more.

But there are also women who, conscious of their quality as active subjects, search for creative participation in the religious rites. Numerous young women, and women of middle age, show up actively in the preparation and participation of religious rites. This position as protagonists has changed the religious experience of the celebrations for them: the symbols acquire great meaning and turn out to be living and effective for them; religious experiences stand for their own subjectivity and emotionality in a much more personalized way. The resulting behaviours are equally more personal and committed. Still these are, without doubt, minority groups.

The cyclical reiteration of this form is not the eternal return that reinforces the experience but the spiral that leaves an open gate to the creative transformation of one's own person and of the reality of one's environment. In this way, religious rites fulfill a *prophetic* function in which the quality attributed to the male passes over to the subjective and social experience of women, who are, in many cases, characterized by radical surrender.

Conclusion

The challenge is there. Each women may decide. To ritualize, to find new symbols, and to name God again might be attractive for some, but others may lack interest in it. Here we have to deal with those women still interested - in a secular Spain that is in many ways either indifferent or controversial towards religion, which means the institutional Catholic Church. For many women, God already does not fit anymore in their subjectivity. For others, the Divine begins to take on other names, other meanings raised by renewed and revitalized experiences. For a large group, God remains the same: a masculine God - we do not know why - who is also not like men because he transcends them. And to a small group of restless and searching ones, God has no name for the moment. All of them are awaiting a path and a process in one way or another.

Notes

1 As is occurring in other places, in Spain there is a diversity of women's groups in relation to the Religious. They differ from one another on the basis of their goals, their activities and some of their characteristics: some are more pastoral, others are more social in nature, others more academic. Generally the groups are ecumenical although most of the women profess to be Catholic so that, in effect (and in actual practice), we encounter few women of other Christian denominations or other religions.

2 In regard to this method in Psychology of Religion I adopt the stance of A. Vazquez Fernandez. "Psicología religiosa," in Cuestiones de Psicología, U.P. de Salamanca, Salamanca 1983, 173-206. See also B. Grom, Psicología de la religión, ed. Herder, Barcelona, 1994.

3 The work of Lene Sjorup, "Women's Lives, Women's Religiosity. Are Women's Experiences Mystical Experiences?" Gender-Nature-Culture, Working Paper (Denmark) 8, 1994, has served me as background for a comparative summary.

4 The studies in psychology of religion which take account of the analytical category of gender, reduce it to the developmental psychology of infancy and adolescence and, in general, are more interesting in regards to the moral development than in regards to this kind of religious experience. See: K. Tamminen, Gender Differences in Religiousness in Children and Adolescents: How do we explain them?, A lecture at the 6th Symposium for the Psychology of Religion, University of Helsinki, June 1994 (unpublished article): ibid., Changing God-Concepts in Childhood and Adolescence: Empirical Results, Methodological Problems, William James Award Address at the Convention of the American Psychological Association in New York, 1995 (unpublished). Other studies are more phenomenological. In return, some studies center now more around the psychological dimension. Cf. Also M.L. Randour, Women's Psyche. Women's Spirit. Columbia Univ. Press 1987.

5 The first hesitant attempt, still in need of revision is my work "Experiencia religiosa de mujer. Notas psicologicas", in: Pastoral Misionera, 178/179 (1991) 75-89

6 A. Vergote, Psicologia Religiosa, Madrid 1975, 46; cf. also for another definition in a theological context: X. Pikaza, Experiencia religiosa y cristianismo, Salamanca 1981.

7 Evidently, there are men who - for innate or developmental reasons - have another perceptive capacity, but this is significantly more common for women.

8 I do not speak of the instinct in the proper sense here, therefore, I have put it in italics.

9 In the rules of psychological functioning, pathology and sanity do not have borders which are perfectly differentiated from each other; it is rather a question of proportion and accents on a same continuum. For example, each person does react *neurotically and transforms reality* in a moment of panic reaction, but we cannot say therefore that this person is neurotic. In the same way we all have a certain schizoid component, the proportion and manifestation of which depends on multiple combined factors.

10 I use the Freudian scheme of instinctual personality (Id - Ego - Super-ego) and the stages (unconscious, preconscious, and conscious). But although I basically use a psychodynamic model, I do not strictly hold to the Freudian or Jungian principles.

11 In my point of view, *empathy* is necessary for the quality of (social and other) actions. But it only precedes in a moment; *sympathy* is more important as an immediate motor of actions.

12 I do not intend to say that it depends only on cultural education. Cultivation of the cognitive dimension is much fuller: it includes that which we call common sense or the capacity of good sense, it assimilates the information that comes from the exterior and the interior of the person, from the events, the relationships.

. . and becomes the capacity for understanding one's own life. In this sense, the cultivation of the cognitive dimension of the human being is very important.

13 Many stigmatized seers can be placed here, even though more factors and dispositions that intervene in the phenomenon have to be analyzed. See for this aspect F. Alonso Fernandez, *Estigmas, levitaciones y éxtasis. De Sor Magdalena a El Plamar de Troya*, ed. by Temas de Hoy, Madrid 1993.

14 The new religious sensitivity explores these possibilities in women and in youth, in other words in those people with less social and political recourses for confronting a difficult future.

15 In my point of view, this is the authentic Christian religious experience.

16 Paradox is a generally accepted feature for psychologists (and phenomenologists) of religion. We know the great paradoxes better, for example the *tremendum / fascinosum* of Otto, but there are many paradoxes to which we hardly pay attention in spite of the importance they have in real experience of human religiosity.

17 Cf. my work M. Navarro, *Psicología y Mística*, ed. S. Pio X, Madrid 1991.

18 My result is revealed in the article by Beverly W. Harrison and Carter Heyward, "Dolor y placer: evitar las confusiones de la tradición en la teoría feminista", in J.B. Nelson, S.P. Longfellow, *da sexualidad y lo sagrado*, DDB, Bilbao 1996 (English: 1993)

19 Maybe women's task of *conserving* life has become more excessive. This is also in the process of change because many women, coming from a religious commitment, have become aware of the diverging masculine and feminine roles with regard to the life of the planet and human life. They know that one cannot conserve a life with utilitarian aims and economic, political, and scientific exploitation (cannon-fodder). . . The ethical statements deriving from the contestations of women are stronger. Women know that life cannot be promoted and expanded if a minimal quality is not assured. The relation of quantity-quality and context has come to the foreground and has led many women to change their religious attitude to a conserving role.

20 My book *Las siete palabras de Mercedes Navarro,* ed. PPC, Madrid 1996, describes my own bodily and sensory experience. One may especially look at the word *sintiendo y queriendo.*

21 I do start to discuss the moral negativity with which passion is impregnated, especially when it has to do with a passion that is experienced by and exciting for women. The reduction of passion to the field of sexuality has been very devastating in the context of Christian religious experience. In reality it was only a defense mechanism in front of its power and the perception of its threat. The rationality (predominantly) of male knowledge is a defense front against the unknown world of affects and emotions. In Christianity, *passion* has also been applied to the suffering of Jesus - thus concealing its positive power and energy that guides to the construction of the kingdom of God, and, in conclusion, to resurrection.

22 Cf. B. Grom, Psicología de la religión, ed. Herder, Barcelona 1994.

23 There would be much to say about this. It is enough for me to think about the *sacrificed* women that the institutional Catholic religion has produced in Spain, the majority of them serious women who came to this world to suffer for the fact of their nature and *because God has wanted it so*, and the bitter and resentful lives in which they have been terminated. Living a satisfactory and pleasant life meant my mother's generation to leave the Church. The moral and religious intolerance of many Spanish people in all regions, as well as the terrible and cruel control that they can establish over others (exeptionals) who allowed themselves to live, is one of the features that our best writers have portrayed. It is enough for me to think for example about the figure of Ana Ozores in the novel of Carín, *La Regenta.*

24 Without doubt, it would be interesting to study the content of free or spontaneous requests (*plegaria*), or of prayer of petition (*oracíon de peticíon*), because then we could see that the themes that occupy the majority of these prayers (*plegaria*) are the ones of everyday-life. Women's pragmatism characterizes the content of the petitions. The concrete and daily life is in them full of its problems, needs, difficulties, pains. . .

25 Amongst the practicing Spanish male orders there is no such control. The men are usually more liberal, behave with great confidence amongst themselves, and manifest in this way a great personal security and a much more elevated self-esteem. Amongst women, especially in conservative groups, villages or religious communities, this control may become a torture. In most occasions liberty, creativity, and initiative is reduced. . . and the religious rite is fossilized and each time made more and more rigid.

26 However, her presence is not *visible.* It is one of the terrible paradoxes that continue to exist in the Catholic Church, the religious confession of the majority in Spain. The institution does not frame itself according to the importance of the empirical fact of female presence. Much less it does question its sense, and, especially, its indirect influence of the religious significance of these rites. A good way to conceive what I say is simply to imagine all these rites without women.

27 Cf. the work of Buitendijk, etc.

28 How do men experience the cyclical nature of the Christian rites, specifically Catholics? How do they articulate their cyclical religious experience with the message of progressive linearity of the prevailing paradigm?

Ursula Rudnick

The Body of Christ: Discipleship of (Un)equals
Lutheran Perspectives from Hanover

Reflections

Much of the Spiritual Context has to do with the place, I grew up in and the family from which I come. Therefore, I will sketch it with a few lines.

I grew up in Hannover, in the North of Germany. The people of this landscape tend to be rather introverted. This area is by tradition a Protestant / Lutheran ohe, going back to the 30 year war in the time of the Reformation. Catholics and Jews were a rather small minority till the 30s of this century. After the Shoah there was only a tiny Jewish community left. Since many refugees were coming from the East, the number of Catholics multiplied. It is only since the late sixties with the advent of "Gastarbeiter", that other religions are coming into the picture as well. A few years ago, a Buddhist temple opened in Hannover.

At the school which I attended, there were only a few Catholics, perhaps 5 out of 28 children. There were no children of other religions. Not yet even children with "no" religion, children coming from families who had left the Church.

My family belonged to "the" - not "a" - Church, paying dues but not attending services. We did not go to Church for Christmas because my parents felt that only going for Christmas would be hypocritical. I was taught "Lutheran religion" in elementary school - confessional religious education in public schools is a German particularity. My very early memories are not good ones: I disliked the prayer of the teacher. About the "why" I can only speculate: whether it was because I sensed some kind of hypocrisy or whether I was just not used to prayer. At the Gymnasiun I was clearly a non-believer. Those miracles told in the Bible simply seemed ridiculous to me. How could they have possibly happened!? My solution was: they did not. Like almost everybody else of my generation I attended confirmation class, and I agreed to being "confirmed" because I did not want to make trouble. Yet, Church became a place for me where I could ask questions - mainly existential and intellectual ones - and where I was not questioned about my beliefs. Thus I was drawn to theology. . . Much has happened since then and I have learned a lot.

I encountered meditation only very late: the first experience were the "Schweigestunden", when I was about sixteen. It was in the early 1980s and many people were afraid that Germany could be the battlefield of yet another war. Thus people came together on Friday afternoon, standing in a circle in the city, doing nothing but keeping silent. Then I found it very difficult to keep silent for over an hour. Over the course of time, this has changed, I have come to like silence in services - this is the place where I encounter it in my tradition - and most often I do find that the period allotted to silent prayers is kept to short, as though there is a fear of this silence. Above all. prayer for me is public prayer. I rarely pray when I am by myself. And if so, it is most a sentence, generally a wish for something to happen or not to happen. - In Sunday morning services I often find that the prayer is very abstract and thus becomes difficult to sustain emotionally. When I hear the word "love" in connection with "Christianity", I sometimes get very angry. If "love" means the sentiment of the heart, an emotion, I think it is mistaken to take this as a term to characterize the Christian tradition and its most important values. Love should be seen not only as a sentiment, but as a deed that includes working toward justice.

Sunday Morning in Hanover

It is Sunday morning in Hanover, Germany. Two women are cleaning the altar in the Church of the Redeemer. While cleaning, they are talking:

Gunda: "Come on, Ilse, we have to hurry, soon the service will start. Look at all the dust, it is the dust of centuries. But two women like us will manage to clean it, well at least we will raise some dust....

I wonder if today more people will come than usual. Today they are celebrating the service of the decade. Our minister, pastor Krull, said that this service has been prepared only by women, and there is not even a woman minister."

Ilse: What did you say? The service of the decade? What on earth is that?

Gunda: "Oh, that is difficult to explain. I have to look into the brochure."

Reads from the brochure. "The goals of the *Ecumenical Decade 'The Churches' Solidarity with Women'* are:

- to empower women to question oppressive structures in their respective churches, societies, and worldwide;

- to recognize the contribution of women to churches and congregations in all areas;

- to make visible the ideas and perspectives of women in work and in the struggle for justice, peace, and the integrity of creation;

- to move the churches to liberate themselves from oppressive teachings and practices such as racism, sexism, and classism;

- to encourage churches to undertake actions in solidarity with women.[1]

Now, did you get it?"

Ilse: "More or less. I think it means that we women are able to do more than make coffee. We are also able to create services and we even should do this with the support of the Church government."[2]

At first, the visitors are amazed: has the cleaning not yet been finished? Then they become aware that the play of these women is already part of the service. It is the annual service which is dedicated to *Ecumenical Decade "The Churches" Solidarity with Women."*

Spirituality needs its vessels, be they theological reflection, poetical prayer or the constitution of the church. In this article I shall describe and analyze the Evangelical Lutheran Church of Hanover, to which I belong, from the perspective of women's work, influence, and representation in the church. Special focus will be on the changes the decade has brought about.

In debates about the nature and form of the church, the ideas of St. Paul played an important role, especially concerning women's role in the church. The church, the *ekklesia*, is not only an incidental collection of individuals, but a community: the community of *Agiois,* Saints, as Paul addresses those who see themselves as the followers of Jesus Christ.[3]

Elisabeth Schüssler-Fiorenza assumes a discipleship of equals for the early followers of Jesus: "The gospel affirms in various ways that Jesus' call to discipleship has precedence over all other obligations, religious duties, and family ties. Jesus did not respect the patriarchal family and its claims, but replaced it with the new community of disciples. When his brothers and mother asked for him, he replied, according to Mark. "Who is my mother? Who are my brothers? And looking around at those sitting in the circle about him he said: "Here are my mother and my brothers. Whoever does the will of God is my brother, my sister, my mother." (Mark 3:31-35). "[4]

Furthermore, Schüssler-Fiorenza sees this egalitarian understanding best expressed in the baptismal formula of Galatians 3:27-29: "For as many of you as have been baptized into Christ have put on Christ. There is neither Greek nor Jew, there is neither bond nor free, there is neither male nor female; for ye all are one in Christ Jesus."

She elaborates: "All Christians are equal members of the community. Galatians 3: 28 is a pre-Pauline baptismal formula that Paul quotes in order to prove that in the Christian community all religious-social distinctions between Jews and Gentiles have lost their validity... Just as Christian Jews remained racially[5] Jews, so women remained biologically female although their patriarchal defined gender roles and subordinate status were no longer of any socioreligious significance in the Christian community."[6]

Even if one contends with Schüssler-Fiorenza, that these texts do not necessarily mirror daily practice[7], her basic thesis is also supported by scholars who do not work in a feminist framework, such as Jürgen Roloff.[8] Furthermore, and most importantly, these texts are open to the understanding that *today* the church ought to struggle for and strive towards becoming a community of equals.

In the Lutheran tradition, it is important to listen to Biblical voices, but also to take Luther's ideas into consideration. In the *Confessio Augustana*, the confessional documents of 1530, the importance of the existence of the church is stressed as well as its character as the community of the believers and saints.[9] The biblical image used is that of the body of Christ as described in Ephesians 4:4 : "There is one body, and one Spirit, even as ye are called in one hope of your calling." In discussions about women's participation in the church, the two images used in the letter to the Ephesians and to the Galatians recur again and again.

When I was a student, the Lutheran Church in Germany represented for me the "heart of darkness" in regard to feminist thought. My image of the church and its congregations was that women in positions of influence and power were underrepresented and that the theology lived and handed on in congregations was conservative, with no room for feminist thought.

After having lived and worked in this church for six years, the image has changed. No doubt, some facts have changed, yet my perception of the church has also changed. In the beginning I was outraged when I heard stories like the following: A minister was not allowed by her superior to substitute "God" for "the Lord" in the aaraonite blessing. Several of such examples made me think that the whole church is like that, which proved to be a wrong conclusion. Working in it, I have learned to see the niches in which there is freedom and room, which have to be taken by the members of the body of Christ.

Here are some statistics about the Evangelical-Lutheran Church of Hanover, which basically covers Lower Saxony in Northern Germany. The church consists of about 1400 congregations with 3.2 million members.[10] Those attending church services and church groups are over-proportionately women.[11] Of those who are doing voluntary work for the church - 90.000 people - more than 70% are women.[12]

Almost 24,000 people are doing paid work, many of them part time. A large number of women - about 5000 - work in child-care centers. There are about 950 deacons and social-workers, of which 50% - this is an estimate - are female. Of the 2200 ministers now nearly 20% are female, yet on the next level of hierarchy, that of Superintendenten, the immediate supervisor of the ministers belonging to one church-circuit, there are only 3 women out of 76. Among the regional bishops, the Landessuperintendenten, there is no woman and thus, there is no woman in the Bischofsrat, the council of regional bishops. Also the bishop, Horst Hirschler, is male. In Germany, however, there is at present one woman-bishop, Maria Jepsen, working for the Protestant Church of Nordelbien and in other churches some regional bishops are women.

Politics are made by the synod, the church parliament, an important institution of influence and power. Since its last election in 1995, about 35 % of the members are female.[13] Yet it should be stated that this is a voluntary task which is not paid.

The most important body to execute the policies decided upon by the synod is the Landeskirchenamt, the church office. They do not only execute policies but also decide upon the policies themselves. Its decision-making-body consists of ordained clergy and lawyers, among which there are only two woman out of 17.

Quite a few things have changed over the past ten years. In some areas women have gained access to clerical power and influence: their numbers have risen significantly in the synod, among the church-elders and in the ministry. In the early eighties less than 10% of the ministers were women. However, on certain levels of church leadership - namely those positions which are paid more than regular a minister's salary[14] - women are chronically underrepresented, often with figures of far less than 10%. Looking at the structure of posts held by women and men, one can well speak of a glass ceiling which runs between the ministry and the subsequent higher positions. Enough of numbers and statistics!

Non-Institutional Church Groups: Women's Groups in Congregations

The 1400 congregations of the Hanoverian church present a very diverse image. To a large extent, the Lutheran church in Lower Saxony is still a *Volkskirche* (church of the people) which means that about 40% of the inhabitants belong to this church. Traditionally, in most areas the Catholic or the Calvinist churches as well as Judaism lead a diaspora existence.[15] Only with the advent of foreign workers 25 years ago, has the picture become more pluralistic.

The concept of *Volkskirche* entails that people belong to it by tradition and that it is an umbrella for a multitude of theological ideas and piety. The Lutheran Church of Hanover includes congregations that are evangelical, and thus very conservative, yet there are also very liberal churches. The individual face of a congregation depends on its local tradition and its present lay- and clergy-leadership. Since this church is minister-centered, the minister can exercise considerable influence on the parish.

Almost all congregations have women's groups, whether they carry this name or not. A number of groups call themselves - or are called by others - *Seniorengruppen*, (groups of elderly people) although often these groups are *de facto* women's groups. In many cases those who are working with these groups are not aware of this fact and thus do not undertake any gender specific work with these groups. These groups are rarely attended by couples, but often by women who are widowed. Of all groups these are the most traditional ones: this pertains more to form than to content. (Their format seems to be a universal one in the Hanoverian church: the meeting begins with a biblical meditation, then coffee is drunk and a presentation is given. The end is marked with a prayer and a song.) Elderly women who want a challenge and are still very active tend to choose other groups.

Other groups are made up of children and mothers who have chosen to stay home: these groups often have an informal exchange of opinions. As a group they tend to focus on questions connected with the religious and general education of children. The impressions gained from interviews are that members of these groups are rarely interested in reflecting their role as women. They seem to wish social contact with other mothers and a release from the daily routine and stress which they experience.

A third category of women's groups is that of groups that are neither defined through their role - as the mothers, nor through their age, but share an interest in a common theme, be it literature of feminist theology. Often - but not always- these groups are made up of mainly middle-aged women. The founding of such groups may be due to ministerial impulse or the initiative of some congregates. In a small town, Bergen, a group of women who were dissatisfied with the Sunday morning worship of their congregation, decided to found a *women's liturgy group* when their minister reported about the feminist liturgies she had experienced. Together with the minister, women prepared and celebrated monthly liturgies which they felt touched their core.

One strength of such groups is that they are connected with a congregation and that they help mainstream feminist theology. This process is, for instance, quite visible in Burgdorf: When the local feminist group created their first Sunday morning service, celebrating the decade and calling for realization of its goals, a big discussion with quite some friction ensued. After a number of years, however, the services of this group have become more and more accepted, and with them feminist theology.

The oldest and perhaps most influential of the groups with a feminist agenda is the Hanoverian *FEM*-group which was founded by Johanna Linz and Elke Möller in 1981. The motivation to found such a group was to be able to work on feminist questions in Hanover and not having to drive somewhere else to do this.[16] Elke Möller describes it as "something that was due." Thus, the group grew fast. Suse Bergengruen, a participant, describes the group: "The group was and is a place where women do not have to guard their tongue but can say whatever they want."

This group drew, and still draws, its members from all over Hanover and is not connected with a specific congregation. In the beginning, the members' age ranged from 18 - 75, now there are only few young women participating. At present there are about 120 names on the mailing list, although only 25-30 women come to an individual evening. Women who are not able to attend still want to keep in touch with the group. The group is ecumenical, it even has members who do not belong to any church. It is not connected with either a congregation or an institution, so that it is not bound by anything.[17] Furthermore, it was important to the organizers that the group was not a private, but a public enterprise.

The group meets once a month: the evening starts with a communal dinner, then information is exchanged, and a theme is studied and discussed. In the beginning, matriarchal religion as well as biblical stories were analyzed and discussed from a feminist point of view.

Living spirituality was an important point on the agenda: on the 13th. of every month, a public liturgy was celebrated in the ruins of a church destroyed in World War II.

Since its inception, the group understood itself as a political group. Thus, they demonstrated against the stationing of cruise-missiles in Germany, they protested against a military fair in Hanover, they were active in the boycott against South Africa and fought against restrictive laws on abortion. While there were still two German states, the group also had contact with a women's group in Magdeburg, in the former GDR. One of the latest activities is a regular silent demonstration of women wearing black, to draw attention to the women's situation in Bosnia.

Besides taking an active stance in social politics, the group also wanted to bring about changes within the church. The local group has played an important role as a pressure group to lobby for women's interests in demanding changes in the structure of the church. For instance, when, in 1988, the election of a new bishop came up, members of the group campaigned for the election of a woman-bishop, collecting several thousand signatures. A walk-in into the synod during the election was organized and each member received, together with a rose, a text containing the following words "Born as a woman, liberated by Christ, called to be God's daughter, I am suffering from a church where male dominion is a painful daily experience... I am dreaming of a church in which the siblinghood of men and women is really lived."[18] The result was predictable: a man was called to the bishopric. Yet, the consciousness of the public has been raised: a women can become a bishop.

Elke Möller describes the group as an emotional anchor. Participating in the group means being together with women who "are interested in this church". It means finding resonance for one's own ideas of faith and theology, it entails an exchange with others who think similarly, and perhaps the most important point: it means receiving strength to carry on in this church, which often enough is alienating and painful.

Women's Reformation Day

On October 31, the day on which Lutheran churches celebrate and commemorate the Reformation, the first *Women's Reformation Day* took place in 1987. All women who "are interested in the church and who want to change it"[19] were invited. The group, who had prepared the day, stated in the invitation: "We (a group of unsatisfied church-employees) no longer want to be represented or ruled over by men.

We aim at strengthening women's position in the church and changing the church at the same time, so that we can recognize ourselves in its forms and contents..."[20] Among the organizers were women of different professions: ministers, deacons and others. Members of the FEM-group were also among them. For the first time, members of different professions got together to articulate their interests which were already stated in the invitation:

- analyse women's suffering in the church
- to achieve acceptance of feminist theology
- to call for a Frauenbeauftragte, a woman monitoring discrimination against women
- to discuss a quota which reserves a number of seats for women.[21]

The day began with a bible study, which was followed by an exchange of experience about working in the church in small groups. After lunch, three themes were dealt with simultaneously in different groups: the role of feminist theology, women and power, pros and cons of the quota and a Frauenbeauftragte.[22] From these groups, further ideas for the continuation of the struggle resulted. The day ended with the nailing of theses, as Luther allegedly did more than 500 years ago. The theses were formulated spontaneously by women: some were criticizing, others were encouraging. Altogether, the day was a success: 300 women came to participate, thus indicating that many women felt a similar alienation as did the organizers of the day.

In 1996 the 10th anniversary was celebrated. Looking back, a number of goals have been reached. Women are aware of what pains them in the church, and have no difficulty naming them. Looking back, Sabine Sundermeyer states that the Women's Reformation Day put an end to individual loneliness and connected women with each other. Furthermore, feminist theology has gained acceptance, which does not mean that it is universally appreciated. A department for the "Renewal of the Relationship between men and women" has been installed, yet the woman who is presently holding this job did not have the endorsement of either the FEM-group nor the Women's Reformation Day or any other women's organization or group in the Hanoverian Church. But it seems that over the years she has gained acceptance. The system of having a women's quota, which has been adopted by the major political parties in Germany, has not been introduced. Yet, the number of women participating has grown immensely, whereas in some areas it is still lacking - as was described above.

Institutions by and for Women in the Hanoverian Church: The
department for renewed relationships of women and men

Following a long struggle, in which members of the *FEM*-group and
women from the Women's Reformation day were involved - the synod
decided in 1989 to create a new department for the "renewed
community of women and men" (*die erneuerte Gemeinschaft von
Frauen und Männern*). They stressed the following arguments:

- Women and men are created in the image of God. As the church,
they form the body of Christ. Existing injustices cause difficulties in
living this community of women and men.

- State law proclaims that women and men are equal. This law has
led to formal equality in a number of areas. Yet the numbers show that
women are not represented in policy making bodies according to their
numbers.[23]

The department consists of three women: a minister, an assistant
and a secretary. The head of the newly created department is part of
the highest body of the church-executive and it is her task to monitor
the "renewed community of women and men" in whatever area women
are concerned. Thus, whenever women or the relationship of men and
women are concerned, it is her task to intervene. Yet, since every
question has to be discussed with her colleagues, the course of change
is slow. According to Dorothea Biermann "the path of consultation is
hard and laborious, yet it entails many possibilities."[24]

The following tasks are formulated by the department itself:

- making visible the different situations in which women live

- to honor women's achievements

- to help men to reflect upon their role

- to further the use of inclusive language

- to support women's theological studies

- to create conditions for combining work and family

- to draw attention to those who do voluntary work and to improve
  their conditions[25]

Asked what she considers to be her achievements, Biermann
declines to answer, since every policy that has been decided upon -
such as the use of inclusive language in church-publications - does not
carry her signature, but is the work of the complete executive body.

Nevertheless, several achievements can be noted: The (almost)
universal use of inclusive language in church publications. The concept
of "gender" slowly gains recognition as a legitimate category of

analysis. The introduction of gender training is scheduled for the first time this year. Furthermore, each church-circuit is supposed to have a local ombudswoman, who monitors discrimination against women.

As a future goal, Biermann sees the task of developing a concept of leadership that contains more flexibility and that takes gender into account.

The department often receives criticism: from those who cannot perceive its necessity, as well as from women for whom matters are changing too slowly. Elke Möller, member of the FEM, criticizes the structure of the department. Being part of the executive body means that there is very little the department can do by itself, for each action it has to win the approval of the colleagues. Furthermore, she states: "It is so domesticated. It is not what we originally wanted."

Das Frauenwerk

The institutional roots of the *Frauenwerk* (Women's Institution) reach back to the beginning of this century. In 1930 the platform of the then *Frauenhilfe* (Women's Aid) gave importance to caring for mothers, poor people, and wayward young women. At the same time, women were educated for taking on these tasks.[26] The institution stressed that it had nothing to do with the women's movement of the time, for they put at their center of activity the service of women for society.[27]

The structure of the *Frauenwerk* is one of its strengths: the basis is formed by women and women's groups in the 1400 congregations of the Hanoverian Church. Each church circuit, consisting of 10- 20 congregations, has a team of two or three women, doing voluntary work, who help organize the work in the congregations. The next level is that of the *Sprengel*, a local unity of about 10 church-circuits, of which there are eight in the Church altogether. Each *Sprengel* has a full-time *Frauenwerk* position which offers seminars and creates programs. The *Landesstelle* represents the *Frauenwerk* to other Church institutions within the Hanoverian Church and outside of it. Furthermore, it offers a number of different activities, which are advertised in its annual program. Till the middle of the eighties, five different areas of activities were stressed: 1. Seminars helping women to be active in their local congregations, 2. Seminars and other activities reaching beyond local parish work, such as seminars on political questions and contacts with other women's church groups. 3. Furthermore, providing centers where mothers could relax and take a rest. 4. A center for "family education", where fathers are also welcome, and 5. The preparation of the Women's World Prayer Day.[28]

With the change of leadership in 1988 when Ulrike Denecke, who considers herself a feminst, became head of the *Frauenwerk*, a change of content came about. Although all of the traditional areas of work, which are partly institutionalized, still exist, others have been added. Whereas the traditional work of this institution has been focused on women with families, has the *Frauenwerk* in the nineties puts the stress on the pluralism of relationships in which women live. Thus, programs by and for women living by themselves have been developed. Another focus is the work with physically challenged women. "Different forms of living" also includes lesbian relationships, however this has not been made an issue.

Seminars on rhetoric and communication and courses that transmit knowledge and faculties necessary for the work as a church-elder have also been added to the program. The theological work focuses on the Bible, which is approached with hermeneutics that are best described as existential-linguistic. In a first step, translations are checked and compared with the original, then women freely share interpretations, associations, and phantasies. The assumption of these hermeneutics are that the Biblical text has an immediate message and that every participant is capable of interpreting the text, something that is shared with the Bible interpretation of liberation theology.

Those working in the headquarters see themselves as feminists. Yet, the institution does not give itself an explicit feminist appearance since it wants to give room to all women in the church, to the more conservative ones, as well as to the feminist ones.[29] Feminist elements have entered the work, without necessarily explicitly naming them. Among them - most importantly - giving space to women to find and express their own faith. Not to confront them with "the truth", but letting each women find her own truth, be it in the interpretation of the Bible or in the celebration of liturgies.

Besides preparing the annual Women's World-Prayer Day, a booklet is published every year to enable women in congregations to celebrate a service calling to mind the goals of the *Ecumenical Decade*. Unlike the material published for the Women's World Prayer Day, the material for the decade is compiled by lay-women and clergy from the Hanoverian Church. It focuses on a Biblical text, it does not include a complete service, yet lots of different materials such as: historical information about the text, stories connected with the theme, different methods of appropriating the text and liturgical elements. The purpose of the booklet is to enable women to create a service of their own.

The head of the *Frauenwerk* Ulrike Denecke states: "The aims of the decade are also my aims. It is important to me that women in the

Frauenwerk become who they are. That they notice their talents and express them. For me, the gospel is empowerment."[30] Celebrating the service of the decade women can experience their own strength. Denecke adds: "Faith becomes part of life, women become more self-confident and experience the specially female forms of spirituality."[31]

Furthermore, Denecke considers it important that the decade is a world-wide undertaking, for "it makes women realize that other women are involved in the same struggle and it connects women throughout the world."[32] Furthermore, Denecke stresses that new themes - such as violence and economics - have entered the discussion.

The Sunday of the Decade

As part of the Ecumenical Decade "The Churches' Solidarity with Women" the Hanoverian Church designated one Sunday a year as the *Sunday of the Decade*. It also pays for the booklet published by the *Frauenwerk*.

Often the service of this Sunday is prepared by groups of women. There are no exact statistics as to how many congregations actually celebrate this Sunday. Depending on the area, estimates range from anywhere between 10 to 40 % of all congregations that are actively celebrating services commemorating the *Decade*. There are much fewer congregations celebrating the *Sunday of the Decade* than the *Women's World Prayer Day*. This has a number of reasons: one of them is that the tradition of the World Prayer Day of Women is longer. Another reason that there are still many women for whom the challenge of creating a complete service looms too large.[33] Furthermore, for a number of congregations it is a radically new concept that lay-members of a congregation prepare and celebrate a Sunday morning service. Grete Schaer, head of the *Frauenwerk* office in the *Sprengel of Lüneburg* reported the following exchange. In a conversation about the celebration of this Sunday, one minister stated: "I will adopt the texts, I assume that this is in your interest." This man clearly did not understand what the Sunday of the decade is about.

Some women experience the decade as a "monstrous, complex thing."[34] This is already mirrored in its name: nobody ever calls the *Decade* by its full name: *Ecumenical Decade Solidarity of the Churches with Women*. People just call it "the decade", a term which has to be explained and whose content is not obvious, since a decade only describes a time-period of ten years. The title is abstract, and according to Ingrid Ganser, head of the *Frauenwerk* office in the *Sprengel of East-Fresia,* "it has nothing to do with the women living in the countryside."[35] According to her, there are still many women in her

Sprengel, who have never heard of it. Thea Kregel, head of the *Frauenwerk* office in the *Sprengel* of Stade, states: "One has to practice the decade without naming it, for the title is the unhappiest formulation that possibly could have been found."[36]

Furthermore, Grete Schaer detects the fear of questioning patriarchal structures in which many women are rooted.

Generally speaking, women who are active in women's work will most probably know of the *Decade*. Yet, men who are serving in the church as elders or in other functions, may have heard it, and then forgotten it again. People who do not belong to a congregation will probably never have heard of it.

Whether or not the service is celebrated depends largely on the women who are living and working in a congregation: if they take up the idea of celebrating the Sunday, in most cases the ministers will not object. If there are women-ministers in a congregation, they themselves will probably take up this Sunday.

Dorothea Biermann compares the *Decade* with the Conciliar process on *Justice, Peace and Integrity of Creation*, which is often seen as something coming from the outside. It can be spread only if people at the grass roots level make it their own and thus work for its acceptance. According to Dorothea Biermann, it is impossible to realize such a program from the top of an institution.[37]

Conclusion

In 1995, Protestant and Catholic churches in Germany invited a team of eight women and men from different countries and churches around the world to evaluate the process of half the decade. In their report, they state: "Among women, the team found a lot of impatience and tears, frustration, and hopelessness regarding the church as an institution. However, we also found satisfaction and pride with the progress made in certain areas."[38] Then the report names the successful steps: the ordination of women, women's desks that have been established, and the growing number of women in leadership positions.[39] Others can be added: The general consciousness of male and female church-members has changed: women's capacities are seen and the necessity of participation of women in all church-matters is generally recognized - although with a certain ambivalence.[40]

On the whole, feminist theology has gained acceptance. Although there is no chair of feminist theology at a university in Lower Saxony, courses are taught and it is possible to choose topics from feminist theology for the theological examinations.

The *Decade* has supported a process of renewal. However, most important were the women who pressed for changes. The goals of the *Decade* helped to provide a justification for the demands of a thorough transformation.

The *Decade* called for the churches to be active in their support of women: the activities of the church-government are quickly named: the synod created the *Department for the Renewal of Relationships between Women and Men* and instituted an annual Sunday service celebrating the *Decade* which will remain as a *Women's Sunday* after the end of the *Decade*.

The report continues: "Although we understand the pain of women and men who would like to see more and quicker progress, it was our feeling, as a team, that there could be more recognition and celebration of the progress which has been made over the last couple of years."[41]

A certain tiredness among women can be observed: After climbing the mountains, there is now "the effort of walking on the plain." - as Nora Borris, a minister, aptly puts it. The thrill of the beginning, when feminist ideas and theology were new, is no longer there. According to Elke Möller, in the late eighties so much seemed possible: the church listened to women's demands. A hearing took place, a book on women's experience in the Hanoverian Church was published.[42] A complete renewal of the church seemed possible. This has not happened. Therefore, many women who were active in this struggle, feel disappointment rather than joy.

In the future, it might be more difficult for women to press for more changes because the fight over the distribution of money has become much harder in recent years, and, with it, the work. Almost everywhere - and also in the church - money has to be saved and positions have to be cut down. When there was more money, it was easier to consent to "a kind of extra" - as women's issues were considered by some. Nowadays, it is not a question of this *and* that, but of this *or* that.

I return to the beginning: Spirituality and ecclesiology are not only connected, but intertwined, they are even interdependent. For expressing my spirituality, I need a community of believers: members of the body of Christ. It is not sufficient to be a Christian on my own and by myself: I am in need of sisters - and sometimes also of brothers - to celebrate, to mourn, to praise or to undertake social action. The church provides me with a framework in which to live and strengthen my spirituality.

Sometimes I am asked why I chose to remain in this church which at times has little to do with the church of my vision. Why not leave the church and found a Women's church? There are women - and men - in the Lutheran Church of Hanover whose dreams and visions are similar to my own, there are sisters with whom to cry and laugh together. Furthermore, I believe and I am convinced that there is room for the realization of Women's Church as part of the church at large. I see elements Women's Church already realized in the activities of many women's groups, in the celebration of liturgies, in the struggle for justice and peace and integrity of creation. It is upon us women to make use of the room which the church provides, making it our own, occasionally fighting for it, but often just taking it.

Services as the one which I described at the beginning show the transformation that has already occurred. Who would have thought ten years ago, that such a service would take place in any church on a Sunday morning

And a final argument for not leaving the *Volkskirche*: Groups which started out with a reformatory program, like the Pietists, and who secluded themselves, have often become extremely conservative over the course of time because they stayed together with only those who shared their vision. Nowadays the Pietists form the right-wing of the church. Yet, the never revolutionary *Volkskirche* was open to change over the course of centuries. Although the process of change is a slow one and painful at times, I think that it is very healthy, in the long run, to have to interact with those who do not share my vision, for believing and living one's faith is an ever changing process.

Ecclesiological sentences have three dimensions: They are statements of faith, statements of hope and statements of action.[43] The sentence: *Women and men - created in God's image - form the body of Christ, as a discipleship of equals*, contains all these elements. This sentence is a statement of faith, because outside of a Christian context, this statement would make no sense. Furthermore, it is a statement of hope, for as we have seen, the Lutheran Church of Hanover has not yet become a discipleship of equals. And last, but not least, the statement is a statement of action, for it motivates women - and hopefully men also - to strive for further transformation of this church. Having decided to live and work in this church, I believe in its capacity for transformation and renewal. Spirituality provides the bread of empowerment necessary for the journey that will not end.

Notes

1 Ökumenische Dekade Solidarität der Kirchen mit den Frauen (1988-1998).

2 Berndt, Gunda, Garms, Ilse. Scene: Cleaning Women. Unpublished manuscript. Hanover: 1996.

3 "The early Christians considered themselves as those who were called and elected by God, as the saints of God." Schüssler Fiorenza, E. Discipleship of Equals. A Critical Feminist Ekklesialogy of Liberation. New York: Croassroad, 1993. 96.

4 Ibid.

5 To me, a Christian in Germany, speaking of „Christian Jews" who remained „racially Jews" conjures up the ideology of the Nazis for whom Jews who converted to Christianity remained Jews who had to be murdered. The modern concept of "races" and particularly a Jewish race goes back only to the 19th century. Therefore it seems to be inappropriate to use this language if the intended message was that the Jews remained Jews ethnically. Furthermore, it should also be questioned whether at this early stage of the Jesus' movement, it is appropriate to already speak of "Christians."

6 Ibid., 177.

7 Roloff questions whether equality was always realized: „ Natürlich kann man mit gutem Grund fragen, ob die paulinischen Gemeinden in ihrer empirischen Vorfindlichkeit wirklich dem entprachen, was der Apostel in Gal. 3.28 und Phil. 2.5 als Realität proklamiert, und auch, ob er nicht selbst in manchen Äußerungen ... dahinter zurückgeblieben ist." Roloff, Jürgen. Die Kirche im Neuen Testament. Göttingen: Vandenhoeck & Rupprecht: 1993. 95.

8 Quoting 2. Kor 5:17, Roloff argues that the new being in Christ has to be understood eschatologisch: „Und zwar dient die Formel „in Christus" durchweg dazu, den Ort der eschatologischen Zukunft in der gegenwärtigen Erfahrung der Christen zu umreißen.... Es trifft zu, daß Paulus in Gal. 3:26-28 die Wirkung der Taufe als ein Eingegliedertwerden in einen räumlichen Bereich darstellt, den er mit der Formel „in Christus Jesus" umschreibt... Das räumlich verstandene In-Christus-Sein kann demnach nicht aus der Vorstellung einer seinshaften Verwandlung der Getauften in Christus hinein erklärt werden. Es geht hier nicht um eine physische Identifikation mit Christus. Das bedeutet jedoch, daß das In-Christus-Sein nur ekklesiologisch verstanden werden kann. „In Christus" bezeichnet bei Paulus da, wo es im räumlichen Sinn gebraucht wird, jenen geschichtlichen Bereich, in dem Menschen ihre Christusbindung in konkreten Lebensbezügen verwirklichen und der durch das Miteinander von an Christus gebundenen Menschen gestaltet ist. „Die Formel „In Christus" impliziert eine Sozialstruktur."...

Und zwar ist diese Sozialstruktur für Paulus eine empirische Realität... Das bedeutet aber, daß die christliche Gemeinde der Ort einer wahrhaft revolutionären Veränderung aller Verhältnisse ist." Ibid. 94f.

73

9 "Es wird auch gelehret, daß alle Zeit musse eine heilige, christliche Kirche sein und bleiben, welche ist die Versammlung aller Gläubigen, bei welchen das Evangelium rein gepredigt und die heiligen Sakrament laut des Evangelii gereicht werden." *Die Bekenntnisschriften der evangelisch-lutherischen Kirche.* Herausgegeben im Gedenkjahr der Augsburgischen Konfession 1930. Göttingen: Vandenhoeck & Rupprecht: 1982. 61.

10 Among the members, 1.5 million are male, 1.7 million are female.

11 The numbers are drawn from different statistics. Some numbers are actual, others are a few years old. To facilitate the reading, I have rounded them.

12 In the Hanoverian Church there are 80.310 people doing voluntary work. However, there is no statistical information available as to how many of these are women.

13 A majority of candidates is elected for the synod, yet a minor part of about 25% are specialists called into the synod. Of those who were elected, almost 50% were women.

14 In Germany all ministers basically receive equal pay. It does not make a difference whether one is the leading mister of a big church or a part-time pastor of a small village congregation. The exact pay depends upon the age (there is an automatic rise every two years), family-status, and if one has children. This means that women are *not* discriminated against on the level of income.

15 This goes back to the peace treaty after the religious wars in the 16th century when it was decided that the populace of a certain area would have the religion of their ruler.

16 Interview with Elke Möller, December 20th, 1996.

17 Diese „Unabhängigkeit" war uns wichtig zum einen, weil wir Interesse gerade auch an Frauen hatten, die nicht den Zugang zur herkömmlichen kirchlichen Arbeit haben, und zum anderen wollten wir nicht Auseinandersetzungen provozieren, ehe wir selbst Genaueres wußten. Wir hielten Konflikte für durchaus wahrscheinlich, die wir zum damaligen Zeitpunkt nicht produktiv fanden." Elke Möller, Initiativgruppen von Frauen in der Kirche. In: Lingscheid, R. Wegener, W. *Aktivierende Gemeindearbeit.* Stuttgart: Kohlhamer. 1990.

18 Flyer. Hannover: 1988. Ann Kathrin Szagun.

19 Flyer. Einladung: 1987.

20 Ibid.

21 Ibid.

22 Brochure: *Frauentag auf dem Mühlenberg in Hannover am Reformationstag 1987. Texte. Berichte.* Hannover: 1988.

23 Aktenstück Nr. 133 b der 20. Landessynode, Blatt 6.

24 Interview on December 10th. 1996.

25 Brochure published by *Landeskirchenamt*, Hannover. 3.

26 40 Jahre Frauenwerk Der Ev. Luth. Landeskirche Hannovers. Geschichte und Aufgaben. Hanover: 1981. 6.

27 Otte, Birgit. *Dekadegottesdienste: ein Konzept instituionalisierter Frauenarbeit in der Evangelisch-lutherischen. Landeskirche Hannovers.* Unpublished manuscript. Hannover: 1995.

28 40 Jahre Frauenwerk, 21.

29 Otte, Dekadegottesdienst, 9.

30 Interview vom 11.12.96.

31 Ibid.

32 Ibid.

33 Interview with I. Ganser.

34 "Die Dekade ist ein komplexes Monstrum." Interview with Ingrid Ganser.

35 Interview with I. Ganser.

36 Interview with Thea Kregel.

37 Interview with Dorothea Biermann.

38 Report. Teambesuch in Deutschland in der Mitte der Ökumenischen Dekade *Solidarität der Kirchen mit den Frauen* 1.-10. Februar 1995. 3.

39 Ibid.

40 This is visible in the work on the renewal of the book of worship: after the publication of a draft, a lot of criticism was raised against its non-inclusive language and its one sided (male) images of God. As a consequence, women were called to participate, yet often feminist prayers were rejected. Therefore, whether or not the book of worship will contain pluralist images of God remains to be seen.

41 Ibid.

42 Hieber, Astrid, Lukatis, Ingrid. *Zwischen Engagement und Enttäuschung. Frauenerfahrung in der Kirche.* Hannover: Lutherisches Verlagshaus, 1994. This study presents an analysis of about 4000 questionnaires of women who report on their experiences with the church.

43 Moltmann, Jürgen. *Kirche in der Kraft des Geistes. Ein Beitrag zur messianischen Ekklesiologie.* München: Kaiser, 1975. 363-365 Berndt, Gunda; Garms, Ilse. Scene: Cleaning Women. Unpublished manuscript. Hanover: 1996.

Eleni Kasselouri

Women and Orthodox Spirituality

Reflections

I was born and grew up in Thessaloniki, a beautiful city in Northern Greece, well-known to all of you as one of the most important places of early Christianity. The majority of the people in Greece are members of the Orthodox Church. The Orthodox tradition is strongly connected with our lives, our ideas, our own history. My family is a traditional Greek Orthodox family with an active spiritual life, and the small Church St. Constantinos and Eleni is my second home. I meditated here for about 10 minutes every day from 8-14 April, 1996, during Holy week which is a very meaningful and unique period of prayer and spirituality in the Orthodox tradition.

I came to the decision to study theology late, when I was 17, after the death of my brother Constantinos. It was this tragic event which led me to search for answers concerning the meaning of life and death, justice and discrimination, love and power, pain and fear, good and evil. Today, after the years, many of my questions are still without an answer.

As I am sitting in the small Church of St. Constantinos and Eleni, I can see all these icons of saints, women and men, around. There is a kind of 'democracy' there, where "there is no male nor female". Above all over the Altar, there is the icon of Mary, His Mother, our Mother and the Father's Mother, a dimension which is usually forgotten in the Orthodox daily practice. Mary is a symbol of love, sacrifice, power and courage. She is "the more honorable than the Cherubim and the more glorious beyond compare than the Seraphim". She is the one who "delivered Adam from sin and she gave joy to Eve instead of sadness."

Orthodox Spirituality

Orthodox spirituality is conditioned by two historical factors: *the biblical* and *the Hellenistic.* It was frequently called to give answers to questions such as: What is God, evil, sin, Grace, Salvation? Thereby it is always situated between two extremes: (1) 'nature', i.e. the timeless and the motionless, and (2) 'history', i.e. the renewed and the ever-progressing.

All the various forms of spirituality and life in the Orthodox tradition have sprung out of such a dynamic and dialectic tension, the consequences of which have, in fact, affected especially women but generally concern the whole body of the Church[1]. A prominent place in this variety of expressions of the Orthodox spirituality is held by the *monastic* and the *liturgical* expressions which were historically connected to two tendencies of Christian ecclesiology: the *therapeutic* or *cathartic* and the *eucharistic* or *liturgical*[2].

Before proceeding to a presentation and a short analysis of these trends and their effects on the life and the course of the Church[3], I consider it necessary to describe the place of Orthodox women inside the ecclesiastic community, i.e. how they participate in the life of the community, how they create circles of love, how they are developed morally and spiritually, and of course how their role, the uniqueness of their nature and the diversity of their gifts are understood.

The female element

The theology and spirituality of the Orthodox Church are strongly influenced by the baptismal confession of Gal. 3,28 "There is neither Jew nor Greek, slave nor free, male nor female". These instructions were never betrayed by the Church, at least on a theoretical level. The Church created a "Democracy of Heaven" where the doctrine was left untouched and the ideal of equality within her, as a proleptic manifesto of the Kingdom of God, unhurt. The female element is present in the spirituality of the Orthodox tradition influencing the atmosphere of worship and liturgical gathering.

The liturgical texts and, especially that of the Divine Liturgy (Eucharist), make no discrimination or depreciation whatsoever, not only between human persons, but also in regard to the whole creation. The first words after the consecration of the Holy Elements (Bread and Wine) are dedicated "exceptionally" to Theotokos, Holy Mother of God. And this is followed by the deacon's reminder that the whole community, together, is offering "the reasonable worship" on behalf and in favor of the universe and its intercession for "all males and females".

The icons of the Church, where the Divine Liturgy is held, are basic elements for people to taste the future world and the kingdom of heaven while still on earth. In this area icons of female saints are placed next to the male ones, having equal value and having as a center, over the Holy Altar, the Blessed Mary, whom the praying community praises as "one more Honorable than the Cherubim and by far more Glorious than the Seraphim".

Maria has a special place in Orthodox worship and spirituality. Completely human, she becomes the representative of the whole of humankind and of the whole human nature. Through the "maternal female element" that she represents, according to P. Evdokimov, the believer feels "a strong nostalgia of the kingdom of Heaven, long before s/he meets the priest or the bishop". The "Church of the Holy spirit", despite a clericalism that sometimes absorbs it, is full of the female presence, Theotokos[4].

Among the countless liturgical names of Maria are those which express the course to the fulfillment, to perfection. Maria is "the gate to heavens", "the gate to salvation", "a staircase to heaven", "a bridge that carries people from earth to heaven".

When the religious old lady in Dostoyevski´s novel "The Possessed" describes Maria as "watered soil" she only wants to point out the maternal element using the secular figure of the nursing earth that gives birth to new realities. And Maria, having freely and absolutely accepted her destiny by saying "May it be to me as you have said" (Luke 1,38) she becomes the watered soil that gives birth to a new world for the whole creation.

The female presence is also important in the calendar. Apart from the great number of holidays dedicated to the Theotokos, the recollection of the work and offerings of holy women are every day a point of reference for the Orthodox person, either male or female. What is more, although the New Testament does not mention, at least not explicitly, the existence of a female apostle, the Orthodox Church perceives a number of women as "equal to the apostles" including Mary Magdalene, Thekla, Helen, the mother of emperor Constantine, and Nina, the missionary and matron saint of Georgia.

If we also examine the practical side of the expression of spirituality in the community, we must mention two institutions that have strongly influenced the church's life, at least while they were valid. These are the institution of the deaconess and of the "spiritual motherhood".

The institution of the deaconess was very important, as we gather from our sources in the life of the Church during the first centuries. From the 9th-10th century its importance was diminished until it became just a title of honor, whereas in the 12th century it was driven to complete elimination. The question of re-establishing this institution has already been asked in modern Orthodox discussions. We do not talk, of course, about a formal re-establishing but about a creative restoration which will be in accordance with the needs and the new state of the Church[5].

"Spiritual motherhood" is a term that basically describes the ministerial duty of spiritual guidance and is mainly connected with the gift to intercede and to prophesy, gifts that are considered feminine by nature. Until now, of course, in Orthodoxy we mainly spoke about spiritual "fathers", the well-known *starets* of the Russian Orthodox spiritualism. But the history of the Church confirms the existence of women who were responsible for spiritual guidance. In "Gerontikon" there are references to three mothers. Besides, the first collection of maternal words, the so-called "Miterikon", was published in 1200 AD The written material of the tradition and history of the Church, especially those of the monastic life, is very rich in this kind of references[6].

Facing the richness of spiritual life and of theology, one is very sad to witness the survival - due to inertia rather than a strong belief based on faith - of ceremonies, widespread customs and prohibitions that created discriminations against women, that darken the spirituality of the Church and are traumatic or inconceivable not only to women but also to the younger members. We refer to the exclusion of women in certain periods of their biological cycle and after childbirth - which on the contrary is considered a blessing - from participating in the mysteries, and the prohibition to enter the Altar, behind the iconostasis - a prohibition extended even to the new-born girl. We also refer to the exclusion of women from the act of worship, e.g. their participation in the sermon. And of course it remains very difficult, especially within the ecumenical framework, the problem of non-acceptance of women to the priesthood, something which could mean that they could even reach the rank of the Bishop.

Nowadays a theological reflection on those matters is indispensable and Orthodox women have the right and duty to participate in it[7]. Living in a European and global community which search for a new perspective and unity, Orthodox women are called to make their own choices and give their witness[8].

If we leave out the women of Diaspora who embrace the Orthodox tradition consciously and in mature age, most Orthodox women are brought up in societies with a culture deeply influenced by the Orthodox tradition. This fact makes the formation of an Orthodox ethos easier, but at the same time it includes the danger of the emaciation of the faith. So, instead of a free, conscious and continuous participation in the eucharistic community and spirituality, many women are driven in a fossilized faith, full of fear, fanaticism and old-fashioned views.

On the very opposite side, however, there are women who accept and respect the influence of Orthodoxy on their cultural identity but in practice are indifferent on the Orthodox way of life, witness and spirituality.

The lack of knowledge and education, correct spiritual guidance, deep and profound understanding of the liturgical texts and substantial pastoral function is the main reason for the above situations. There is also a lack of understanding of the very essence of the "Church" and a human disability to realize the mystery of spiritual experience and piety and to adapt it to a new situation. In addition, the Church "has exploited" women in practice for centuries[9]. In other words, women are given only secondary, i.e. of practical significance, jobs (cleaning, preparation of the celebration etc.), which might have their importance but in general exclude them from the decision-making process.

Nevertheless, the presence of a great number of Orthodox women, who are graduates of theology and other fields of advanced study, and who struggle to witness their eucharistic / ecclesial identity and proclaim the real message of the Gospel participating creatively in the spiritual life of the Church, creates a new reality; this is the optimistic and positive side of the current situation. The zeal, the faith and the dedication of many of these women could effectively contribute to the renewal of parish life and Church life as a whole, especially if greater attention were paid to them, and if their charismatic and theological ability in their work of teaching, in their ministry, and in their pastoral care for people would be supported sufficiently and encouraged by the leadership of the Church.

At this point, we must refer to the progress made in the field of studies about the role of women in the Orthodox tradition.[10] The problem of full and creative participation of women in the social and spiritual life of the Church is no longer something "external" but has started to become an "internal" issue. This "internalization" has more the meaning of the revision of ideas and experiences and opening up forgotten prospects and horizons of the Orthodox tradition. [11] However, a situation and a way of life and thought cultivated systematically for centuries does not change easily. Fortunately, this situation is no longer an insurmountable obstacle for those who fight to establish a new reality and way of participation in the Church with the purpose of making her the authentic community of all sons and daughters of God.

In order to give a fair explanation of the above situation, one has to bear in mind the sort of ecclesiology and spirituality that developed in the Orthodox East. Imposed by historical factors it allowed the beginning and development of such ideas, prohibitions, exclusions and practices.

Eucharistic or liturgical spirituality

The understanding of Orthodox spirituality does not only depend on the various trends, but also on the connection they might have with the historical reality and the situation in which they were born. That is, what we call Orthodox spirituality is not simply the outcome of an established ecclesiastical way of life, but very often a conscious or unconscious dialectical tension between expressions of spiritual life and the completely opposite worlds that they usually represent.

In our introduction we referred to the two basic trends, the short analysis of which might give us an explanation of the woman's place in the life and spiritual expression of the Orthodox Church today, which although on its theoretical level and theology retains all authentic elements, expresses the baptismal confession of Gal. 3,28, as well as the model of the community of the inner dynamic of the persons of the Holy Trinity. Some of these elements in every day life, if they are not totally abolished, have become weakened.

The eucharistic or liturgical spirituality, basically biblical and connected with the messianic beliefs of Judaism, comes as a result of the conscious understanding of the eschatological identity of the Church.

The Church is understood as the new Israel, the Royal priesthood, the holy nation of God during the last days, eschata. It experiences, after the Resurrection of Christ and especially after Pentecost, the eschata every time it assembles "to it", mainly that is to celebrate the Eucharist. Its members are invited to holiness, not as individuals but as collective reality. The spirituality, which is the outcome of such an understanding of the Church, has a *dynamic, radical* and *collective* character. In it, a pyramid-shaped structure of the ministerial duties does not make any sense, but instead a unanimous participation of all the people is shown through a conciliarity at all levels (sobornost). Every self-centered or individualistic idea is by definition incompatible since the community and the relational character comes first. A natural consequence of this situation is the active presence of the female and the enrichment of the life of the community with the special talents and characteristics bestowed on women. Inside this community "all the people are ministers" [12].

Since the third century AD, mainly under strong pressure exercised by Christian gnosticism and platonism, a new content has been given to ecclesiology and further more to spirituality, first by the Alexandrine School of Catechism, which is considered by modern Orthodox researchers not only "as a change but as an overthrow" and is called *therapeutic or cathartic*[13].

The Church is no longer an image of the eschata but of the beginning. The original state of things is described as perfect and what follows it as a kind of fall. The importance of the incarnation in this system is considered to be very little, while its difference and deviation from the biblical eschatology is a basic characteristic. Therefore, it ceases to be a historical reality and becomes a sort of a primordial idea which functions more as a sanatorium ("θεραπευτηριο") of souls. This spirituality is connected with monasticism chronologically and historically.

The consequences of such a spirituality can be well-understood. The worship in the Church, the ministerial duties and its institutions, lost their importance as images of the future things. What becomes prominent is a self-centered sort of salvation, where the soul tries hard to return to the state it had before the Fall. The "come, Lord" and "μαρανα θα" of the first Christian communities is replaced by the unceasing prayer and the struggle with the demons of the flesh. Even the understanding of the central point of the spriritual life of the Church, the Eucharist, was somehow affected. From a collective procedure it soon becomes soon an expression of individual worship and salvation, and a symbolic act of union with and dedication to God. The pyramid-shape construction of the body of the Church separates people into those who are more perfect spiritually and those who are inferior, creating relations of subjection and dependence, while the continuous struggle for liberation from the passions of the flesh leads to the formulation of theories which have nothing to do with the original meaning of the Gospel. Women, naturally, have started being considered a source of evil and the unclean, views that are usually found and derived from the Old Testament, before the coming of Christ. Thus the need for a continuous expiation, which of course means a marginalization of women, is more and more stressed. Fields in which they could develop their talents successfully and to the benefit of the whole Church, due to those beliefs, are excluded. It is, of course, to be admitted that in more recent years most of those rules and prohibitions are flexible or obsolete. But their formulation and even more, their official preservation are still an expression of a spirituality which often causes bitterness, sadness and confusion for the largest part of the members of the Church. All these are the result of the widespread idea that therapeutic spirituality is *the only* authentic expression and definition of the Orthodox tradition.

However, the truth lies at the opposite side. The theology of Orthodox spirituality is based, perhaps exclusively on the eucharistic/ liturgical ecclesiology[14]. And it is obvious by the fact that the identity of the Church has a social and not self-centered character, which is connected and derived from the One Trinitarian God, who is unity and plurality at once, the One and the many. The Orthodox community has as its model and prototype our Triune God, and as a result the relationships between the members of this community to be clear, vivid and blessed by the Holy Spirit, i.e. charismatic, just like those between the persons of the Holy Trinity. In this framework the idea of ecclesial consciousness and ecclesial morale is more clearly understandable. It is neither about the morale of an individual A or B but it is about the experience of the acts of the Holy Spirit through the charisma bestowed on all baptized members of the Church. If this is missing for some reason, then the Church becomes a hierarchical body fossilized into external power, and it acquires the characteristics of a secular society that is dominated by the idea and logic of the power, unfortunately losing the sense of being a community, the Body of Christ. Additionally, tradition must not be imposed from outside but consists inside of the Church, as we ought to live ethically in order to teach correctly and not the other way around[15].

Therefore, every sort of authentic spirituality, even monasticism, the most venerated among Orthodox, must exist according to the ecclesial / eucharistic criterion in order to be authentic. That is to be able to be determined as a spiritual state of an authentic community. These views, which more and more are adhered to in the Orthodox world, are perhaps the only way-out to a renewal in Orthodox spirituality which is so necessary and important for all the members of the Church, men and women.

Conclusion

Nowadays, since our world needs "unity" and "community" as much as ever before, the *eucharistic/liturgical* criterion acquires a special meaning and significance. In the multiplicity of the creation, the recognition of the special characteristics of women has as a result their full and free participation in the economy of the salvation. The Eve of theology is the woman of history; with her special characteristics she can help humanity not only to be raised spiritually but also to reconcile: "in order to be brought to the complete unity" (John 17,23).

Notes

1 See S. Agouridis "History and Orthodox Spirituality", Theology and Opportuneness, (in Greek), 1996, p.p. 39-48, esp. 40

2 See P. Vassiliadis, "Eucharistic and Therapeutic Spirituality", Lex Orandi, (in Greek), 1994, p.107

3 The term "Church" is used with its theological meaning i.e. the community of people of God and not with its institutional meaning

4 For more information see Evangelos Theodorou, Le Feminism des textes liturgiques Orthodoxes, La mere de Jesus-Christ et la Communion des Saints dans la Liturgie, Conferences Saint Serge, XXXII Semaine d´Etudes Liturgiques, Paris, 1985, Edizione Liturgiche, Roma 1986, pp. 267-281

5 P. Evdokimov, La Femme e le Salut du Monde, Etude d´Anthropologie chretienne sur le charisme de la Femme, 1958, pp. 320-329

6 See Kyriaki Karidoyanes-Fitzgerald, "The characteristics and nature of the Order of the Deaconess" Women and the priesthood, ed. Thomas Hopko, 1983, pp. 75-95. Also Evangelos Theodorou, "The Ministry of the Deaconess in the Greek Orthodox Church" The Deaconess, World Council of Churches, 1966, p. 29

7 A few efforts of such importance are made under the initiative of the Orthodox Churches or the World Council of Churches. We will characteristically refer to Convention at the Monastery Agapia in Rumania (1976), at Rhodes (1988), at Orthodox Academy of Crete (1990) . All of them emphasized the necessity, significance and importance of a more creative and active participation of women in the worship.

8 See d. Koukoura "The Role of Orthodox Women in Modern Secular Society" Kath´Odon 9 (in Greek), 1994, pp. 37-45

9 The 25th conclusion of the Inter-Orthodox Symposium in Rhodos points out and admits this reality while recognizing these facts, which witness to the promotion through the Church of the equality of honor between men and women, it is necessary to confess in honesty and with humility that owing to human weakness and sinfulness, the Christian communities have not always and in all places been able to suppress effectively ideas, manners, customs, historical developments and social conditions which have resulted in practical discrimination against women. This may be the most important and sincere conclusion of the conference and a good point for reflection. See Genadios Limouris (ed.), The Place of the Woman in the Orthodox Church and the Question of the Ordination of Women, Tertios Publications, 1992, p.29

10 Especially in the Theological Faculty of the University of Thessaloniki, there are some courses about the recent research and reflection of feminist theology. Additionally, there is a great number of young women theologians who are writing their dissertations in this field.

11 See Eva Adamziloglou, Is Feminist Theology possible in the Greek Othodox Tradition? In: ESWTR-Yearbook, Vol. 4 (1996), p.18-27.

12 See N. Lossky Femmes et hommes dans l' Eglise which is an Orthodox approach of the issue of ministerial duties, an announcement at the Conference of the Section Faith and Order at Lima (1982), at S.O.P. Appendix No 66

13 See J. Zizioulas, Issues of Ecclesiology, (in Greek), 1991, p.28

14 A further analysis of the two trends, their consequences as well as their authenticity as a genuine expression of their Orthodox spirituality in the articles of p. Vassiliadis, "Eucharistic and Therapeutic Spirituality" as above (in Greek) and "La pneumatolgia ortodossa e la conteplazione", Vedere Dio, Incontro tra Oriente e Occidente, EDB Bologna 1994, pp. 83-97

15 See N. Matsoukas, Dogmatic and Symbolic Theology, (in Greek) vol. II, 1988, p.435

Susan Roll

When From Our Exile:
A Woman Between Two Continents

By the rivers of Babylon
there we sat and wept,
remembering Zion;
on the poplars that grew there,
we hung up our harps.

For it was there that they asked us,
our captors, for songs,
our oppressors, for joy.
"Sing to us," they said,
"One of Zion's songs."

O how could we sing
the song of Godde
on alien soil?[1]

Exile is a state of unhealed fracture: a perpetual flat note, a sour chord. Exile is a fragmented, disjointed, raw-edged existence.

Exile can be internal as well as external. External exile might refer to a physical or geographical distance from an environment in which one "fits" comfortably, an environment in which one feels at home, whether that might be a matter of national boundaries, culture, language, or simply familiarity with the setting. One could speak of exile from one's homeland to a foreign land; exile from one's home culture to a foreign culture; exile from one's house, flat or room to another residence; exile from one's family or from one's network of close relationships. Exile tends to imply a potentially transitional state of affairs in which one is not where one wishes to be, but will return at some hoped-for point in the future. Yet exile might not have been forcibly imposed by circumstances beyond one's control; it could also have been freely chosen, perhaps temporarily, perhaps permanently.

Internal exile, on the other hand, can almost be said to form one aspect of the spiritual tradition of Europe, and most certainly of women. Internal exile is the insidious awareness of disjunction or alienation from oneself or within oneself. The raw edges rasp against each other in one's own being. And because it is in the nature of a dualistic bipolar split to shift either to one side or the other, never remaining value-neutral, one pole or the other will be experienced as the disjunct one, the one which is preventing integration, healing and wholeness. This could result in what feminist analysis has come to call "colonization of consciousness" : instead of identifying one's own ideas, thoughts and experience, one thinks and feels what one has been conditioned to think and feel. One might live with a sort of double-consciousness, a simultaneous awareness of being both subject and object, a consciousness turned back double upon itself. What others say about oneself exerts hegemony over what oneself might say, and this false consciousness shapes (or misshapes) one's own perception. Not only dualistic but multiple disjunction might occur: one exists in several environments, none of which is "home."

But this is all very abstract: what is personal is not only political (another dictum of feminist analysis), but considerably more colorful, immediate and interesting. The present writer returned to the United States in June 1995 after ten years in Belgium, spent in attaining a doctorate in liturgy as well as pursuing research and teaching in the faculty of theology of the major Flemish Catholic university. The position in Belgium had finished and so had my visa, but fortunately there was a job offer at a Catholic diocesan seminary in the United States which started right when the Belgian position finished.

I am in fact an American citizen. So why does this feel like a particularly difficult and difficult-to-explain form of exile? Every day I struggle to keep the pain, mourning and resentment at bay. There is a paradoxical sense that I really should be grateful for where I am and what I have today: a full-time academic teaching position in my own field at graduate level, in a small friendly institution with a good supportive atmosphere, a reasonable teaching load, summers free, living in a cozy flat in a lovely village and driving my familiar old car, living not far from my family of origin in a region I know from childhood, speaking my native language every day.... I should fit. But I don't. Day by day, minute by minute, I have to work at belonging here. And the raw edges grate.

Europe is in my bones. That did not just happen during the ten years in Belgium; I had made four trips including two lengthy stays before I began graduate theology studies in 1985, and Europe has been in my bones a very long time. When I packed up my Belgian life in twenty-four boxes and had it shipped to the United States, a whole depth-dimension dropped out of my being. I had lived in an environment with much deeper roots in a rich cultural past. In the park or along the street I could walk up and run my hand over old stones which formed part of a wall from the 16th century, or the 12th century, or the 3rd century, and know that I was linked with generations and generations of persons who passed by these same walls. As a Christian I was living much nearer to the deep roots of the original historical context of the church, and my spirit was nourished by this nearness.

Moreover there was daily fascination, excitement and challenge in the cultural and linguistic "surfing" I had to do. I shifted back and forth continually from English to Flemish, and into French or German when necessary, not terribly fluently at times but with a vibrant sense of participation and connectedness to a great richness of communication patterns and ways of thought and expression. I learned to adopt complete sets of social graces appropriate to different European cultures, not like a chameleon but as a personal challenge to grow and expand my horizons. I joyously (most of the time!) welcomed other persons quite different from me into my life, and was in turn generously welcomed into theirs.

Even among the sizable community of foreign students, visiting professors and their family members in Leuven, a complex and dynamic sort of community was formed in which practically everyone fit, precisely because no one fit. We were often strikingly different from each other in our history, talents, educational background, age, profession, gender and (particularly pertinent in a theology school) our approach to church and to spiritual roots. We learned to cherish each other's uniqueness as a gift, and to modify our stereotypes.

An enormous analogy can be made to the historical experience of Christian women, foreigners in the formal structural tradition of the church, inside-outsiders who are supposed to fit, or pretend to fit, and yet do not. On the surface we "should" fit in the patriarchal tradition: after all, Christ came to save all "men." We should be happy and grateful for the generations of spiritual riches that we do have, and in fact there *is* much to be grateful for: women mystics and poets, or women of wisdom we have personally known, for example.

But the emerging consciousness of women points to deep underlying flaws shooting through the entire fabric of "the" Christian tradition. The entire official version of our tradition has been built upon androcentrism, or male-normativity: the unspoken assumption that what is male is normatively human. Women's consciousness has been colonized such that we have tended to think what we were taught to think, in flat two-dimensional linguistic categories disconnected from the complexity beneath. One result has been the classic reduction of our identity to sex-roles defined from outside ourselves, either "mother" or "virgin."

At present women are less and less inclined to work hard at "belonging here." Some feminist thinkers have spoken of "the culture of women" to point to the place women occupy on the invisible underside of national or ethnic cultures. This culture of women, in all its rich variation, has had up to now no history or language of its own. Yet in a sense, as women, "all of us fit because none of us fit," and this outsider-culture potentially links us to ages of wise, faith-full women.[2] Paradoxically, the more we claim our history and the more we learn a new language and speak it, the greater the overt misogyny, the threats of rape or abuse, and aggressive attempts to marginalize and silence us. Sometimes it seems we are more in exile than ever.

> *Als God ons thuisbrengt, uit onze ballingschap,*
> *dat zal een droom zijn.*
> *Als God ons thuisbrengt, uit onze ballingschap,*
> *dat zal een droom zijn.*[3]

The old stones of the Beguinage in Leuven testify to the ingenuity of women to create a space of safety and dignity within a historical period and a social environment which offered women neither. Each little home has a little garden, there are grassy common areas, and a disproportionately large baroque church dominates one side of the complex. The paving stones of the walkways jut upward from their sand foundation: biking is bumpy and walking hazardous for those with light shoes or unsteady stride. Yet generations of uncommonly determined women made a living and a life within the stone bounds of this community.

> Beguines—lay women pledged to poverty, chastity, manual labor and communal worship lived in all-female, self-governing communities. In addition to the spiritual reasons... there were also economic reasons for the spread of this movement in certain regions. There was in the 12th and 13th centuries a surplus of females in the population, which made many women unmarriageable. It did not require a dowry to join a beguinage, as it did to join a convent, and this fact may, according to some historians, explain the rapid spread of the Beguine movement. Beguine communities not only offered sanctuary and a new lifestyle to single women, they also promoted the reading of the Bible in the vernacular, which increased the potential

for unschooled women to express themselves religiously. ...several Beguines became celebrated mystics.[4]

For women, living within patriarchy is an exilic nexus, a perpetual alien existence. There are ways to do it, however, which potentially transform exile-within-the-environment into a supportive, educative, even mystically illuminative state.

Cherchez la Sagesse, puisq'elle se laisse trouver,
Invoquez-la, puisq'elle est proche.
Que les méchants renoncent á leur conduite,
Et les pécheurs á ses projets.
Qu'elles reviennent á la Sagesse qui en aura pitié,
Et á nôtre Dieu qui pardonne généreusement.
Car mes pensées ne sont pas les vôtres,
Et vos façons d'agir ne sont pas les miennes,
dit la Sagesse.
Mais autant le ciel est plus haut que la terre,
Autant ma conduite est supérieure á la vôtre,
Et mes pensées surpassent les vôtres.[5]

While on retreat at a women's monastery in the Ardennes, I discovered a version of Isaiah 55 which uses "la Sagesse," wisdom, instead of "le Seigneur." When read this way the entire passage is suddenly transformed into a richer, more profound, more cohesive vision. Wisdom here is a quality with an existence of its own, apart from wise persons. This Wisdom feels emotion and is moved with compassion; she invites and allows intimacy; she is infinitely transcendent yet cannot be identified with the distant dominative transcendence of the traditional Father-God. Wisdom both permeates and hovers beyond our own limited minds and often petty spirits. When I read this familiar passage substituting "la Sagesse," I feel safe.

Women living in particular situations in which we do not feel safe, whether from violent abuse, verbal belittling, the emotional instability of an active alcoholic or addict, or any form of intimidation or manipulation, might resort to a range of coping mechanisms. In denial we might block out the painful reality, refusing to see what we see or to hear what we hear. In obsession we might struggle within the vivid fantasies we compulsively create, to vent our rage, to punish the aggressor, or to change the aggressor with just the right words. We might project blame everywhere, on anyone or any circumstance, just to have a focus; and if we can blame ourselves, we might somehow hope for the power to change a chaotic situation into something manageable. When we rationalize, we can make senselessness seem to make sense. When we can stay mentally busy, we don't hear the hollow echoes.

All of these are forms of mental exile to escape a dangerous and threatening environment, and to anesthetize the pain. We risk losing touch with the taproot of reality buried in our psyches in order to survive. We block our inbuilt capacity for discernment and obscure the inner voice of wisdom. When I try to force myself to believe things which I sense are not true, I divide my own consciousness and numb the subtle workings of wisdom. I have at different times in my life bent my mind inside out to force myself to see what I was under pressure to "see," and so to resolve the pain and ambiguity and guilt. Instead of returning I tried to deny exile by visualizing and projecting a false "homeland." But I never fit there either.

One lets go of denial only when one is strong enough, strong enough to act and think with courage. Courage can mean to live with awareness, in two or several realities at once: one's authentic lived reality, and the structured imposed "reality" outside oneself which does not grant credibility to that experience. Courage means that I can at least tell the difference, whether or not it is safe to speak it. Courage can mean actively choosing one's options from among several, living no longer as a victim or a marionette, but continually measuring the conditions and the possibilities. One can accept exile temporarily, for a greater good, or to protect oneself until one is strong enough, with faith that when the time is right, a way will clear.

> Conduct yourselves reverently during your sojourn in a strange land.
>
> Realize that you were delivered from the futile way of life your fathers handed on to you...[6]

As a lay woman professor of liturgy in a Catholic seminary, this is what I try to do: to live reverently, in a strange land. Just *to be*, here, is a sign of contradiction. When my appointment was announced but before I arrived, seminarians were heard to declare with outrage that they would *never* take a course from a lay woman. Well, they all have me for Liturgy in their first year and Sacraments of Healing in their fourth. I train seminarians in effective proclamation of the scripture readings, and work hard to help them overcome their resistance to using inclusive language. I have spent hours with a few who are upset by women's liturgy. I participate in the canonical vote with the other professors to determine whether each candidate will be recommended for ordination. I *am*, here.

As a child I loved liturgy. I sang in the children's choir directed by my aunt, accompanied on the organ by my uncle, from the age of eight. I grew up in liturgical vestments, close to the altar. As a university chaplain I found liturgy planning was my favorite part of the job. Yet just as I live now, moment by moment, in sharp exile from the deep roots of history and culture which anchored my life in Europe, so do I live in exile from myself as female, every moment I spend in worship and prayer with male texts, patriarchal formulations, or clerically-centered liturgy. Each year it becomes harder for me to sit through the liturgy of the Easter Vigil, as I perform a running hermeneutic on the texts and the symbolic configurations, uncovering different levels of the subliminally sexualized, "woman-unfriendly" substructure of this liturgy. Every insight strikes me with the force of a body blow delivered as if by violent physical abuse. Is my presence at the Vigil, teeth gritted, witnessing to a contradictory truth, or does my presence rather suggest that I am willingly participating in collective denial?

On the third Sunday of Easter, in cycle A of the readings, we hear the wonderfully, wickedly subversive text, "Realize that you were delivered from the futile way of life your fathers handed on to you..." Through mutual support among women, feminist theological methodology, a thoroughgoing hermeneutics, and listening attentively to the authentic voice of wisdom, I struggle to believe that I am indeed delivered. I fall into step as one of many travelers on a journey of freedom from the futility handed on by our fathers.

Just to *be*, in the words of A. J. Heschel, is a blessing. Just to be, as an authentic person who stands serenely in her own light, implies, if not reconciliation of alienated opposites, at least holding them in creative dynamic tension. To be is to be journeying, to be is to construct a provisional home in transit. The return from exile, however longed-for, is not an endpoint, but a phase in the journey.

Notes

1 Psalm 137, verses 1-3; The Grail (England), The Psalms. An inclusive language version based on the Grail translation from the Hebrew (Chicago: G.I.A. Publications, 1983): 200. The present author's interpolation of "Godde" reflects a usage growing among feminists involved in the spiritual.

2 The question of whether women can be said to form a distinctive culture is important for the development of what is meant by inculturation of the gospel, as well as that of the liturgy. To speak of "a" culture in this sense should not imply a universalizing paradigm, but rather the coming-to-voice of a heretofore unrecognized culture comprised of a multiplicity of voices. See Cobi Van Breukelen, "Vrouwvriendelijke liturgie in de rooms-katholieke kerk," Tijdschrift voor Liturgie 76 (1992): 184, and Teresa Berger, "The Women's Movement as a Liturgical Movement: a Form of Inculturation?" Studia Liturgica 20/1 (1990): 56-59.

3 "When from our exile God leads us home again, we'll think we're dreaming..." Text based on Psalm 126 by Huub Oosterhuis (trans. Redmond McGoldrick), © 1974, TEAM Publications.

4 Gerda Lerner, The Creation of Feminist Consciousness, (New York and Oxford: Oxford University Press, 1993): 77.

5 Isaiah 55: 6-9.

6 I Peter 1:17b-18a; New American Bible, Lectionary for Mass (New York: Catholic Book Publishing Company, 1970): 109 and 1096.

Anne Hunt Overzee

Shadow Play

Here in the Scottish Borders we have a respite between snow and more snow. The mild January weather is both a blessing and a curse; it brings a foretaste of spring and also a epidemic of 'flu'.

It is this inherent ambivalence that renders the natural elements particularly valuable resources for coming to know myself, my environment, and Christ. They provide me with a vehicle for perceiving the inter-relationships I sense that there are between them. And they teach me not to underestimate the importance of difference of perspective and the art of creating balance. All these things I test out in my work as a contemplative psychotherapist working with myself and others in the context of a structured relationship.

I have an instinctive preference for ordinary, tangible learning tools and when in the 1970's I discovered Hindus and Tibetan Buddhists in India using the natural elements of earth, water, air, fire and space[1] as reference points in transformation meditation and ritual practices, I decided to study and experiment for myself. Later on in my life when I was researching Teilhard de Chardin's descriptions of his view of the relationship between Christ and the earth, and his reference to Christ as *l'Elément universel*[2], I was inspired to begin to re-vision Christ in terms of these eastern models of relationship. In the process I realised that what many eastern 'pictures' of the divine include that I missed is precisely this ambivalence. In addition, I missed the sensuousness of many such descriptions which balances the emphasis in certain meditation traditions on apophatic language, and a resistance to focus on images in favour of present sense-based experience.

Where I live now, in a remote Scottish Borders valley, the natural elements have assumed a compelling place in my daily life. In the winter, for example, my day revolves around the fire, hot food and persuading my car to start (there's no public transport) to take me to work along often treacherous narrow roads. I think this grounds me, and it certainly makes me aware of the very real dangers as well as benefits of certain weather conditions.

Recently, when re-reading some early Celtic Christian texts, stories of the lives of the first known missionaries in northern Britain, I found myself making an imaginative connection with these early pioneers who were for ever challenged by storms and winds. Record has it that St.

Cuthbert was able to master the elements as well as communicate with wild animals.[3] Such mastery reminds me of eastern notions of creating balance within oneself and in one's relationships as an expression of wholeness. More recent Scottish material, in the form of chants and prayers from the Highlands and Islands, the *Carmina Gadelica*, witnesses to a similar concern with the elements. Invocations and popular Catholic songs refer to a worldview which is simultaneously fearful and superstitious as well as being deeply optimistic about the potential for Christ consciousness - as I would call it - in nature and everyday objects.

In what follows I describe something of my recent explorations in connecting the elements with my understanding of Christ, and I go on to outline several contexts for the work which seem important as reference points going forward.

Groundwork

Since 1993 Caroline Mackenzie, an artist and friend, and I have been travelling to each other's homes to meet and work together regularly. In between meetings we have been developing the themes arising from the work on our own. The overall intention has been to enquire into our experience of the elements as women, and how this enquiry affects our sense and vision of the divine. In practice, this has been an immensely challenging and enriching experience for both of us. What I shall say about it is of course my own reflection on the work and represents an opportunity to locate it in relation to the European Society of Women in Theological Research (ESWTR) which served to inspire our project in the first place.[4]

For the first year Caroline and I chose to focus on one of the natural elements each time we met. By that I mean we took earth, water, fire, air and space as the subjects for our enquiry. Every two months we met in one of our homes. We evolved a particular structure which became the basis of a two or three day retreat. Some of the main aspects of the practice as a whole included the following: locating the element in our immediate environment and meditating on it; an imaginative exploration of the element using sound and artwork; and developing both contemplative and ritual practices which enable us to connect our experience, and the personal 'stories' that emerged to contextualize this , with our devotion to Christ and our wider communities.

The succeeding two years have involved depending this practice and focusing on the elements in relationship with one another. Having spent two months of the first year exploring one element (on a personal

Fig. 1. *Fire and Water in Opposition*
Fig. 2. *Water's Boundary*

daily basis as well as when we met together) we were ready to allow contrasting elements to 'meet' one another. This took the form of evolving a structured way of selecting two elements for each meeting and taking it in turns to represent each one. We designed a way of bringing he two together in a very direct way by dressing in masks and costumes and improvising a coming together - or not, as the case sometimes was! A dialogue was opened up which proved to be very powerful. And the one particular meeting of elements which touched us both most was of 'fire' and 'water'. We had known that astrologically we were connected with water and fire signs individually, but had not foreseen the impact of enacting our own relationship in this way.

At the time we both found that our own relationship to each element created a sense of 'shape' to our individual identity, and to how we are in relationship with each other. For example, when I was 'fire' (dressed in my own or Caroline's fire mask and costume) I connected with fiery aspects of myself and related to Caroline as 'water' from those aspects as they emerged at that time. What proved to be so powerful for us both was the experience of wearing each others masks, playing in them, and perceiving aspects of ourselves in the other. We tended to project onto the other what we did not like or value in ourselves, and then found it very difficult to relate to those qualities. We experienced the ritualised mask-play as healing to the extent that we were able to embody for each other as well as ourselves qualities we reject (in ourselves and others); having a kinaesthetic sense of being in a particular mask and costume really helped us identify different 'elements' in each other's make-up. The strangest experience was to see the shape of ourselves, the shape we rarely glimpse or allow, standing or dancing before us. The shadows of our experience took on flesh and blood as we met our hidden self in the other.

We allowed these meetings to conflate with rituals and periods of silence which held Christ more centrally in focus. There was a mutuality of influence, between the rituals which had the more inter-personal structure to those which focused on our relationship with Christ. We began to perceive one through the filter of the other; our language and understandings in one context ran over into the other. Holding both was the underlying experience and symbolism of the element:

You have come from water
In your mother's womb

Your body is made of water
Water is life

Fig. 3. *Water baptising or cooling Fire*

Will you receive your passionate water nature?
Will you receive your frozen fear nature?

Will you receive your water nature
which sparkles with Christ's life and consciousness? ... [5]

As we developed the work our relief grew at connecting up in a very direct and tangible way our sense of who we are with Christ and our daily experience. We began to realise that our enquiry was providing us with a vehicle for 'remembering' in the sense of 'putting things together' the often disparate and separate aspects of our lives. Christ took on different 'shapes' and 'colours' as we viewed Her or Him[6] from the perspective of earth, for example, or fire. When working on water, Caroline's blue costume and mask reminded us of an earlier painting she had done, *Calming the Storm*, in which Christ is depicted as a dancing blue Indian woman. We began to allow these new shapes of Christ to emerge, using images as icons for meditation. The potency of this cross-fertilisation of perspectives had an effect of changing and confusing long-held reference points in our sense of who and what we and Christ are.

Contexts

My everyday work as a psychotherapist is one of the main contexts for my research and reflection. And if 'spirituality' is not about a life that is 'other' but rather about the whole of life at depth[7], then my work is fundamental in its ongoing challenge to me to deepen, to meet and acknowledge what arises through and in relationship.

The form of psychotherapy I practice, Core Process Psychotherapy, is based on a deep understanding of human personality process and human potential which draws mainly on Buddhist psychology and awareness practice. The frame of reference underpinning what is viewed as a joint awareness and healing process between therapist and client, includes the assumption that it is possible to develop at the core of human experience. I have found that through bringing this awareness to the ways in which we hold the shape of our past experience in the present moment, possibilities for change can arise. Such a perspective supports an intention to reverse what could be called an 'endarkenment' process, in the sense that our ongoing de-selection of attitudes, feelings, sensations, - moving into relationships, actions and thoughts - as being unacceptable or unwanted, is gradually revealed as we bring attention to the moment to moment process of being in relationship with another, and with ourselves. In this context, an enquiry into who and what we are keeps coming back to relationship: we live in a relational world of experience which we are more or less aware of, depending on how 'in touch' or in contact we are with what is happening. A sense of solid or substantial 'self', which in many cases is a healthy state of affairs, is not the whole picture as it unfolds within such a joint enquiry. Sometimes we find that we have come to believe that what we have selected as acceptable and wanted in our experience is actually who or what we are. (And we defend this belief to the hilt, even perceiving the world in relationship to it). In Buddhist psychology it is precisely this self-identification, based on attachments (what we've selected) and aversions (what we've de-selected) which is understood to lead to pain and suffering in our experience, as we remain fixed in our self position and expect the world to move and change around us. Healing then, involves deepening into a sense of self which is both bounded and open, separate and in relationship.

I suppose it is the power of such a joint practice which has both inspired and challenged me so much during the last ten years, since I formally completed my doctoral studies in comparative theology[8]. It has provided me with a ground from which to come back to my earlier faith formulations and perspectives. Any theological reflecting I do now, needs to be contextualised within my psychotherapy practice, which is at root, a contemplative practice[9]. And my sense of Christ has been questioned, stretched, and revised as the last years have passed. Above all things, I return to the notion of person as elements in relationship, and Christ too as in some sense comprising relationship.

In agreement with the idea of faith being the substance of things hoped for, there are Tibetan Buddhist practices which, translated into certain forms of psychotherapy[10] involve uncovering what is termed 'brilliant sanity'. Any notion of substantial 'essence' is here viewed rather in terms of inter-relationships between given aspects or constituent 'elements' of who and what we are. Each 'family' or elemental form is characterised by qualities, and related to specific colours, shapes and psychological or emotional dispositions. To use an example from the elements I referred to earlier, the water 'family' is associated with one aspect of our fundamental 'brilliantly sane' and wise nature which is mirror - like and of essential clarity. This quality is connected with the colour blue, with a narrow shape, and with the emotional energy of anger. Fire, on the other hand, is associated with a discriminating aspect of wisdom, with compassion - or aggression, - and with the colour red. In two forms of psychotherapy based on teachings from the Vajrayana traditions of the Kagyü and Nyingma lineages[11], the trainings of psychotherapists involve very specific practices of viewing oneself, others, and the universe in these elemental and relational terms. Also, of course, in terms of parts in relation to the whole.

One of the features that I take with me from this approach is the assumption that there is an unconditional health or wholeness in every moment, every emotion or person - even if (and especially if) I cannot see it. There is here a holding together of the powers for 'good' and 'bad'. An emotional energy like anger, for example, can both be destructive and a form of wisdom. What we do with the energy is the crucial thing. These days I am reminded of Teilhard de Chardin's elemental view of Christ and the cosmos and wonder whether viewing Christ in this way would allow for the holding together of both 'light' and 'dark', a destructive as well as creative potential.

Also, there is a connection for me between the feminist concept of 'hearing into speech', described by Anne Primavesi in her article, "A Tide in the Affairs of Women"[12] and the psychotherapeutic function of listening to another with my whole being - which in Core Process terms means with all the senses, with my body as well as at subtle energetic levels , with my cognitive mind but above all with the 'big mind' - the heart. The roots of any epistemological theory are, in this context, to be found in this seemingly subjective practice of 'knowing in relationship'. I say 'seemingly' because as any meditator will tell you, the more you listen in depth to your own experience, the more you gradually meet with transparency and resonance, which confuses the conception of 'mine' and 'yours'. In both feminist theories of knowledge and in Buddhist psychotherapeutic practice, the starting place is subjective experience.

A significant context for my work as a psychotherapist is my relationship to both Christian and Buddhist spiritual traditions. In fact it is my familiarity with several spiritual 'cultures'[13] of India, that gives my European Christian context a disjunctive and displaced quality. This is a fundamental part of my experience. For as long as I can remember I have been drawn to both my non-conformist (Baptist) Christian heritage, and the path which that led me to study Theology and be baptised in the Catholic Church as a young adult, _and_ to what feels like an equally strong Indian heritage. This latter influence resulted in my studying Hinduism and Buddhism alongside Christian Theology (both at undergraduate level and through all subsequent areas of research), and to my living in India for several years, researching at depth spiritual practices used within Hindu and particularly Tibetan Buddhist traditions. It is the relationship between these two strands of my religious experience that is critical. Historically, links were made along the way through my being baptised in an Indian (not British) Catholic cultural context (in the 1970's), through my chosen areas of academic research, - which I have always described as 'comparative theology'[14] - and through my own personal practice which incorporates aspects from both Christian and Buddhist spiritual traditions. The other side of this, however, is that I do not feel completely at home in either European Christian contexts, such as my local Church, for example, or in European inculturated Buddhist contexts, which are sometimes quite robust in defining themselves in contradistinction to what are perceived as Christian European values and practices.

"You can't ride two horses at once!" I have been reminded by spiritual teachers/ directors on both sides of the fence. Of course, that is true. And yet it seems that there are certain 'givens' in my life, based on choices I have made at some level, which I am seeking to hold in relationship rather than deny or let go of. I am not sure that I would have set out to create this situation consciously at all! It seems as if my own path involves an attempt to integrate, in my being, my body, experiences arising from contact with radically different - but not perhaps mutually exclusive - spiritual traditions.

There are, of course, others in Britain whose experience has points of overlap with my own. A number of people in the Church lived in India, for example, as a significant part of a missionary or Church worker ministry. Most of the individuals I have met in this context are deeply involved in their Christian commitment, and integrating their 'Indian' experience takes the form of work in multi-faith communities or in academic or theological training situations There are also people who align themselves with particular groups, such as the Christian Meditation Centre, as a vehicle for their spiritual growth. And today in Britain there are increasingly large numbers of people who are themselves Indian Christians living in Europe. Sugirtharajah, in his *Voices from the Margin*, gives an excellent collection of critiques of Eurocentric assumptions, practices and concepts in the field of Biblical enquiry in his anthology of post-colonial discourse from writers in the South[15]. Teaching at Selly Oak Theological Colleges he is giving a voice to emerging suppressed voices of Indian dalits, women and indigenous people, for example, who 'continue to be subjected to hermeneutical forgetting by mainstream biblical scholarship'[16]. He offers a new critical tradition within the heart of Britain. Referring to the Indian feminist and deconstructionist Gayatri Chakravorty Spivak, he re-images the margin as a centre of critical reflection, rather than a site 'opposed to the centre or as a state of peripherality'[17].

All of these contexts are of significance for any open-ended critical reflection in European theology. The historical events of British colonialism in India make it a necessary challenge for us to learn to listen to experiences arising out of this colonial situation. The discourse expressed in *Voices from the Margin*, for example, is ours to acknowledge and dialogue with.

My own position here is both inside and outside such a dialogue. Where I 'come from' is in itself a margin place where Buddhist as well as Christian experiences conflate, displace one another, and live in dialogue. I am not in the position of someone whose Christian faith has grown out of an oppressed social situation or whose parents' spiritual tradition has been denied or rejected as a result. I come rather from a people who have perpetrated such situations. And historically my own formation as a person owes a lot to a culture other than my own. If I were to name others whose position I identify with to some degree, - people whom I could look to for some sort of modelling - they would be the Frenchman Swami Abhishiktananda (Henri le Saux) or Bede Griffiths, a British monk who lived out his British-Indian integration in a particularly radical way[18].

I qualify their significance for me because however deep and radical their respective 'border' paths, I look especially to women in the field of spiritual or inner growth, for ways of living and being that connect more personally with my own vision. Mostly it is through friends that I find such connection. It is a Scottish woman who, after a period in robes as a Buddhist nun, created an on-going experiment of a Buddhist based form of psychotherapy in Britain; an American friend and Buddhist practitioner has inspired me through her continuing daily dialogue with her Catholic upbringing and Sikh husband; and it is the artist referred to earlier, Caroline, who through her painting and sculptures brings to life the very real challenge of 'inculturating' Indian spiritualities within Britain. All of these women maintain an essential clarity about their own roots and relationships with traditions, and somehow create small 'cells' of awareness within their respective local communities which are both self-sufficient and yet seek to feed and be nourished by the existing religious communities, such as Buddhist centres or Churches. And this is happening here in Britain, not in India, where both Abhishiktananda and Father Bede chose to live out their visions. I take heart from this , and feel privileged to count these and other close friends as members of my own 'sangha' or community on a shared path[19].

One point I want to make about my own experience of living at the interface between two different spiritual traditions, is that it can feel isolating, painful and even de-constructive. It is as if the pull of the two paths counter-balance one another, and can run contrary to any intention to hold them together. I am referring here more to the social and cultural aspects of my experience, such as the fact that there is a large Tibetan Buddhist community nearby and several Churches, but there is no 'place' other than my own home which can hold the two 'forms' together. It sometimes feels as if the relationship I have constructed between them can only exist in myself, and the place of holding is my body,

Heidi Singh, in an unpublished paper given at a Los Angeles Catholic-Buddhist Conference in 1984 writes of the pain involved in living out what is often referred to as 'inter-religious dialogue': "I don't believe anyone who enters into dialogue, at any level, is prepared for the transformation of one's own theology and perception of both self and community, which occurs over a period of time".[20] The question that arose for her then was, 'how does the Christian maintain that Christian identity in the face of the greater Reality?' For me this touches the experience of becoming somehow less solid, having a less sharp delineation of attitudes, beliefs and names for things. Singh describes how the 'gnawing' of this question at her heart, which is fundamentally painful, has become 'a consuming liberation, an unbinding'. She acknowledges, however, that for many, such conflict remains an all-gripping pain. While I would not describe my own experience in either of these ways, it is the case that living in a margin place is by definition a place of separation and differentiation as well as a place of contact. And in my experience it can have a desert-like feel.

Re- Visioning

As I go about my day, which always starts with re-lighting the fire and putting the kettle on, and usually involves travelling to work and returning late, it is as if I am continually remembering and re-visiting someone I once know, but whose face is no longer clear to me. Perhaps the features will become clearer if I continue remembering:

When a person dies, they leave behind, for those who knew them, an emptiness, a space, the space has contours and is different for each person mourned. This space with its contours is the person's likeness and is what the artist searches for when making a living portrait. A likeness is something left behind invisibly... [21]

In one way, the task of seeing again in the present is a letting go of the past through acknowledging what was and is no more and what remains. I shall no longer see myself, my environment and Christ as I did before - before I left home, before I lived in India, before I began to view my inner work in terms of psychotherapy, and so on. And yet a 'likeness' remains which is both a reminder of what I have lost and also a 'space' in relation to which my present experience can make itself known. In fact it is these 'invisible' imprints from the past which inform my current perceptions, and give them flesh and blood.

In Indian *bhakti* and particularly tantric spiritual practices, there are traditions of meditation which are compared to 'remembering' the divine. Often the divine is visualised in a specific form and meditated upon in ways which connect the devotee with the divine through the iconic image. 'Be one whose mind is placed on Me', says Krisna to Arjuna, 'That is, have your mind fixed well on Me without interruption like a stream of oil...'[22]. The Hindu theologian, Ramanja, describes this meditation practice as a kind of seeing, and also a form of knowing. It comprises a 'mental energy', of the nature of remembrance, which renders the divine 'immediately present' to the devotee through a form of 'direct vision'.

My situation is rather like trying to do a simple meditation practice of 'remembering' but without having an iconic image, a visual form, for the divine. Yet there is a forgotten 'likeness' which seems just out of sight. I can only get on with my life, my work, and trust that holding open the 'space' as possibility for seeing things in ordinary ways moment to moment is enough. I may never see a 'form' which embodies the divine likeness I seek to remember.

Notes

1 This is the way that the elements are named in Tibetan Buddhism. In other traditional cultures they have been named somewhat differently; as earth, water, fire, wood and metal (Chinese), for example, or as earth, water, fire, air and ether (Greek).

2 'Note sur "l'élément universel" du Monde', Oeuvres 12 (Paris: Editions du Seuil, 1965) p. 393; see also Oeuvres 4, Le Milieu divin (Paris: Editions du Seuil, 1957) pp. 137-41.

3 Bede, Life of St. Cuthbert trans. by J.F. Webb in The Age of Bede ed. D.H. Farmer (London: Penguin Books, rev. 1988) pp. 55-56; 70-71.

4 It was during a Channel crossing after an ESWTR Conference in Leuven in 1993 that Caroline and I embarked on this project.

5 This is an extract from a ritual Caroline and I created in the context of a retreat on 'water' (March 1994).

6 It is significant that in the context of this enquiry the images we evolved become more gender inclusive, to the point that we realized that in certain ways we were viewing Christ as woman rather than man.

7 Philip Sheldrake, Spirituality and History: Questions of Interpretation and Method (London: S.P.C.K. 1991) p. 52.

8 The Body Divine: the Symbol of the Body in the works of Teilhard de Chardin and Rámánuja (Cambridge University Press, 1992).

9 I trained at Karuna Institute (England) in Core Process Psychotherapy. This is a discipline based on Buddhist psychology and awareness practice, the therapist's role being that of reflector and facilitator of awareness. The client is viewed as the 'object' of bare or sustained attention, in which our body, feelings and states of mind are used to explore our unique process. The work is viewed as a joint healing and contemplative practice.

10 In particular, Core Process Psychotherapy and another discipline I know of which locates itself in Chogyam Trungpa's lineage of Buddhist and Shambhala traditions from Tibet. See Karen Kissel Wegela's article, 'Contemplative Psychotherapy: a Path of uncovering Brilliant Sanity' in the Journal, Contemplative Psychotherapy of Naropa Institute, Boulder, Vol. IX (1994) pp. 27-52.

11 I am referring here to both the Naropa Institute discipline and that started by Akong Rinpoche at Samye-Ling Tibetan Centre in Scotland, which is called Tara Rokpa Therapy.

12 Ecofeminism and Theology: Yearbook of the European Society of Women in Theological Research, Vol. 2 (Kampen: Kok Pharos, 1994) p. 14.

13 I am adopting Philip Sheldrake's description of spiritualities as cultures (op. cit. p.59) which seems particularly appropriate since he goes on to examine examples of marginalisation in terms of cultural conflicts.

14 In doing so I am deliberately widening traditional confessional definitions of theos and theos - language.

15 Sugirtharajah refers to such writers as 'third world' and explains that this is a socio-political designation of a people who have been excluded from power and authority to mould and shape their future. Ed. R.S. Sugirtharajah, Voices from the Margin: Interpreting the Bible in the Third World (London/:New York: SPCK/Orbis, 1995), p.8.

16 Ibid., p. 4.

17 Ibid., p. 2.

18 These two remarkable men immersed themselves in the contemporary life of Hindu India. They knew one another, and for a time lived in community together. But Swami Abhishiktananda chose to settle in the north, spending years in the Himalayas as a sannyasin, and Father Bede lived at Shantivanam in Tamil Nadu, an ashram that has been a foothold in India for many European 'seekers'. For an introduction to Swami Abhishiktananda in English, I recommend James Stuart's book, Swami Abhishiktanada: His Life told through his Letters (New Delhi: I.S.P.C.K. 1989). Bede Griffith's A New Vision of Reality: Western Science, Eastern Mysticism and Christian Faith (London: Collins, 1989) is a good introduction to his life and thought.

19 The term sangha (Sanskrit) has different levels of meaning, but in its most current usage refers to the Buddhist community of monks and nuns. As one of the three 'Jewels' in which practitioners take refuge, it is highly valued. It is said that when the Buddha was asked which of these 'Jewels (namely buddha, dharma and sangha) were most important, he said, the sangha.

20 Heidi Singh, 'The Pain of Dialogue: Implications for Catholics involved in Interreligious Encounters', p. 3. The Conference was entitled, The Concept of Transcendence in Buddhism, and was co-sponsored by the Buddhist Sangha Council of Southern California and the Archdiocesan Commission on Ecumenical and Interreligious Affairs.

21 John Berger, 'Steps towards a small Theory of the Visible', Tate, Issue 11 (Spring 1997), p. 44.

22 Ramanuja's Commentary on the Gita, Gitabhasya trans. M.R. Sampatkumaran (Madras: Prof. M. Rangacharya Memorial Trust, 1969) p.286.

Caroline Mackenzie

Fire and Water Woman
Background to the Images

Four of these drawings are done in soft pastels. One, 'Fire and Water acknowledge each other', is a water colour. The pastels are done on A2 cartridge paper (59.4 cm x 42 cm). The water colour is much smaller (27.5 cm x 19 cm) and done on water colour paper.

The immediate source of inspiration was the experience of the meeting between Anne's 'Fire' mask and costume and my 'Water". Interestingly, the pictures actually depict what I remembered of Anne wearing the mask and costume I had made and me wearing hers. Although, 'Fire and Water Woman' was the first picture that I drew, in terms of my own understanding, it was the last, that is, the end result of our 'playing'. It shows a state of integration which I am still in the process of trying to realise.

While these drawings were created spontaneously over a short period of time, they belong within the wider context of my work, which goes back twenty years. The 'mythic' quality is inspired by Hindu icons. For example, I see now that 'Fire and Water Woman' originates from figures such as Hari-hara, that is Vishnu and Shiva conjoined as a single deity, or from the image called 'Ardhanari' where Shiva (male) is conjoined with Parvati (female). This androgens figure is seen from the point of view of what it feels like to be a man integrating the feminine side.[1] By contrast, my images try to express the experiences of integration from the view point of woman as subject.

Another important source for these works is my association with Christians, particularly Catholics, who are involved in 'inculturating' the Gospel within the Indian context. If I consider where the first mask came from, I can trace it back to the picture mentioned by Anne which shows Christ as a woman calming the storm (Mk 4:36-41). I know that the way I have used my imagination in this interpretation owes a lot to Indian theologians such as Anand Amaladass.[2]

The transition from the picture to the mask owes its origin to some of Jyoti Sahi's ideas about art as a sadhana or spiritual practice. Jyoti Sahi is an Indian Christian artist who has been very influential in the debates about inculturation. Although I studied with Jyoti in India for

Fig. **4**. *Fire and Water acknowledge each other*

Fig 5. *The Fire and Water Woman*

several years, interestingly it was during an Art Retreat given by him here in Wales that I actually learned to make masks. Jyoti's work in Europe is sponsored by various Christian mission organisations such as 'Missio' (Aachen, Germany) and U.S.P.G., and is seen as being an expression of 'Cross-cultural Mission' or 'Partnership in Mission'.

One of the important features of inculturation in India has been the value given to *folk culture*.[3] There has been an effort to re-work traditional festivals. I have been inspired by these ideas to create festivals here in Europe. Since the past three years, I have organised a Maypole Festival in my village. This has been an opportunity for people to come together and create a context for bringing out the creativity of people who are not professional artists. The original impetus for the first 'Water' mask was this Maypole Festival. The fact I chose to make 'Water', was probably influenced by the meditations I had been doing with Anne. However, the mask was not first of all made for our work but for the festival. The form the mask took was related to the much earlier oil painting. It was interesting that the original woman Christ appeared to me *as an Indian*. Part of my motivation in making the mask and costume was my struggle to realise the possibility of this form of Christ here in Europe. For some reason, probably connected with the process of projection and shadow, it was easy for me to create the Indian woman Christ, but much harder to integrate this in the West.

To sum up, - these pictures have arisen primarily as a response to the work with Anne. Therefore, the basic context is of women working in Europe. However, the background to my creative process lies in Hindu iconography and Indian Christian culture and theology.

Notes

1 cf. Wendy Doniger O'Flaherty, Women, Androgynes and Other Mythical Beasts, University of Chicago Press 1980

2 cf. Anand Amaladass, Philosophical Implications of Dhvani, Experience of Symbol Language in Indian Aesthetics, Vienna 1984.

3 See for example the work of anthropologist / theologian J.J. Pallath, Theyyam. An Analytical Study of the Folk Culture, Wisdom, and Personality, New Dehli 1995.

Ulrike Wiethaus

Mechthild von Magdeburg's Mystical-Poetic Language:

An Inspiration for Women's Spirituality and Sexuality Today?[1]

> Christianity has fostered a discourse of power based on the control of sex rather than a discourse of service based on the power of love.
>
> *Mary Condren*[2]

Spiritual Beginnings

My first contact with medieval holy women was sensual, embodied, direct, magical. I had the good fortune to spend most of my childhood near the home of St. Mechtildis of Diessen-Andechs, Bavaria. In the wooded hills near our school a sacred well exists in her name, the Mechtildis Brunnen, that is renowned for healing illnesses of the eye. As children, we actually tried the water, believing it to be charged with supernatural power. Our little town's magnificent Marienmünster hosts St. Mechthildis' skeleton in a glass sarcophagus, less attractive to me then because it seemed tainted with adult aesthetics, bandaged and stifled by adult piety. Much more interesting was the stone, firmly embedded in the church wall, that Mechtildis used as her pillow: her head had carved a soft deepening into the surface, and it was said that to touch the stone would heal any headache. As children we could touch the stone whenever we liked, without prescribed ritual or permission, and ponder what it meant to fall asleep on it, willingly. What an outrageous use of a simple stone! So one could do things adults would disapprove of and still be respected by them!

In my child's mind, then, a holy woman was more like a benevolent fairytale being, a Frau Holle who acted as an iconoclast, who gave generously, who could heal unconditionally, who was connected to elemental forces: water, stone, the towering beech trees that still grow around Mechtildis' well, the smell of rotting leaves turning to earth at the foot of the trees. A holy woman also demanded a type of respect not given to anybody else; her power was of a different order, as old and direct as that of nature. Through the stone and the well, she was inviting sensual knowledge of her presence: one could touch her essence, smell it, drink it, taste it, hear it in the soft bubbling of the water, see it in the fine grains of the pillow stone. Mechthildis offered me an aesthetic of saintliness and of feminine sacrality lost in the theological discourse of the seminary and the academy that I studied much later; how lucky I was to have absorbed these sensuous layers of truth when I was still a child, when I still believed that magic was never far away, when light and darkness and the seasons of nature were pregnant with meaning.

Holiness is not only an ethical experience, it is aesthetic and sensuous as well. This is what it shares with the experience of sexuality.

Introduction

Mechthild von Magdeburg lived from ca. 1208 until ca. 1282/97. Revered as one of the strongest voices in bridal mysticism, she is a prominent spiritual foremother "to think back through". Bridal mysticism is a distinctly medieval religious path based on the love language of the Song of Songs in which Christ is courted as bridegroom and the soul is conceptualized as his bride. Both men and women followed this path. It is therefore a legitimate project to ask whether and how the tradition of bridal mysticism as exemplified in Mechthild of Magdeburg's text *The Flowing Light of the Godhead* is suitable as one of many resources for women's spirituality today.

At first glance, however, the question posed in the title of this article should be answered with a clear "no". Mechthild was a medieval religious woman, possibly a Beguine, who practiced asceticism, rejected most of society as corrupt, and more than likely never experienced sexual intercourse. She fiercely believed in the superiority of chastity and, we may assume from the high value that she placed on marriage as a spiritual estate, thought that of the wide variety of human sexual behavior, only marital heterosexual sex was appropriate. Her world-view was thoroughly medieval. For example, she was suspicious of Jews and advised others not to live with them. To her, Christianity was the only true faith, and she pitied all those who lived "outside" Christendom. Furthermore, feudal social structures were unquestioned by Mechthild except for excessive accumulation of wealth among the nobility. Her language is steeped in the courtly culture of her times, and she shows clear biases in favor of "valiant" knights, "beautiful" young ladies and against "coarse" peasants, "lowly" animals, and "heathens". These attitudes are of little help today as we stand up for social justice and equality and struggle to overcome heterosexism, cultural hatred of women's bodies and attitudes and laws that limit women's rights for full reproductive freedom, freedom from sexual violence, and full personhood and citizenship as mothers. Few of us today would choose the monastic and ascetic lifestyle as an expression of our spirituality. For the most part, contemporary spirituality embraces life in the midst of society, not at its margins, and affirms sexual and sensual activity in as broad a range as possible rather than rejecting it.

To better understand the relationship between constructions of female sexuality and spirituality, however, it is useful to put it into a historical perspective; understanding its origins and historical development helps us devise strategies for resistance to abuse and exploitation. In this respect, the cultural landscape of the Middle Ages is crucial for at least two reasons. For one, we see exclusively female institutions—convents, beguinages—with relative autonomy support the production of texts that testify to women's imagination and spirituality, often valued as equal or superior to men's. These texts help us construct an authoritative tradition that challenges the patriarchal insistence on exclusively male spiritual traditions. Secondly, we also witness the simultaneous rise of another set of highly influential literature that contributed to the sexual and spiritual oppression of women for centuries to come—the penitentials and the scientific texts on gynecology. Defining women's sexuality as dangerous and women themselves as inferior became a commonly shared "scientific" and "theological" outlook among learned male writers in general. Looking back through the centuries to the Middle Ages, we can clearly see the seeds being sown that led to the sexual demonization of women, the heresy and witchcraft persecutions in subsequent centuries, and the exclusion of women from the   ecclesiastical formation of Christian spirituality.

Mechthild's writings thus demonstrate how women insisted on defining Christian spirituality on their own terms, but they also absorbed the misogyny of her times: the human body is sometimes described as good, sometimes as bad; she denigrates menstruation as "that curse". Her female self is split between baseness and nobility.

She rejects the "world" yet her language cannot do without its images, people, and customs. To summarize: in search of a female lineage of Christian spiritual teachers, Mechthild left extremely valuable writings; we must be aware, however, that she wrote and taught as a medieval person. Her truths are not timeless; we declare them to be so only if they mirror back something of ourselves.

How then is Northern European/American female sexuality and Christian spirituality different from Mechthild's? Due to the historical impact of secularism, science, and the feminist movement, women today can articulate and fight more strongly the misogyny and oppression within the churches that occurs on every level. Descriptions of cultural/spiritual reality shaped by women rather than by men (as happened in the past) are growing, as is the level of education among religiously engaged women; also, more women intentionally create a woman-affirming "Woman-Church", women's groups that meet regularly and experiment with woman-centered liturgies, selections and interpretations of biblical texts, etc. Oftentimes, non-Christian spiritual resources are welcomed and the ecumenical, inter—religious boundaries are wide open. Through the impact of feminist activism, women encourage each other to name and fight sexual violence and to develop a life-affirming approach to female sexuality that honors differences such as sexual orientation, marital status, age, or disabilities. Spirituality is becoming a patch-work of traditional and non-traditional techniques, inspirational texts, and loosely patterned communities; both the *vita activa* and the *vita contemplativa* are respected, and ecstasies and trances become integrated in liturgical language, music, and ritualistic celebrations.

These developments are exciting and encouraging. Yet when we study history, we realize that Western women's lives throughout the centuries are marked by advances followed by setbacks. In every era women were forced to re-invent a discourse of woman-affirming values and ideas, and to re-discover practices in all aspects of life that protect and enhance women's well-being. For this reason—the never-ending fragility of women's liberation within a patriarchal system—we must conserve and re-member women's achievements and insights from the past to help us to preserve and strengthen our present and to build a long-lasting bridge into the future for our children and our children's children.

Mechthild of Magdeburg's Spirituality: A Textual Interpretation

Rather than discussing *The Flowing Light of the Godhead* as a whole, I will offer a close reading of a representative text to illustrate Mechthild's teaching and spiritual understanding of the Christian tradition. Here is my translation of the text I chose[3]

> *Of the Soul's Journey to Court through Which God Reveals Himself.* When the poor soul arrives at court, she is wise and well-mannered. She happily gazes at her God. Oh, how sweetly she is then received! She is silent and boundlessly desires his praise. So with great yearning, he

shows her his divine heart. It resembles red gold burning in a large fire of coals. He then places her in his glowing heart. When the high prince and the lowly maid-servant embrace in such manner and are united like water and wine, she experiences an annihilation of her self and loses her self as if she could not extend herself any further. He, however, is lovesick for her as he has always been because (his desire) neither waxes nor wanes. So she speaks, 'O Lord, you are my beloved, my desire, my flowing well, my sun, and I am your mirror'. This is a journey to court by the loving soul who does not wish to be without God.

This short text on spirituality and sexuality is extremely rich in theological and mystical content. Due to the complexity of the images, the narrative functions on several levels simultaneously, for both a contemporary and, we can assume, a medieval audience. On a physical, material level, a woman describes first the arrival of the female protagonist at a place which is foreign to her; then an intense sexual union between a man and woman; during the union, the woman recognizes the psycho-emotional state of the man and names it by defining the relationship between herself and her partner. The male partner is not given speech.

On a social level, the narrative describes dramatic changes in status: first, the male, although benevolently inclined toward the female, is described as possessing higher status than the female ("hoher Fürst", "geringe Magd"""[4]); in medieval society, their sexual encounter was judged to be highly unfavorable to the female, since she can never expect the relationship to become legalized as a marital union and her children to be acknowledged as legitimate members of their father's family. The social inequality between the two actors, however, is challenged by the emotional vulnerability of the male—he is subject to his desire for the female; his lack of speech, and the female act of naming her partner with status-neutral metaphors that defy social categories: desire, flowing well, sun, mirror. Love and female speech suspend social inequality. On a theological level, the rich images work in two ways. One can very well argue that the text is an exploration of the claim in 1 John 4: 16 that God is love. "Thus we have come to know and believe the love which God has for us. God is love; he who dwells in love is dwelling in God, and God in him." Whereas the first letter of John stresses that love is the essence of a Christian *community*, Mechthild interprets divine love through the lens of the Song of Songs, as a personal and intimate encounter between a lover and her divine beloved. This psycho-sensual encounter does not exclude community, but it adds em-bodied, sensual depth to the religious insight.

In the Song of Songs, verse 5:8, lovesickness is assigned to the bride, however, and not to the bridegroom as in Mechthild's narrative. "I charge you, daughters of Jerusalem, if you find my beloved, will you not tell him that I am faint with love?"

Mechthild does not simply reiterate 1 John 4:16 or the Song of Songs, however. Similar to Beatrijs of Nazareth and Hadewijch, two other medieval women mystics who practiced and taught bridal mysticism, she offers several radical departures.

The philosophically abstract notion in 1 John that God is love is enlarged to accommodate certain dimensions of *bodily knowing* God. Yet for Mechthild, sexual ecstasy and orgasmic swooning are only one aspect of sensual exploration of a theological insight. Equally important are sensations implicit in elements of the natural world (water, fire, light), and of the realm of emotions: desire, lovesickness, letting go, trust, respect for oneself and the other, self-esteem. Also, it is not just the human person who experiences the divine holistically. The Divine as well is *known* as sensual and emotional, close by and vulnerable, generous and passionate. This is a far cry from dominant "cold" understandings of a Divine being that is distant, unfeeling, and disembodied (though male!). And because of love and mutually shared sensual embodiment, the Divine and the human meet on equal footing.

Secondly, in a biblical text that is seemingly gender-neutral and that because of that seeming neutrality allows for a hermeneutical bias that privileges the male voice in scriptural interpretation, Mechthild re-inserts a female protagonist, a female voice, a female perspective and - most audaciously! - puts this female agent on center-stage. She thus forecloses any patriarchal usurpation of scriptural exegesis that intends to render women invisible or secondary to men and male agency. This bold strategy is reinforced by privileging the female persona with the opportunity to speak. The ontological power of the Divine, metaphorically expressed as masculinized high social status, does not give itself up to an idolatrous worship of masculinity (as Mary Daly has convincingly demonstrated in traditional uses of male God-language) since what is metaphorically masculine is also described as vulnerable (driven by desire) and faithfully loving.

What about sexuality as such? Whereas the emerging medieval genres authored by male theologians display great hostility and suspicion toward sexuality in general and women in particular, Mechthild's ecstatic mystical theology is only minimally affected by these tendencies, especially in her early books. As she gets older and, we may assume, becomes more exposed to and influenced by her

Dominican confessor(s), we find more expressions of mistrust of sensuous knowing and the body itself, yet never a denigration of femininity in the way a St. Bernard of Clairvaux, widely regarded as the key propagator of bridal mysticism in the twelfth century, develops it in his writing and preaching. For Mechthild and other female authors of the bridal mystical tradition, sexuality provides a highly valued language to understand the relationship between the Divine and women, between the Divine and men. In the realm of spiritual experience, Mechthild seems to argue, one cannot do without resources of knowledge embedded in sexual experience.

But is that just sublimation, that is, a pious re-emergence of repressed sexual desire? After all, Mechthild was committed to a life of chastity. I think that the answer depends on one's view on the separation between the body and the mind. Sigmund Freud, an heir to post-Enlightenment thinking, assumed a very rigid boundary between both. For medieval people, the boundary was soft and just beginning to emerge as a hard and definite divide in the High Middle Ages. The soul was imagined as a human body, endowed with five senses. The body was understood to have its own "mind" and "will". For Mechthild, as for many other medieval authors, the soul was a body, and the realm of spiritual imagination was therefore by necessity sensual. For her, no distinction could be drawn between experiences in the physical realm and experiences in the spiritual realm. That division is uniquely ours. For medieval people, the world was one, and the world was made flesh. A legitimate question arises at this point: but what about the heterosexual scripting of Mechthild's interpretation? How can a lesbian Christian relate to this text and not feel rejected? The soul's crucial recognition of the nature of the Divine, her supreme theological insight moves beyond gender, beyond heterosexual romance yet without giving up sensuality and embodiedness: the Divine becomes "my beloved, my desire, my flowing well, my sun". This naming invites a re-naming of what it means to be human: the soul becomes a "mirror', that is, she transforms herself, too, into a "beloved", into "desire", a "flowing well", a "sun". The experience of "annihilation of self" breaks down dichotomizing registers of individuality through a shattering experience of communion: one becomes a self in the religiously most profound way by losing one's boundaries of self.

Conclusion

In the beginning of the essay, I stated that if we look at Mechthild's "actual" (in our sense of the word) life experiences as a celibate ascetic, she could not offer us anything useful for constructing a life-affirming spirituality and sexuality. It is my thesis, however, that if we look at her experiences in the realm of lived, experienced faith, which were deeply real to her and her medieval followers, we can glean a number of insights and principles that might be useful to women's communities today: the insistence on bringing female perspectives to the foreground and giving them their full due; this entails the emergence of an image of the Divine as vulnerable and embodied, sensuously knowing us. In other words, we cannot simply operate in a post-Enlightenment paradigm and insert women into it, thinking that this would improve our spiritual health. The paradigm needs to be changed from bottom up; and most threatening perhaps is the necessary return to an older Christian notion of the divine - to a sensuous God, a sexual God, a hot, tender, faithful, erotic God. A God who is not prudish. From Mechthild's perspective, we need a holistic theology and spirituality that honors bodily knowing and experiencing as much as complex intellectual theologizing; that honors the valorization of sexuality as a language about the ground of all being, about connection. We need the confidence that women possess deep-rooted authority as teachers and are affirmed in their authority by the Divine; the knowledge that ultimate reality is grounded in love, not judgment, in intimacy and belonging, not isolation and distance, in self-esteem, not self-hatred, in abundance, not scarcity, in process and transformation, not stagnation and status quo, in mystery, not platitude.

Notes

1 Background Reading to my article: Alison M. Jaggar and Susan R. Bordo, eds., Gender/Body/Knowledge. Feminist Reconstructions of Being and Knowing (New Brunswick and London: Rutgers University Press, 1989); Haunani-Kay Trask, Eros and Power. The Promise of Feminist Theory (Philadelphia: University of Pennsylvania Press, 1986); Ulrike Wiethaus, ed., Maps of Flesh and Light. The Religious Experience of medieval Women Mystics (Syracuse: Syracuse University Press, 1993); Christiane Mesch Galvani, tr., Susan Clark, ed., Mechthild von Magdeburg, Flowing Light of the Divinity (New York and London: Garland Publishing, 1991).

2 Mary Condren, The Serpent and the Goddess, p. 185

3 Book One, Chapter 4

4 English: high prince, low maiden

A Prayer for Solidarity and Hope
In the Struggle Against Women-Hatred and Sexism

Reader: O Great God!
Hear this humble prayer!
Hold us steadfast in your way
     of soothing, gentle, loving kindness.

People: Open our ears to hear the lament of women
     to enter into its long and sad song
     coming to us through the voices
     of women and girl children worldwide
     today and through the ages
Open the hearts of menfolk
     and their sister-kin who cannot hear.

Leader: Release the tongues of those who will not speak
     against the social sin of sexism
and the suffering it creates for all women and men
a grief yoked through webs of greed
to the harm of animals,
the destruction of plant life
the wasting of our water ways
the devastation of the planet
Energize those who long to act in women's behalf
but who wait in the wings
silent and afraid.

People: O Great One God!
We believe you are at work in our world
revealing Yourself through acts of courage of women
     through acts of solidarity by men with women
     In the struggle for justice.
We believe the time to act is now
It is wrong to wait for better times
for more companions or consent
or an easier route.

Leader: The moment is now as You, O Great One God,
turn evil situations
of woman-hatred into goodness, justice, and love.

People: We believe one day all tears will be wiped away.
True peace and true reconciliation will come.
In you, they are assured and guaranteed.
This is our prayer and our hope. Amen.

Carol Winkelmann

Annie Imbens-Fransen

Digging Up Women's Sources
Of Wisdom And Strength
In the Quest for Women's True Spirituality.[1]

Song of the Bird, True Spirituality
The master was asked, 'What is spirituality?'
He said, 'Spirituality is that which succeeds in bringing one
to inner transformation.'
'But if I apply the traditional methods handed down by the
masters, is that not spirituality?'
'That is not spirituality if it does not perform its function for
you. A blanket is no longer a blanket if it does not keep you
warm.'
'People change and needs change. So what was spirituality
once is spirituality no more. What generally goes under the
name of spirituality is merely the record of past methods.'
Don't cut the person to fit the coat.
                                        Anthony De Mello[2]

Different sides to spirituality

After considering many women's stories about their daily lives and reflecting on my own experiences - especially during my study of theology and my work in theology and pastoral care for women - as a white, Western, middle class, married woman with a Christian background, I discovered two different sides to spirituality.

First, *spirituality* is a stimulating and empowering source of strength and insight that grows as we become more receptive and realize our abilities and limitations. Inner strength stimulates us to open our eyes to the structures, mechanisms, and limitations in our society that support unjust practices and relations and to the suffering they cause. Spirituality also cultivates our insight, self-esteem, strength, courage, creativity, and sensitivity to truth, justice, beauty, and love, which are the necessary instruments or attributes for transforming ourselves and our societies and for creating a better life for all beings. This quality is conveyed through words, attitudes and gestures, paintings and sculptures, music and dance, and poems and stories. Biographical stories express how and where we find hope, strength, perseverance, vitality, and joy in daily life, even under difficult circumstances.

This view on spirituality emanates from texts and stories from my Christian heritage and from many women s stories. Two biblical texts have acquired a special meaning to me. The first answers the question: What is needed to inherit eternal life or enjoy the fullest possible existence? According to the answer, we should love God, the supreme being, wholeheartedly, with all our soul, all our strength, and all our mind, and we should love our neighbour as we love ourselves. (Luke 10:27). The second text is a story about a widow who was involved in a lawsuit. The judge who heard her case neither feared God nor respected people. After refusing for a while, he finally granted her justice. The widow succeeded in convincing this judge of his obligation to dispense justice by repeatedly telling him: ' "Provide me justice against my opponent." She persisted until the judge sighed: "I have no fear of God and no respect for anyone, yet because this widow keeps bothering me, I will see to it that she gets her rights. If I do not, she will keep on coming and finally wear me out." This story advises us how we should believe and pray. It also expresses the power of justice and the wisdom and strength of a woman who knew how to obtain her rights before an unjust or corrupt judge. (Luke 18:1-8).

Besides spirituality as a stimulating source that increases insight, self-esteem, strength, courage, creativity, as well as our sensitivity to truth, justice, beauty, and love, there is another destructive side to spirituality. This is often overlooked or denied and not seen to belong to the field of spirituality, because it does not accord with our desires and expectations of how spirituality should be defined - if not dominated and manipulated by people who have the need to control and disempower others. In reality, spirituality is not only developed and used to create practices and relations between people that are just.

Studying theology and receiving instruction exclusively from male teachers made me aware of male domination in Christianity and mainstream theology. I discovered that mainstream theology marginalizes and ignores women and children and their experiences, problems, feelings, interests, insights, and talents and imposes androcentric and patriarchal views about God and the world's creation and ideal order on women and children. Mainstream androcentric theology views reality on the basis of the experiences, feelings, and insights of men who consider themselves superior to women and children.

Androcentric spirituality also figures in biblical texts and stories from my Christian heritage and in their androcentric interpretations. The texts Ephesians 5:22-33 and 1 Timothy 2:11-15 are notorious. In the first text wives are told to submit to their husbands as unto God. This text fosters inequality in relationships between husbands and wives.[3] The second passage prohibits women from teaching but has them study in silence instead. It explains the cause and manner of the violation of women's human right to freedom of speech in Christian tradition: because Adam was created before Eve, and because Adam was not deceived, while Eve was deceived and became a transgressor. The passage concludes that women will be redeemed through childbearing, 'provided they continue in faith and love and holiness with modesty'. As long as texts and ideas such as these are interpreted as God's law by people raised as Christians, they stimulate acceptance and justification of women's subordination.

The impact of androcentric, patriarchal spirituality on women

My realization of androcentrism in mainstream theology and Christian tradition led me to become a feminist.[4] I began teaching about *Women, Religion and Society*, and *Reading the Bible with Women's Eyes*. I wrote articles including: *The Myth of Male Superiority, and the Image of God* (1981); *Thecla, an Apostle Besides Paul* (1981); and *Women and Spirituality* (1983). From that moment, women started telling me about incidents in their daily lives, their problems with their religious education, and their experiences with sexual violence and incest. Hearing these women's stories increased my awareness of the negative and harmful spiritual contents of mainstream androcentric theology for women. Here, men with androcentric patriarchal views claim exclusive authority to interpret reality and present their ideas about God and about the world's creation and ideal arrangement according to God's Will. This theology and spirituality encourages women to accept the role and tasks men have designed for them and have presented to children, women, and men as representative of the order created by God for centuries.

Several research projects revealed how destructive and oppressive androcentric, patriarchal Christian thought and spirituality can be to women. The study *Christianity and Incest* led to the conclusion: 'When Christian upbringing is seen from the perspective of patriarchal premises, the experience and teaching of Christianity makes girls easy prey for male family members. This religious education complicates the woman's or girl's ability to overcome the effects of sexual abuse'.[5]

This study, pastoral counseling, and contacts with over four hundred sexually abused women with religious conflicts led to the conclusion that the way these women experienced God greatly affected their chances of recovering from the traumatic aftermath of the abuse. These women were burdened with a destructive image of God. During their childhood they internalized the male-constructed patriarchal image of God that reinforces male power over and aggressive behaviour toward children and women. Their frequent associations of their fathers with God reveal the destructive potential of patriarchal thought processes and structures in Christian churches. Many women, whether they had been abused or not, recognized their own religious experiences and feelings in the analysis in *Christianity and Incest*. The stories of these women raised as Christians motivate my thesis: Sexual and other physical violence against women and girls is a physical violation of women's self-identities. Patriarchal Christian theology and evangelism signify a religious violation of women's identities.

Further qualitative research enabled me to answer the following questions: How do images of God arise during women's lives?

Does a correlation exist between the way women experience God, their self-consciousness, and their perceptions of other individuals?[6] The study *God in de beleving van vrouwen* (God in Women's Lives) is based on interviews with a random selection of women who were raised as Christians, and analyses of five samples from contemporary literature.[7] The study explored the possibility for women, raised as Christians in a culture dominated for centuries by an androcentric and patriarchal view of God, to love God 'with all thy heart, and with all thy soul, and with all thy strength, and with all thy mind, and thy neighbour as thyself' (Luke 10:27).

The interviews revealed that when viewing God as a person during childhood, God was predominantly seen as male and as the Father. The ways women learned to believe in God as a Father, however, differed remarkably. This study both confirms and complements Mary Daly s statement: 'If God is male, then the male is God.'[8] As these women progressively idealized their fathers and associated their idealized fathers with God, they increasingly learned to suppress and deny their own and other women's experiences, feelings, insights, and abilities. They forfeited both their space and their freedom to interpret reality and their own experiences and to learn from other women's perceptions and interpretations of reality. Two women who associated God with their mothers had greater respect for and confidence in themselves and both their mothers and their fathers. Their images of God stimulated them to support women and children, to care for their well-being, and to struggle for their rights.

An analyses of the five samples from contemporary literature revealed a correlation between these women's images of God, their self-consciousness, their perceptions of others, and their vitality. They also revealed five moments in the course of their social and spiritual development.[9] At each moment the women asked themselves different questions. The literature analyzed reveals common elements throughout the five stages of this quest.

In the *first moment, or the moment of doubt and discord,* the individual doubts the purpose of her life and raises questions that reflect her way of life. These questions may range from 'Does my existence serve a purpose, given my present way of life?' to 'Given my present way of life, how can I lead a meaningful existence?'

In the *second moment or moment of introspection,* individuals explore their identity and find ways to cope with their present situation.

The *third moment is the critical moment of insight and faith or of doubt* regarding others and one s own abilities and opportunities. While this stage may be a turning point in a woman's life, it may also strengthen her resolve to pursue her original course of life. During this stage, she realizes how she would like to continue her life. At this critical point in her quest for a sense of purpose, other individuals (both people close to the woman and strangers and outsiders) help her acquire new insights or reinforce old ones. Here, the woman discovers her deepest motivations and sources of strength. At this point, women experience God in different ways. A woman may feel helpless and dependent on the approval of others - especially of men and fathers - and of God the Almighty Father. The second possibility is that a woman no longer wants to believe in God, as she has never sensed that God was on her side. Alternatively, a woman may find a faith in God and sense that God is her ally after all. This third experience gives the woman strength and self-confidence.

The *fourth moment or moment of hope, or of despair* is another moment of introspection. Individuals wonder about reality and ways to cope with it, given their options and limitations.

In the *fifth moment or moment of being or of not being,* women define their purpose in life. This answer determines their subsequent approach to life, as well as their actions until they begin to question the meaning of their lives again. The outcome of this stage is determined by whether these individuals base the continuation of their lives on actual daily circumstances (such as being a black or Jewish woman in a society permeated with racism, colourism, fascism, and sexism), or whether they focus on fantasies and desired ideal conditions. In the first case, women can devote their energies to depicting and abolishing such injustice and oppression and may take pleasure in improving or changing these circumstances. In the second case, their lives are driven and consumed by their utter helplessness and their sadness about the misfortune and injustice afflicting them.

Both studies highlighted the impact of religion dominated by androcentric spirituality on women, children, and men, which is destructive and disempowering for women and children and stimulates men to aggressive and dominant behaviour toward women and children.[10] Women and men, theologians and religious leaders, have internalized this destructive androcentric spirituality which stimulates male domination over women and oppression and suffering among women. I will illustrate this statement with two examples. The first one is from Joan, a survivor of incest: 'My father had very 'Christian' ideas about women. He thought women should be submissive, obedient, servile.'[11]

The second one is from Aruna Gnanadason. She quotes a priest - as 'a voice of the church' - who is counseling a woman being battered by her husband 'every single day of her married life': 'Go back to him ... learn how to adjust to his moods ... don't do anything that would provoke his anger ... Christ suffered and died for you on the Cross ... Can't you bear some suffering too?' Instead of receiving refuge and moral and spiritual support, this woman is advised 'to learn submissiveness and obedience in a distorted relationship and an abusive marriage.'[12]

While exchanging my research results with people from different religious and cultural traditions, women and men from all over the world started telling me stories about their own religious and cultural backgrounds. Some stories were depressing, others liberating. Exchanging our stories based on experiences from our different backgrounds allowed us to identify basic themes in our assorted traditions. We recognized the oppression and neglect of women and our insights, feelings, and capacities. Women and some men acknowledged the destructiveness of androcentric patriarchal thought processes and spirituality in their religions and illustrated their views with stories and books they recommended or sent to me.[13] This exchange convinced me that in all male-dominated religions, men use religion to affirm their power and control over women.[14] The effects of this male religious and spiritual abuse of power over women are neglect, mutilation, and rape of women and children's minds and of their bodies, spirits, and talents, as well as denial and concealment of this violence against women and children.

Women's issues and mainstream discourse and research

Liberating women from mainstream spirituality in a Christianity which is destructive for us requires a greater understanding among both women and men of its impact on women, children, and men and the willingness to transform mainstream spirituality into a stimulating and creative force conducive to equality between women and men. This objective is quite ambitious because of the extended tradition in mainstream discourse, research, and publications of ignoring women and women's insights; marginalizing 'women's issues, and discrediting women's studies research and publications as ideological or political.

As women were excluded from academic circles until recently - at many Western universities and faculties until the late 1960s or early 1970s - they lacked the opportunity to rectify, differ, call into question, or elaborate on the androcentric view. 'For centuries, men were thus able to research, concur on, and determine what was human, male and female; what needs to be researched and what does not; what is relevant and what is not; which conditions must be fulfilled in order to be considered academic and objective; which methods are academic or scientific. This situation has caused wrong conclusions to be drawn and incorrect information to be passed on.'[15] This traditional attitude renders androcentric researchers and publishers unwilling to read and publish findings from women's studies. Male colleagues persistently neglect research and publications on women's studies. Publishers and editors justify their rejection of manuscripts on remarkable grounds, such as God's awareness of society's ongoing effort to avoid confronting reality and the consequences of rape.

My description of mainstream discourse and research is based on my work and research on 'women's issues' . Repeated responses from women and men from different disciplines and religious and cultural backgrounds clearly indicate that the mechanisms and problems I describe are not exclusive to Christian, Dutch, white women. Rather, they characterize research on and by all other groups of people that became 'outsiders' in mainstream academic, religious, and theological discourse, dominated by white, Western, upper-middle class, male scholars, and spiritual and religious leaders.[16] The situation necessitates mutual communication - as should be the case in every field of research - about questions such as:

> *Who determines which research is conducted?*
> *Which issues and problems are included in mainstream research, and which are excluded?*
> *Which methods are acceptable, and which are not?*
> *Which views are ideological or political, and which are not?*
> *How did this situation arise?*
> *How can we change this situation on behalf of the outsiders and the insiders?*

Interreligious and intercultural dialogue on women's spirituality

Having spent years hearing and analyzing stories revealing extensive destructiveness and suffering because of the androcentric spirituality in Christianity, I felt the need to focus on aspects of Christianity that are inspiring, encouraging, empowering, and liberating for women. Different responses to my previous research stimulated me to start a research project on women's true spirituality. My first reason concerned the frequent requests from incest survivors and women with religious problems to write more about positive aspects of religion. Many other women expressed a desire for publications on religion that viewed reality from a feminist perspective. Second, upon meeting women and men from different religious and cultural backgrounds, many women told me that they considered similar research within their culture both important and inspiring. Sometimes they asked me for advice. These women made me realize that if women's views on Christianity can be studied and the religion's destructive aspects singled out in a manner understandable to people from different cultural and religious backgrounds, then revealing its positive and inspiring qualities and communicating and comparing the results with people from other traditions must be possible as well.

After being invited by different organizations to share my views on women's spirituality, I decided to start an *interreligious and intercultural dialogue on women's true spirituality*. The stories I had heard from women and men about their traditions contained inspiring and liberating elements that taught me that every culture has tales about wise, strong, and creative women. I remembered the books women had recommended about women's stories and women's spirituality.[17] In China, information about Chinese women's research, history, and general circumstances had been difficult to obtain. Scholars at every university we visited there answered our questions about women by stating: 'In China women are not oppressed.' Months later I received a letter with a hand-written text in Chinese characters. After translation it proved to be a lecture written in 1904 by the Chinese woman Qiu Jin (1875 - 1907). The text appeals to Chinese women to fight against the injustice done to girls and women in Chinese society. She describes in detail the impact of the subjugation of girls and women throughout different periods of their lives. Referring to Chinese scholars she writes: 'These awful scholarly recluses said: 'The man is respectable, the woman subordinate. Her ignorance is her greatest virtue. The wife must obey her husband's commands.' Qiu Jin continues: 'We women must rebel against this nonsense'.[18]

Women are now meeting each other across the restrictions placed in their paths. We are becoming aware of our prejudices and ignorance about our different traditions and are sharing our views on spirituality. All over the world women know the flaws and attributes of our religious and cultural traditions. We know that our traditions need to change to stop the worldwide psychological, physical, and sexual violence against women and children. We also have thoughts, ideas, and knowledge regarding the transformations necessary to create a world in which women enjoy respect and opportunities to apply their talents toward improving life for all beings.

I have designed a questionnaire to enable women all over the world to participate in this dialogue. The dialogue is intended to improve insight into women's spirituality and views of religion and God in different religious and cultural traditions; to discover differences and similarities in women's spirituality; to improve the situation of women from different cultures, religions, colours, races, classes, and sexual orientations by exchanging the information gathered for critical reflection about our different traditions; to collect, reveal and create women's stories conveying liberation and empowerment for women in different traditions; to use women's knowledge based on our experiences and interpretations of reality to devise new theories about religion and spirituality; to avoid using androcentric and patriarchal theories to interpret women's experiences with religious and cultural traditions; to cultivate spirituality and religion in a manner that encourages, empowers, and liberates women from different traditions and ensures respect toward all beings.

The expertise of feminist, womanist, mujerista, and Asian theologians - who stress the importance of critical reflection for women's spirituality in our different religious and cultural traditions - will serve to draft guidelines for analyzing the interviews featuring various perspectives on and forms of women's spirituality.[19]

The feminist theologian Ursula King, a pioneer in the dialogue on women's spirituality, describes women's spirituality as 'a struggle for life'.[20] She believes that spirituality is not separate from women's lives and experiences but deeply interwoven with women's struggle for survival, including resisting and overcoming violence. She defines spirituality as a force for survival, an inspiring resource in our struggle and resistance, a powerful tool, and a method of transformation. She believes that the very act of living is nourishing and strengthening and harbours great energies for renewal and sustenance, for rebirth and continuing growth.

She stresses critical reflection 'on our situation as women and asking ourselves where we can find the energy, the power of courage and hope, the inspiration and zest for life to carry on our difficult and important tasks of transforming ourselves, our societies and our churches' and share our life's experience with younger women. She mentions three different resources of spirituality: the deepest depth in ourselves; the inspiring elements of hope, courage and faith that women can find in every religious tradition and in 'women's great spiritual heritage'; and the sharing of contemporary women's awareness and experiences.[21]

Sister Mary John Mananzan explains that Philippine women adopted a feminist perspective on spirituality as they started to reflect on their personal and social experiences as women and on their struggle against their oppression, exploitation and discrimination. 'This spirituality is nourished by their growing understanding of their self-image which has been obscured by the roles that have been assigned to them by a patriarchal society.'[22] This understanding influences their personal relationships and the collective consciousness that is growing throughout their struggle. Women's emerging spirituality is therefore not just a vertical relationship with God or shaped by prayer alone but integral and influenced by relational experience and personal, interpersonal, and societal struggle.

Women's struggle, new insights, and the release of creative energy have achieved a new focus on and new expressions of spirituality. As a result, Philippine women's spirituality is creation-centered rather than focused on sin and redemption, holistic rather than dualistic, risky rather than secure, joyful rather than sombre, active rather than passive, expansive rather than restrictive, more given to feasting than to fasting and to letting go than to restraining, more like Easter than Good Friday, vibrant, liberating, and colourful. The holistic aspect of spirituality gave rise to a new phenomenon: 'the reclaiming of the contemplative heritage of Asia's great religions'.[23]

Women's and children's situations in today's society enable women to develop, create, and voice true women's spirituality. This spirituality reflects an awareness of women's experiences, concerns, insights, and capacities, of the suffering of women and children, and of the structures that cause this suffering in our society. It stimulates our struggle against domination, neglect, and exploitation of women and children. It inspires respect for our different religious and cultural traditions. It is inspiring, encouraging, empowering, and liberating for women, it is serious and joyful and radiates inspiration, moral wisdom[24], creative energy, and the virtues needed to imagine, create, and sustain a better life for all beings.

Underneath or beyond the dominant Western and androcentric view of spirituality lies the spirituality hidden from women and all other outsiders. We can rediscover our underground spiritual heritage. We can voice the ignored and forgotten stories about strong and wise women, their survival in difficult circumstances, and their use of their wisdom and strength. We can share these gifts from our different traditions with others to stimulate each other in spiritual growth.[25]

Notes

1 I am indebted to many women, men, and organizations for their encouragement in cultivating my views on women's spirituality over the past two years. I specially wish to thank: Mary Phil Korsak and the women from the subject group Spirituality at the 1995 Conference from the European Society of Women in Theological Research, Höör, Sweden, August 18-22, 1995; the Dutch women from the spiritual academy Brahma Kumaris for the opportunity to participate in the dialogue on women's spirituality at the conference The Four Faces of Women, Mount Abu, India, March 1-7, 1996; Judith van Herik and the women and men I met in China through the Citizen Ambassador Program, Religion and Philosophy Delegation, June 13-28, 1994; the women and men I met in South Africa through the Citizen Ambassador Program, Education, Science and Technology, November 4-17, 1995; the Association for Religion and Intellectual Life for the invitation to participate in the 1996 Coolidge Research Colloquium and for exchanges with Nancy Blackman, James Breeden, Gila Gevirtz, Michael Gillgannon, Kirsten Stammer Fury, Ghazala Munir, Carol Ochs, Emilie Townes, Jane Rinehart, Carol Winkelmann and Thomas Wyly. Preparation of this article was funded by the Wetenschappelijk Onderwijsfonds Radboudstichting.

2 Ghazala Munir read this text to me when we exchanged our views on women's spirituality.

3   See also: Rosemary Radford Ruether, Mary - The Feminine Face of the Church. Philadelphia, 1997, p.24.

4 'Feminism points out the obvious but previously overlooked fact that Christianity is one of the many religious traditions in which it has been the males who have 'named the sacred' from the view point of their own male life experience. Like Narcissus of Greek mythology, the male has looked into a pool which has made the religious tradition a reflection of himself. This is what feminists mean when they call the received tradition 'androcentric': it embodies the perception of the entire world through 'male-colored glasses'.   Elizabeth Dodson Gray, Sunday School Manifesto. In the Image of her? Wellesley, Mass, United States, 1994, p .9.

5 Annie Imbens & Ineke Jonker, Godsdienst en incest. Amersfoort, 1985/Amsterdam, 1991. Christianity and Incest. Minneapolis, Minn., United States/Tunbridge Wells, United Kingdom, 1992.

6 Annie Imbens-Fransen, God in de beleving van vrouwen. Kampen, 1995. Befreiende Gottesbilder für Frauen. Damit frühe Wunden heilen. München, 1997.

7 Etty Hillesum, Het verstoorde leven. Dagboek van Etty Hillesum. 1941-1943. Bussum, 1981. Maureen Dunbar, Catherine - The Story of a Young Girl Who Died of Anorexia. Harmondsworth, United Kingdom, 1986. Anne Benjamin, Winnie Mandela. Ein Stück meiner Seele ging mit ihm. Hamburg, 1984. Nienke Begeman, Victorine. Amsterdam, 1988. Marilyn French, Her mother's Daughter. 1987.

8 Mary Daly, Beyond God the Father. Toward a Philosophy of Women's Liberation. Boston, 1973.

9 See also Carol P. Christ, Diving Deep and Surfacing. Women Writers on Spiritual Quest. Boston, 1980.

10 Annie Imbens-Fransen, Women - Health - Religion. In: Women, Health & Urban Policies, International Symposium, Vienna, 13-15 May, 1991, pp. 171-175.

11 Imbens & Jonker, p.34.

12 Aruna Gnanadason, No Longer a Secret. The church and violence against women. WCC Publications, Geneva, 1993, p.1.

13 Two titles: Dee Ann Miller, How little We Knew. Collusion and Confusion with Sexual Misconduct. Lafayette, Lousiana, United States 1993. David Johnson & Jeff VanVonderen, The Subtle Power of Spiritual Abuse. Recognizing and Escaping Spiritual Manipulation and False Spiritual Authority Within the Church. Minneapolis, Minn. United States, 1991.

14 'Why is it that everywhere women are dominated? Why do they continue to be submissive? Why is it that on all five continents one finds a quasi-identical situation, different only in its form? Why is it that women always end up doing the domestic jobs?' You can go wherever you want - to America, France, India - and everywhere you will find women in the middle of doing domestic chores: that's a common aspect everywhere. Another thing is that women on all five continents are always subordinate to men. The subordination we're speaking about exists everywhere.' Awa Thiam, in: Alice Walker & Pratibha Parmar, Warrior Marks. Female Genital Mutilation and the Sexual Blinding of Women. New York/San Diego, 1993, p.284-285.

15 Annie Imbens-Fransen, Research on Women and Health in the Netherlands. in: Information in a Healthy Society. Health in the Information Society, Eindhoven, 17-20 November, 1993. (Ed. Ad van Berlo, Yvonne Kiwitz-de Ruijter.) Knegsel, 1992, pp. 202-209.

16 Michael Gillgannon used the word 'outsiders' while explaining that my research and analyses are important for all people excluded from mainstream discourse in theology and philosophy. James Breeden and some other people of colour stressed the importance of my research for people of colour.

17 Women in Sweden, the United States and South Africa advised me to read Clarissa Pinkola Estés, Ph.D. Women Who Run With the Wolves. Myths and Stories of the Wild Woman Archetype. New York, 1995.

18 Annie Imbens-Fransen: Qiu Jin en de bevrijdingsstrijd van Chinese vrouwen. [Qiu Jin en Chinese women's liberation struggle.] In Symforosa, June 1996, nr. 31, p.42-43.

19 Among the womanist theologians, cf. Emilie M. Townes, In a Blaze of Glory. Womanist Spirituality As Social Witness. Nashville, Tenn., United States, 1995.

20 rsula King, Spirituality in a Multi-Religious Household. Women in Dialogue - Voices and Visions of Empowerment. Lecture at the Sixth ESWTR Conference, Sweden, August 18-22, 1995.

21 Ursula King, p.6.

22 Mary John Mananzan, OSB, Theological Perspectives of a Religious Woman Today - Four Trends of the Emerging Spirituality. In: Feminist Theology from the Third World. Ursula King, ed. New York, 1994, p.340-349.

23 Mary John Mananzan, OSB, p.347-348.

24 Emilie M. Townes, p.11.

25 'For where two or three come together in my name, I am there with them.' (Matthew 18:20). 'Honesty among friends is an opening for God.' Anthea Church, Inner Beauty. A book of virtues. Australia, 1994, p.44.

133

Maaike de Haardt

REVERENCE FOR LIFE IN FACING DEATH:
A READING OF MAY SARTON'S "A RECKONING"

*If only the body were as simple as a flower, opening and
fading in an hour or two. For the body it seemed such a
long, intricate process by comparison, whole galaxies of
molecules slowly transforming into what? Going where?*

May Sarton

Introduction

In this article I shall present a reading of May Sarton's novel *A
Reckoning* as a source and an example of a transforming spirituality.
The heart of this novel is the description of the dying process of the
main character. Through this description, the novel is an empowering
and, at the same time, critical force for the development of a feminist
spirituality and theology.

Feminist theologians assert that many women express their faith
and knowledge of God in a language and in stories different from those
which are traditionally acknowledged as spiritual or religious. Rather
than expressing themselves in stories that speak explicitly of God in the
classical terms of the mysterium tremendum and fascinans, as wholly
other or the ultimate concern, women have other ways of expressing
their experiences of the sacred, of transcendence, or of God. Women
tell other stories and use other words to name the sustaining or
grounding power of their lives.

The classical and dominant, often male, religious language and stories refer to experiences and events which are isolated from daily life.
The spiritual writers often describe their experiences as an experience
of discontinuity, as a contradiction of everything that was known and
valued before. It is precisely this disruptive character of the experience
that gives the experience its religious meaning. Antrophologist Victor
Turner used the term 'liminality' to describe these situations and their
function in religious narratives and rituals. "Liminality" is described as "-a
moment of suspension of normal rules and roles, crossing of boundaries and a violation of norms, that enables us to understand those
norms, even where they conflict, and move on either to incorporate or

reject them".[1] These events all take place in the public sphere. In her work on the piety of medieval women, the historian Caroline Walker Bynum has demonstrated that the definition of this concept is biased by gender, Christianity and class.[2] 'Liminality', in this male-gendered sense, has to do with the limits one meets in life. The ultimate limit one has to face, so it is said not only by anthropologists but by theologians as well, is death.

Feminist theologian Rebecca Chopp has argued that religion takes care of the limits of bourgeois existence. She understands these limits as that which the social-symbolic order denies, represses or forgets. Religion, she asserts, describes and prescribes moments of trans-cendence from this social-symbolic order through such terms as awe, mysterium tremendum et fascinans, and ultimacy.[3] But then, Chopp asks, "How can woman being not and not-being, have the "limit-expe-riences" that the religious order requires, when women are already and always outside the limits?"[4] Walker Bynum formulates the same problem in other words when she says that "one either has to see wo-man's religious stance as permanently liminal or as never quite becoming so".[5] Unless of course, one redefines what counts as religious experience or as spirituality.

Feminist theologians point out that the nexus of religious experience, at least for many women and also for a lot of men, is in and through relationships, friends, families, and memories of the dead. For most women, they are lived out in the realm of the private, composed of duty, nurturing, preparing, waiting, taking care. These experiences of 'everyday life', are the necessary condition for spiritual or religious experiences. In every day life we can find what is traditionally called "forces of being larger than the self." Carol Christ has convincingly des-cribed women's spiritual quest in her now famous *Diving Deep and Surfacing*. She says: "Women's spiritual quest concerns a woman's awakening to the depths of her soul and her position in the universe. It involves asking basic questions: Who am I? Why am I here? What is my place in the universe? In answering these questions, a woman must listen to her own voice and come to terms with her own experience. She must break long-standing habits of seeking approval, of trying to please parents, lovers, husbands, friends, children, but never herself."[6]

Feminist theologians have a preference for the language of stories, poetry, song, and rituals to criticise the dominant spiritual and theologi-cal traditions and to describe other kinds of religious experiences. It is from this perspective that I shall read May Sarton's novel "*A Reckoning*" as an example of a religious narrative dealing with the ultimate limit of life: death.

However, before turning to the novel, I shall start with a short summing up of the most striking feminist objections to classical theology of death and afterlife. It is this theology that lays the ground for the heavily criticised life-denying Christian spirituality.

With regard to death, feminist theologian Rosemary Ruther states: "The question is not whether men and women share the same mortality; it is whether women have the same stake in denying their mortality through doctrines of life after death, [...]."[7] Although formulated in a negative way, these feminist objections are indicative of elements for a renewed and life-affirming theology and spirituality of finitude and death. Next I will discuss some of these elements, notably the most complex of these: the body, finitude, and the image of God. I shall relate them to contemporary discussions in women's studies. These reflections are the background from which I shall present what is the core of this paper, a reading of May Sarton's *A Reckoning*. In my opinion, we can find traces in Sarton's novel which are critical of classical as well as feminist thinking on finitude and death. They can spark creativity in the search for an authentic spirituality in dealing with the unavoidable limits of this life.

In a nutshell, the basic problem feminist theologians have with the classical theology of death is its strong emphasis on immortality and after-life.[8] Almost every feminist theologian, regardless of the differences among them, agrees with the view that Christian spirituality and theology denies finitude and death. Some even say that this applies to all Western culture. What is more: "As a paradox this denial may express a more profound failure of our culture, the failure to affirm life on this earth, in these bodies".[9]

Because it is formulated too schematically and therefore overdone, the theological basis of this classical thinking needs "a doctrine of God's absolute transcendence that correlates with a theology in which this earth, this body and this life are despised, and in which the spiritual goal is to transcend the flesh and its desires and to seek a life after death in which the limitations of finitude are overcome".[10] In this theological model, carnality is equal to sin, and death is God's punishment for sin. Women, nature, and the body are the icons of this despised carnality, sin, and death, and they all need to be overcome.

In contrast to this thinking, feminist theologians stress that death is an indefeasible or natural part of life and that we must learn to love this life that ends in death. No feminist theologian -as far as I know- explicitly denies the possibility of some sort of individual or collective survival. However, they all are very persistent in stressing that you should not live your life in light of such a possibility, no more than it should be a theological concern to speculate on the possible 'eternal meaning of life', let alone that this should become the focus of the religious message or spirituality.

However, it seems to me that feminists, in rejecting traditional eschatology and in their emphasis and continuous struggle against death as a consequence of injustice and violence, seldom address questions regarding a more 'common' or non-violent death. Whenever they speak about dying and death as the natural end of life, it is called 'good' or 'inevitable' or a 'process of growing' without any references to the (often painful) materiality of the dying body.[11]

In agreement with the general contemporary and feminist emphasis on the body, feminist theologians underscore the importance of (women's) bodies in relation to creation, to immanence, to redemption; they stress the goodness of sexuality and the embodied character of every religious experience and knowledge. The celebration of women's bodies is an important act of self-affirmation and establishes an autonomous religious identity.

Without denying the relevance of this project for political as well as theological reasons, the proud statement 'my body, myself' is strongly contradicted by the experience of all kinds of bodily inconvenience, as long as we have not fully accounted for the ambivalence of the body.

Clearly, feminist theologians are right to criticise the otherworldliness and the life and body-denying features of traditional spirituality and theology. However, despite all their good intentions, in formulating body- and life-affirming alternatives, they have not been very successful in wholly integrating transience and finitude, bodily decay, or suffering from illness and daily dying. To develop and transform a theology and spirituality that fully acknowledge the 'conditions of life', we need to recognise the painful or even paradoxical elements of life as well, even when they are 'not nice'.

Therefore my question is: Under what conditions is it possible to 'celebrate the body' as feminist theologians and contemporary philosophers suggest, while at the same time accounting for the fact that this body can suffer and at a certain moment will decline and die? How should we deal with the fact that a body is ever changing and unavoidably finite without falling into abstractions that have nothing to do with the living body?

In formulating my questions this way, the body again becomes the focus and the centre of a spirituality, and of reflections on finitude and death.

At this point I would like to introduce May Sarton's novel 'A Reckoning'.[12] In this novel, May Sarton tells the story of Laura Spelman's life between the moment she walks up the street, after her

GP told her that she is suffering from terminal cancer, and the moment she dies. In these few weeks between the last winter snow and the first signs of spring, Laura Spelman draws up the balance of her life: "It is then to be a reckoning."(10) Although there are several interesting lines in the novel, for the moment I will focus on the question of the body and identity in relation to death. The message of her forthcoming death alternately scares her and brings her feelings of 'a blessed state', a situation she could not easily define in words. Dying can be compared with "[...] being born, falling in love, bearing a first child.... always there is terror first." (10) It is striking, by comparison with many of the books written by men, that Laura does not view death as fearful, loathsome or absurd, as is reflected in many theological and philosophical works. For Laura, death is not the ultimate limit that should be transcended. In facing the fact that she is dying, her fear gradually diminishes. But this fear is never directed at death itself. In the beginning, her fear stems from her uncertainty about how to deal with the sense of doom she expects of her children, her sisters and others: she doesn't want to deal with *their* fear of *her* dying. Moreover, she fears and is repulsed by the idea of giving up her autonomy and being in need of the help of a nurse.

Even her 'a reckoning' itself, her reflection and reliving of the important relations of her life, generates a kind of fear, especially with regard to her relationships with her mother and her daughter. In the face of all these complex, unresolved, and all too complicated relations, Laura wonders "whether she had the courage."

However, all this fear and uncertainty does not keep Laura from thinking of her death first of all as a great experience. The moment she tries to formulate how she is experiencing her death as a great adventure, she realises she can't put it into words. Here, as in other scenes, the story explicitly balances on the boundary between what can be said and what cannot. It seems to be, what Robert Lifton and Valerie Saiving have both called, a kind of 'ecstasy', an intensity of life for which there is no adequate language.[13]

From the beginning, Laura wants her dying to be an adventure she undertakes in her own way. And without exactly knowing what that means, she is determined to die at home, with as little medical care as possible and related to the fear just mentioned without any of her loved ones.

Although Laura had a Christian religious education, she does not, as in traditional christianity, relate her illness and death to sin, punishment, judgement, no more than she thinks of her dying in relation to an afterlife or to a personal God. Even very common objections in situations of a sudden deadly disease, such as "I do not deserve this", are missing in

Laura's reactions. She simply seems to accept the fact that she is dying, and she only regrets that she is not being given some more time. Her Christian belief was replaced by "the belief she was an organic part of the universe, and that was why she felt so strongly that man, attempting to change the flow, to alter the design for his own purpose, missed the point. This [...] was why she wanted so passionately her own death. She wanted to be the part of a natural process, unimpeded." (38) At the very same moment, she asks whether cancer really is natural, and there is no answer. However, it is important to note that the fact that she accepts her deadly disease does not mean that dying is easy for Laura.

Laura views dying as a kind of ultimate growth or wholeness, a kind of ultimate harmony between mind and body as, so it is suggested, one sometimes experiences in love or work (218). We also find this vision of dying in some feminist, as well as classical theological, reflections on death, for instance, in the work of Mary Grey or Karl Rahner. As I mentioned before, I wonder if this approach, although not intended, is not a reinforcement of the mind-body dualism, by making an abstraction of the actual suffering and disintegrating condition of the body.

Laura's vision appeared to be an illusion, which was to be disturbed very soon: Her cancer is proceeding very fast. This brings a loss of physical power, a loss of appetite and an increasing need for (medical) care. "Dying is turning out to be harder than I supposed, and longer. [...] I had imagined that dying might be like that- coming into a wholeness, but the trouble is one has no strength. It leaks away."(218)

In this process, it is the body that destroys the idea of the wholeness of dying. The body that sometimes seems to be the most terrifying and undeniable other and, at the same time, is the most terrifying and undeniable self. This happens in more than one way. Laura tries to formulate why dying is much harder than she supposed: "I do not believe we wish to leave our bodies, perhaps it is that. Mine is of very little use to me now, but-" (218) It is once again one of the moments that Laura realises there is very little language available for all her experiences.

At another moment, while Laura undergoes the draining of her lungs, she realises not only the decay of her body, but also the distastefulness of this process: "It would be an awful shock for him [her son] to see those bottles filling up with the dark-orange fluid- She dreaded it herself, the visible sign of corruption." (221) Sarton writes explicitly of these moments of physical disfigurement in a sober, clinical way, without any commentary but as a description of a particular situation. That gives these descriptions of visible transience a certain credibility without appealing to a false compassion.

But perhaps the most confusing and disturbing moments are those in which Laura experiences the frightful situation of feeling as if she lives in two separate places, the body and the not-body that she calls her Self. Here we are confronted with the question, mentioned earlier, of the meaning of 'my body-myself' and the relation between identity and body. In the novel, we see a continuously changing and, from more than one perspective, ambivalent way of responding to this question. For instance, when Laura is in the hospital, the impersonal and sheer technical, body-centred treatment gives her the feeling that her "identity reaches zero". This loss of identity is caused by the way other people relate, or better not-relate, to the *person* Laura. They only relate to her body, that is, they relate to her as 'a body'. At the same time, the reactions of her body make her life 'extremely uncomfortable', and she feels completely detached from her body. However, she realises she cannot find herself without "this machine" and she decides that the only solution is to reject this tameless body as irrelevant. (214) It is the same moment she faces the fact that she has to give up her independence and that she cannot make her journey to death alone. She no longer is the only director of her life. "Things were out of control". Her body is out of control, and the way other people react and relate to her is out of control as well. In my opinion, it is striking, and no coincidence, that the process of Laura's relating to her body has a parallel in her relating to other people. The process and the act of dying, of letting go, in all its confusion, disintegration, and pain, takes place within a context of relations.

When she realised that detachment from her body, as well as her detachment from other people, did not work out because, as she says, "somehow we are in our body", she called this experience a kind of revelation: "When I gave up trying to do it alone, a lot of light flowed in." (220) But even this experience does not hold forever; it could not prevent her feeling, for a moment, like a stranger when she is back home again. "But if she was a stranger here [in her own garden], where was home? And who was she herself now? The real panic was a loss of identity, for she seemed inextricable woven into her body's weakness and discomfort, into struggling sick lungs. What essence was there to be separated from her hand, her flesh, her bones? Laura lifted her hand, so thin it had become transparent. Is this I? This leaflike thing, falling away, this universe of molecules disintegrating, this miracle about to transform into nothingness? "(233-234) There is no answer at that moment, and it is the everyday routine of seeing a visitor and having tea that seems to calm Laura's panic and that breaks the intensity of her feelings.

For me, all these different descriptions of identity, and of the way the condition of the body can be a threat as well as a sign of identity, reveals that (feminist) theology and spirituality needs a more differentiated concept of 'wholeness'. This novel ultimately rejects the assumption that seems to underlie the concept of wholeness, that is, that it is health, understood as integrity/wholeness of the body, that is the condition for other kinds of well being.[14] For this reason I question the universal importance of the theological notion of 'healing'. And I would like to mention here the relation that can be found between 'healing', redemption, and the definitive healing and redemption at the resurrection/in the eternal life. The concept of 'healing' can indeed be powerful as an ethical category, as a metaphor directing social change, but ultimately it disregards the factual physical reality of the transience of the body. Contrary to this position, this novel makes it clear why it is important to reflect on another kind of 'wholeness'; a wholeness that has nothing to do with bodily 'healing'. The novel describes a healing -or perhaps it is better to speak of finding an identity- that happens at the time of physical disintegration, fragmentarisation and atomising. It is not the literary 'healing' of the disintegrated body but the healing that consists in the ability to live with this disintegration, to live with and in this body without the urgent need to deny what is inevitable, however, without neglecting the painful or frightening moments of that life. In her ability to bear the ultimate limit of life, Laura Spelman shows an intense spiritual power. Only then, it seems to me, will the feminist plea for reverence for this life and this body include all of this life and all of this body, with its transience, decay, and death.

I find this novel stimulates more systematic reflection on a kind of ability to live living in a complete and all-embracing uncertainty and on the meaning of a confidence to let go of all need to control, but without falling into apathy or despair and without forgetting social struggle. For a time Laura tried to 'keep things under control' in order to keep her identity: but it did not work out.

In traditional theology, this loom of despair is overcome by trying to gain greater control. Therefore, there has to be an explanation for death and dying, and there has to be the certainty that transience, disintegration and finitude can, in the end, be overcome. But, it seems to me that did not work out either.

I want to finish by turning to the novel again:

> "If only the body were as simple as a flower, opening and fading in an hour or two. For the body it seemed such a long, intricate process by comparison, whole galaxies of molecules slowly transforming themselves into what? Going where?"(225)

And after these thoughts, when Mary enters the room, Laura said "I am afraid". [. . .] I don't know how to let go. I don't know what is happening to me. I am scared, scared.[. . .] scared of the dark." And then Mary answers: "'It is all right. The sun is just rising.' It was not an answer, but in a way it was. For the moment the words held a true promise: whatever happened the sun would rise."

Notes

1. Caroline Walker Bynum, "Women's Stories, Women's Symbols. A Critique of Victor Turner's Theory of Liminality", in: Caroline Walker Bynum, *Fragmentation and Redemption. Essays on Gender and the Human Body in Medieval Religion*, New York 1992, 30. Turner in turn, borrowed the concept 'liminality' from van Gennep.

2. Caroline Walker Bynum, "Women's Stories, Women's Symbols. A Critique of Victor Turner's Theory of Liminality".

3. Rebecca S. Chopp, The Power to Speak. Feminism. Language, God, New York 1990, 119.

4. Rebecca Chopp, *The Power to Speak*, 118.

5. Caroline Walker Bynum, o.c. 33

6.Carol P. Christ, Diving Deep and Surfacing. Women Writers on Spiritual Quest, Boston 1980, 8-9.

7. Rosemary Radford Ruether, Sexism and God-talk. Toward a Feminist Theology. Boston 1983, 235.

9. Carol Christ, Laughter of Aphrodite: Reflections on a Journey to the Goddess, New York, 1987,214.

10. Carol Christ, Laughter of Aphrodite, 217.

11. I have made an extensive analysis of this, in my opinion, far too optimistic feminist attitude towards death, in my book '*Dichter by de Dood. Feministisch-theologische aanzetten tot een theologie van de dood.*' Zoetermeer 1993.

12. May Sarton, A Reckoning. W.W. Norton and Company, New York/London (1978) 1981. All quotations are from this edition.

13. Valerie Saiving, "Our Bodies,/Our Selves: Reflections on Sickness, Aging and Death", *Journal of Feminist Studies in Religion* 4 (1988) 117-127; Robert Lifton, *The Broken Connection: On Death and the Continuity of Life*, New York 1979, chapter 2, "The Experience of Transcendence", 24-35.

14. See for instance Sallie McFague, The Ethic of God as Mother, Lover and Friend, in: A. Loades (ed.)Feminist Theology. A Reader, London 1990, 261-269.

APOKRIF

Én Uram, Teremtőm
Mikor engem teremtettél
Szentlelkeddel szerettél
Szent véreddel megváltottál
Fogodj hozzám Úristenem
Fogodj hozzám Úristenem.
Én lefekszem én ágyamba
Testi, lelki koporsómba.

Adj három angyalt a fejemhez
Adj három angyalt a testemhez
Egy őrizzen,
Egy élesszen
Egy elvigye a lelkemet
Krisztus Urunknak a markába.

Megcsengítik a harangot
Kigyülének az angyalok.
Kihágok a kalavári hegyre
Látom a töviseket
Kivirágozva, kilevelezve,
Szebbnél szebben virágozva
Futtatott aranyból.

Beléje ül Szűz Mária aranyos
székibe
Könyökig könnybe, térdig
vérbe.
Miért sírsz Szent Anyám?
Hogyne sírnék Szent Fiam?
A zsidók törvényt tettek,
Hogy szent pénteken elfognak
Rút nyálakkal köpdösnek
Vas kesztyűkkel szabdaznak
Hajad húznak, nagyon
csúfolkodnak

Szent Fiam elmenj a fekete földre
Ádámnak a bűnös fiaihoz
Hírdesd ki ezt a két-három,
Igémet-szómat
Aki ezt az imádságot
Reggel, este elmondja
Kezibe adom a mennyország
kulcsát
S ki el nem tudja mondani
Mennyországnak a kapuján
nem oda bémenjen.[1]

APOCRYPHE

My Lord my creator
The day you created me
With your soul you loved me
With your blood you redeemed me
Stay with me Oh my Lord
Stay with me Oh my Lord
I lie down in my bed
In the coffin of my soul and body.

Place three angels at my head
Place three angels at my feet
One to guard me
One to revive me
One to take my soul away
Into the hands of Christ our Lord.

They ring the bells
The angels gather
I climb the hill of Calvary
I can see the thorns
In full bloom
With beautiful golden flowers

Virgin Mary sits in her golden chair
Up to her elbows in tears, up to her
knees in blood
Why are you crying Holy Mother?
Why wouldn't I my Holy Son?
They have proclaimed
That by Holy Friday you will be caught
They will spit you with their ugly saliva
And torture you with iron gloves
And pull your hair, and mock you.

Go to the Black Land my Holy Son
To Adam's guilty children
And teach them these two or three
Words and prayers of mine
Whosoever says this prayer
In the morning and in the evening
Will get the keys of Heaven from me
Those who cannot say them
Will be banished from the gates
of Heaven.

---

[1]   Erdélyi Zsuzsanna, Hegyet
hágék, Lőtöt lépék; Archaikus népi
imádságok. Budapest 1974

Marianna Király

Toward The Within

This text is an old folk prayer which expresses my feelings of being a Hungarian and a Christian. I heard this prayer for the first time on a CD by a well-known Hungarian folk singer, Marta Sebestyen. I was really impressed by it. I know that in the Reformed tradition this prayer is theologically not correct; especially because of its belief in Mary and the guardian angels. Still, I think this is a very powerful and deep prayer. I can hear the voice of the ancient, pre-Christian Hungarian soul that meets Christianity here. According to folk tradition the angel is like a spirit bird that carries your soul away at night. You travel to another place we can call dreamland. The angel brings your soul back in the morning as you wake: - if he/she did not, you would die. This is just like a spiritual journey.

In this article I would like to talk about my own spiritual journey. This is, at the same time a journey into the world and a journey towards the within. What does it mean to say, "towards the within"? Is it possible to make a spiritual journey towards one's self? When does this spiritual journey start - at birth or before? And when does it end - when we die or after death? There are certain periods in our life when we ask these questions, e.g. when we lose someone who is close to our heart, or when we suffer a serious illness, but also when we experience extraordinary joy and happiness - thus, when the very ground of our being is shaken. I encounter this as a pastor at funerals, weddings, baptisms, and counseling. Personally I experience all these questions and look for answers. I would like to share my responses to these questions by relating my own spiritual journey as a pastor, as well as my encounter with the people whom I met on my path.

When did this journey start? My earliest memory goes back to my childhood, where I always imagined an invisible world that I could not touch and could not see. Later on when I was about seven, I created another world which existed under the piano. I lay there and created a new alphabet and new linguistic codes. Of course, this world only existed at night, when I could be there without being disturbed by anyone.

I fully enjoyed my night-time life. There were angels and spirits. It was full of light and peace. Perhaps I just wanted to escape from the trouble of everyday-life at school and in my family, where I was the only child. But then, I did not know about God, the Bible, and the Church, because at that time Communism was very powerful, and religious education was not encouraged. Parents were genuinely afraid to take their children to Sunday school. As a child I did not know about this sad situation. I only felt that something was missing, that I could not experience my whole environment. I wanted to create a world not only for myself, but also for everybody else in order to become happy and fulfilled.

As I grew older, whenever I couldn't play with other children at home, I started to read books about world religions. I found them fascinating. In school I heard of Sándor Körösi Csoma, who was born in the nineteenth century in Transylvania, and went to Tibet to find the origins of the Hungarians. I really admired him for his resolution, passion and persistence. He became an inspiration and a role model for me and helped me to discover why we are here on earth. I decided to go to Tibet as soon as possible. At age eleven, I started preparing myself in exercises for this great journey by sleeping on the floor underneath my piano, with which I had a special relationship. I also began to watch my diet in order to get strong and I did exercises for survival-training such as standing alone in the dark for a while without getting afraid, or not eating a cookie when I desired it. My parents had already started to worry about me because of my crazy ideas. Later on I came to understand that every one of us has a different vocation, and we need to find our own and not someone else's.

When I was eighteen and started to plan for my further education, I decided to go to the Seminary in Debrecen and study theology. Everyone was shocked. At this time this meant that you would forfeit a successful future in the Communist society. But I wanted to go to the seminary, for I never had a chance to study theology in school. I also wanted to know what communists were trying to hide from the people. Why was it important to keep people from God and the Church? I was very curious about what the seminary would look like. How does it feel to be there? What kind of people are there? What is the Bible and who is God? I did not even think about becoming a pastor. And the professors of the seminary did not accept me at first. They thought I was not ready, which was true. They understood my intentions were good, but they also saw my uncertainty. I was told I needed to experience more of what the Church was about, since I had passed my confirmation-exam only two months before. They suggested that first I should work for a year as a deacon at one of the Church institutions before I started with the Seminary-studies. I decided to work at a church home for elderly women, which turned out to be a great experience for me. Many of the women were members of the Hungarian Reformed churches, and some of them were former deacons. Being around them and talking with them was fascinating for me. At the beginning of my spiritual journey, I learned from the residents who were at the end of their own journey. They had built up their theology in their life-long experiences. The deacons, who we called sisters, had also practically applied their beliefs in very difficult times during the war and after the war, until the communist state closed their institutions. Over the next year, 1986, I learned from the residents about spirituality by listening to their wisdom, and shared experiences of Christ and of the faith. This was heavy spiritual food for me, as I was just like a "baby" in faith.

I wanted to leave the seminary in the first year. I did not find the depth of spirituality there that I had found among the elderly women. I struggled because I could not breathe any fresh air there. In spite of this, I stayed. I studied Hebrew and Greek grammar, doctrines, and Church history in order to "find" God. I did not find God but I kept looking for Him. At that time, I was still looking for God in the world outside myself.

In 1989, in the year of the political upheaval in Hungary - when the Communist party was dissolved - and in my third year at the seminary, I traveled to Scotland. I wanted to see the world beyond the Iron Curtain and to intensively experience the English language. A friend had given me the address of Iona, where a retreat-center had been built at the site of an old monastery, and where I could stay for several months. Immediately I could sense the Celtic spirit that made this place so unique. The volunteers like me, came from all over the world and I felt the size of the planet. I could breath in the spiritual air of the earth. It was the first time I felt comfortable and at home in the church liturgy.

> And we worship to remind ourselves that together we are the church, the body of Christ met in this place. . . And we worship so that we may consciously allow ourselves to be drawn into God's presence, and be changed by the spirit of that presence. Of course, we are always in God's presence wherever we are, at work or at meals or alone, but in worship, we deliberately place that at the front of our minds, and try as much as we can to experience the mystery of God.[1]

At Iona, every day was a different kind of service. Monday the "peace and justice service" and Tuesday the "Healing service". Wednesday the "pilgrimage round the island": we walked to St. Martin's cross, the Augustinian nunnery, St. Columba's bay, the Hermit's cell and so forth. Thursday, there was a "Commitment service". The communion on Friday evening developed into an informal celebration of the week spent together in the Abbey. Sunday we celebrated the morning service. In the evening there was a silent service, which I enjoyed the most.

One of the deepest experiences I had was in the healing services on Tuesday. During the second part of this service, there was "an opportunity for those present at the service to pray for each other and to receive and share in the ministry of the laying on of hands."[2] Thereby we prayed, everyone together, for those who were kneeling in a circle in front of the altar:

Spirit of the living God, present with us now,
enter you, body, mind and spirit,
and heal you of all that harms you
in Jesus' name. Amen.[3]

The first time, I did not dare join the circle. I remained in the pew. It was not because I was ashamed of kneeling down. Rather, I was afraid. Coming from the Reformed tradition, I did not know what was going on here. I felt that there was power present during the service, but I did not know what power it was. After a few weeks of remaining in the pew and listening, I got tired of being scared and I joined the circle for the first time. I was determined and thought, "what comes will come". When I was kneeling in the circle and the pastor put his hands on my head, I felt an unmistakable energy flow into me. My eyes were closed, but I sensed everybody around me as well as an energy present in the circle. It was very warm and intense.

The experience in Iona that really hit me was an encounter with spiritual beings. Then again, perhaps it was just the spiritual radiance of this ancient place that I sensed. One night two of my friends came back from their walk and were shocked to tell me that they had seen a ghost. The whole community became excited about this. I was very curious to find out more. I wanted to meet the ghost, too. I went to the cemetery at midnight on a full-moon. But of course, I could not find it because ghosts do not come when you call them. I was disappointed. A few months later, I went down to Wales in order to work there and then it happened. I stayed alone in the old wing of a recreation center run by the Methodist Church. I always heard noises and steps during the night, and my door was usually open in the mornings. I thought this was a hallucination. One night, I was half asleep, when my door was open. I got up and put a chair in front of the door so that it would not open again. The next morning I could not get up because my back was hurting so much. The medical treatment that I was given was not very helpful. Later on, I talked to the director of the center about what had happened. I told him about my experience in the room and also mentioned the ghost story of Iona. He told me that who ever had stayed in this room had similar experiences. He also told me that according to other people who had known the place for a long time, there was really a spirit in that room. He believed in this spirit, and so did I. Finally, my curiosity was satisfied!

But it was not this simple. For a year afterwards I was seriously ill. I was partially paralyzed below my waist. The doctors wanted to cure me with Western medicine and do surgery, but I rejected it. I believed that this illness had to do with my experience of the spirit. I turned to the Eastern way of healing and went for an acupuncture treatment. This helped me. Reading about Eastern ways of healing, I also learned about Taoism. I understood that the Taoist principle was that everything needs to be in balance. I felt out of balance because of my ghost-experience, and I could only be healed when I brought back balance into my life.

This balance also had to do with my belief in God that needed to be put into the right place. I realized that before my serious illness, I wanted to find God in the wrong place. I had searched for Him in nature, in other people, and in the Church, but I could not find Him there. I had thought I could find Him in the wisdom of the deacons, in my theological studies in the seminary or in monasteries. Still I could not find Him. Because of what I had gone through, I came to the recognition that God is in us. And then another journey started: the journey to my interior life.

After I finished Seminary I was assigned to two small rural communities in one of the poorest areas in Hungary. Before my ordination I was required to serve a practical year. After the safe school years I met the reality of life and words like death, anger, gossip, fight, hate. But also joy became very meaningful for me as a concrete experience. I learned what it is like when you have to support everybody else spiritually, but no one is supporting you. I experienced spiritual emptiness. On the other hand, I learned wisdom from very simple people who had almost no education. And I learned to be very happy about little things in my work. I learned to be gracious when someone says "thank you" for being nice, for paying attention, or for preaching a good sermon.

After my practical year I received a scholarship to Princeton Theological Seminary in New Jersey. The day I received the letter of acceptance was the day of the funeral of my father. I went to Princeton in 1993 with the feeling of leaving behind my past, and starting a new life in another country. Coming to America from Eastern Europe was astonishing. The image of America that I was given through movies and advertisements seemed to suggest a "wonderland". Of course, the reality was very different. In America I found poverty, loneliness, and hard working people, - just the other side of the coin of this image. I felt the culture shock every day. When I wanted to buy milk and bread in a shop, the variety of products were overwhelming. I often felt afraid of doing routine things, but eventually I learned to handle the American way of life.

In Princeton a vast variety of courses were available for me to choose from; for example, "medieval mysticism", which opened a new horizon for me. I already had understood that the path to God is through the interior life. But I had felt alone with this notion. By reading mystical writers and especially the early Christian Scriptures I felt that I was not alone. Elisabeth of Hungary, Bernard of Clairvaux, Hildegard of Bingen, Meister Eckhardt, Angela of Foligno and other mystics were close to me. I felt we had things in common. In their visions and their knowing of God, I found freedom.

After Princeton, my path lead me to become senior pastor of The Hungarian Reformed Church, first in New York and later in Passaic, New Jersey. Being Hungarian in another country, and leading a Hungarian community, is not an easy task. Living in America as a Hungarian pastor, I am not only a communicator between God and my congregation, but also I have to build a bridge between the two cultures. I have to preach in English and Hungarian, and I encounter a lot of older Hungarians whose children have left the congregation in order to settle down as "Americans" at other places. I am also a bridge between the past and the present - past meaning our ancestors' way of living and present meaning the modern world. I found myself cultivating the Hungarian folk tradition and having Hungarian folk music and dancing evenings in my congregation. This is truly a source of my own spirituality.

Looking back on the path I have chosen, I look at it as a journey towards the within. I am certain that others could talk about their own journeys, telling stories similar to mine. What I want to share here is that this journey is a living thing, and always a process; the process of living it, experiencing it, and listening to inner voices. We have to take our time to listen to what is happening in our lives and to see the connections of our happenings; to look at our life as a whole. What happens to you during your lifetime besides your physical body changing in your spirit? Each moment of your life has a purpose that fits your whole identity. You can read it in the book of your life. You can turn the pages of that book. However, I believe that angels lead your finger to read the lines, - just as in the prayer at the beginning.

The angels guard you. They revive you and they can take your soul away into the hands of Christ our Lord.

Notes

1 The Iona Community Worship Book, BPCC Paulton Books 1988, p. 8

2 Ibid., p. 35.

3 Ibid., p. 38.

Gabriella Lettini

Praying With My Eyes Open
A Spiritual Journey

My heart is bubbling over with joy;
With God it is good to be a woman.
From now on let all people proclaim:
it is a wonderful gift to be.
The One in whom power truly rests
has lifted us up to praise;
God's goodness shall fall like a shower
on the trusting of every age.
The disregarded have been raised up:
the pompous and the powerful shall fall.
God has feasted the empty-bellied,
and the rich have discovered their void.
God has made good the word
given at the dawn of time.[1]

For many years, I felt my life was like a broken mirror whose pieces could not fit together. Today, I feel as I used to feel as a child: whole, powerful and alive. Today, I can fully join in Mary's song: in God it is good to be a woman. In this newly found sense of wholeness I experience my spirituality as being in symphony with and participating in the life-giving power of God. When I speak about spirituality I'm thus ultimately speaking about my life itself, in all its different aspects, from my theological studies to my love of the arts, from my political and social activism to my most intimate relationships, from preaching to enjoying the winter sunlight on my skin, from laughing to crying, from sharing to receiving.

This particularly blessed moment of my life is part of a long and quite painful process that is both very personal and contextual but also somehow common, as I learned through the years of sharing my experiences with women of very different backgrounds. For instance, I could tell you about our last Women's retreat in my congregation in New York City[2]. In one of our activities, I first led my group in a guided meditation, where they had to see themselves as a river, thus re-experiencing different situations and moments of their lives. After this moment, each woman was invited to draw for the others the river of her life, putting down on paper particular places and situations, and sharing

151

her own story. This experience has been very touching and empowering for all. First of all, I was surprised by the high level of connection among us that generated a deep sense of trust. As we blessed the space around us, we felt it was truly holy ground. The richness of our stories, about fifteen, was impressive. The blank paper in front of us was soon filled by lines and drawings. We found several points of connection among our rivers. Something that really struck me, and that another woman put wonderfully into words, was the fact that all our rivers, at the beginning, were deep, wide, strong, full of life and energy. But sooner or later, the rivers became creeks, brooklets, some even disappeared and went underground. And here there were stories of abuse, experienced in different forms and degrees, from a systematic sexist and homophobic education to incest, sexual harassment, rape. The strong rivers were no more. Strong children became weak teenagers, who experienced low-self esteem, depression, anguish, repressed anger, sense of unworthiness, guilt and powerlessness. Eros became relegated to sexuality, and was associated with fear, abuse, degradation, guilt. For some women in the group, these feelings tragically led to substance abuse, mental illness and attempted suicide. However, in almost every story, the river was starting to become stronger again, as we were able to get in touch again with our inner strength. We struggled to get in touch with our body-selves, and to be in harmony with our spirits, and now bodies and minds were healing. After years of anger against a male God, we were able to speak with God again, using different images of Her. Our faith had become embodied, and not just mental or spiritual. New kinds of relationship, focused on mutuality and sharing, were at the center of our lives. We enjoyed to be alive, to be part of this universe, to write, to work, to worship, to dance, to sing again, almost as in our early childhood. We were able to think for ourselves, but not just for ourselves. Being members of a very socially aware congregation, we shared a common struggle for justice and liberation for all. I think that this is to experience the different aspects of the erotic, as the power of the God of life among us. Our lives have definitely been touched and empowered by it, even if the struggle with a society that still would like to silence our inner voices and our sources of power is not over.

Maybe many of the women reading this article have somehow recognized themselves in the story of our rivers. Many men might as well, as Western socio-political hierarchical power structures, which I call patriarchy, are abusive and oppressive of their identities as well. But now I would like to tell you more about my own river, so that you can better understand the meaning of spirituality for me.

My river started in an ancient yet industrialized town in Northern Italy: Torino. Among the things that mostly shaped the course of my river I see a very early awareness of the oppressive nature of the patriarchal society in which I was living; being part of a religious minority, the Waldensian church, in a Roman Catholic country, and being part of a struggling working class.

I don't know exactly when and why that started, but I just remember as a child praying with my eyes open. I have glimpses of what I thought at that time, and much of it didn't change twenty years later. I thought that God is here on earth, among us, and not in a special place. I thought I met God through people, through love and care for the others. I thought that God was best met in community, and best served in the everyday struggle for justice and peace. For all these reasons I resisted what I thought was an individualistic temptation of alienating oneself from reality and from others: praying with my eyes closed. Recently, however, I learned that sometimes it is good to close my eyes too.

As a child I always kept my eyes wide open to see everything that was happening around me. I was especially interested in understanding the world of the adults and its power structures. I kept inquiring about what being a girl meant, and about what it would mean to become a woman. Thus I very soon realized that, for the traditional values of Italian patriarchal family and society, being a woman meant, among other things, to have no obvious power in any kind of decision making. What I also quickly learned, is that women can at times get their own way, if they are willing to submit to the so- called "smile prostitution"[3] . That means that traditionally women do not exercise power on their own, but through the mediation of someone else, namely, men, from relatives to state officials or clergy.

I strongly rebelled against this kind of pre-set destiny. In my acts of resistance I often felt alone and misunderstood. However, I found the writings of many feminist and pre-feminist women tremendously empowering. At nine or ten I read the autobiography of Italian writer Sibilla Aleramo for the first time, even though I couldn't grasp every single thing she was saying. But I felt she was giving me the gift of a precious wisdom, the unmasking of Italian patriarchal society. At the same time, her own story of resistance in the face of abuse, her writings, her accomplishments, her intelligent and beautiful face that smiled at me from the cover of her novels never stopped being a powerful inspiration. In the same way, as I mostly lacked strong female models around me, many other women that I never met, novelists, poets, artists and political activists have been like nourishing and inspiring guardian angels throughout all my childhood and teenage years. They are the link to feminist theologies, which I met many years later, and they prepared me for this important encounter.

At the same time, coming from a working class family made me always very conscious that even women are not all the same, as we experience different degrees of oppression, and in many occasions participate in power structures that are oppressive for other women and men. I also understood left activist Rossana Rossanda[4] when she said that she could not feel sisterhood towards Susanna Agnelli, whose family owned the largest Italian automobile company, FIAT, and she identified instead with the overworked male operatives on the Fiat assembly line.

Certainly my early understanding of spirituality was also greatly shaped by my upbringing within the Italian Waldensian church. Being part of a religious minority in a Roman Catholic country, sharing its history of persecutions, being constantly questioned and challenged - sometimes discriminated against - because of my "otherness", forced me to elaborate quite early a strong sense of identity rooted in my faith experience. Today I also see the important role of the very Roman Catholic church in my formation, and not just because I grew up in a culture mainly shaped by it. I also recognise that in order to explain why I was different, I needed to know and understand what I was different from, as a better knowledge of the "other" is quite often one of the few privileges of being a minority.

The Waldensian church originated from one of the Middle Age pauper movements which proclaimed the necessity for the church to repent and to go back to the example of the early Christian community. Such preaching was rooted in a non-mediated reading of the Gospels - for which Valdesius provided a translation in Vulgar French - and in a consequent personal experience of conversion. The Bible was given a practical interpretation: it was about how to live, to be authentically faithful to Jesus Christ. The following comment, written by quite an unsympathetic contemporary of Valdesius, always echoed in my mind from the first time someone read it to me as a child:

> These people have no settled dwellings, but go around two by two, barefoot and dressed in wool tunics. They own nothing, sharing everything in common, after the manner of the apostles. Naked, they follow a naked Christ.[5]

As a child, I used to imagine these courageous women and men. And as I grew up with very few examples of women ministers and preachers, maybe it was the experience of women in the early Waldensian movement[6] which inspired my desire to be a preacher too, one day.

As a child I drew some very important teachings from the history of my church, which still stay with me, even if today I'm much more self-critical and less idealistic: the church of Christ is not about powerful institutions, but about being faithful to the Christ of the Gospel. Faith in Jesus Christ gives new hope and dignity to the last ones, and turns the world of the rich upside down, as in the case of Valdesius, who sold everything he had and gave it to the poor, becoming one of them. To be faithful to the Gospel means to take risks, to give up and share, to follow Jesus' radical example, an example that often leads to the crosses of this world.

As Waldensian historian Bruna Peyrot puts it when speaking about the nineteenth century, Waldensian spirituality was not just about a private and personal relationship with God:

> ...for Waldensian women as for men as well, spirituality had to be practically embodied through an attitude of servanthood towards the other. For the Waldensian woman as for the Waldensian man "servanthood" has always been the foundation of thought and action, a way of living, of thinking, of achieving individual and collective projects. Servanthood became a theological concept: to love others means to love God; it became a sociological concept: to do something for people in need, near or far away from us; it became also an anthropological concept: the self is in constant relationship with the others.[7]

Today, as a feminist theologian, I see the need to look back at this heritage with critical eyes as I recognize the negative outcomes that a theology and an ideology of servanthood has on women. At the same time, I greatly treasure this tradition, which lead me to experience my faith and spirituality as being constantly and critically "engaged" in the social and political struggle for justice and peace.

Because of its history of persecutions, the Waldensian Church in Italy developed a very close relationship with Northern-European Protestant countries, especially with Switzerland and Germany. As they supported my church politically and economically, a subtle pattern of dependence developed, a pattern that even lead our theology to be massively shaped by Swiss and German theology, which was looked upon as somehow "superior". However, I would argue that the radicalness of our own historical heritage kept us from being totally colonised by those foreign realities, thus overcoming the neo-orthodox temptation to grow apolitical and ahistorical, and opening the way to the exciting developments of the Waldensian church in the twentieth century. However, if today the Waldensian church is known in Italy for its often radical social ministry and political involvement for justice, it is because it went through a constant and often painful process of self-critique and discussion. In the Sixties, for many Waldensians their faith translated in taking full part of the political life of the country, and for a large number of them that meant at the time to militate in the Italian Communist Party, a quite courageous and shocking stance in conservative Christian Democratic Italy. The emerging generation of Waldensian theologians became greatly shaped by Marxist class analysis. At the same time, many Waldensian women were also deeply involved in the Italian feminist movement, which fought several important battles for women's determination, in particular for divorce and abortion rights.

This is the reality in which my faith was nurtured, my understanding of the church was shaped, and my sense of calling was developed.

However, almost from the very beginning of my theological training, I started seeing some of the inconsistencies and deep flaws of that theology, and thus also of my church. I started looking at it with new critical eyes, which generated a very painful process, because it lead me to perceive the very same reality that I loved and was part of my identity as also quite alienating and oppressive.

What I came to realize is that my church, with all its claims for radical social change, was in fact a very patriarchal reality, which did not take women's experience in any serious regard. Even the apparent openness to women in the context in which I grew up was deceiving: of course in a Roman Catholic country the fact that my church was open to women's leadership and ordination was revolutionary. But that was also the extent of the "revolution". In fact, our theology and our faith, in their pretence of universality, were mainly rooted in a male perspective of reality, and in a male understanding of God.

At the same time I have to acknowledge that several Waldensian women have tried and are trying to make a difference to the androcentric focus of our church and theology, even if in small numbers and with even less resources. For instance, there are the women of the FDEI, the Federation of Italian Protestant Women. Some groups have a sharper feminist awareness, as *Cassiopea*, a women's collective founded in 1990, and *Sophia*, the Association of Italian Protestant Women in Theological Research, founded in 1992.

Unfortunately, during my theological training at the Waldensian Theological Seminary in Rome in the late eighties these voices were not as strong as today, and they were certainly not well represented at the Seminary itself, where as of today there is not yet a single woman professor. For these reasons I felt quite alienated from my theological training, to the point of seriously thinking about quitting my studies, thus giving up my call to ministry as well. My year of studies in the USA, at Union Theological Seminary in New York City, renewed my interest in theology and vision for the church.

Confronted and nurtured by the strong voices of Feminist, Womanist, Mujerista, Asian, African and Latin American women theologians, I came to a better understanding of the causes of my alienation from church and theology, and sharpened my own critical thinking. I realised that I needed to de-colonise myself as much as possible from the oppression of patriarchal theology and ideology. That meant to re-imagine my God-talk, my Christology, my relationship to the Bible, my ecclesiology, my ethics... my faith. This process involved radical deconstruction of all previous theological assumptions, done with the strong hope that, unpeeling the different layers of patriarchal mystification, I would still find something meaningful in it, the seeds for a new spirituality.

At the same time, the voices of women all around the world suffered from different forms of oppression were a constant challenge to the integrity of my theology, as on several occasions they helped me to avoid to fall in a new version of a myopian Eurocentric approach, the same I was trying to fight against.

In this process of deconstructing, recycling and re-imagining, I find that my theology and faith went through enormous changes, especially in the area of biblical hermeneutics, christology and eschatology. I think it is important to illustrate this development, since it is an important part of my spiritual journey. At the same time, I want to stress the fact that I feel that my theology is still grounded in the most positive aspects of my Italian faith heritage, and in the struggle for justice and peace of the Waldensian Church in Italy. I also want to point out that I believe that theology is done not by individuals, but by communities. However, being an Italian Ph. D. student in the United States puts me in the particular position of being part of several communities at the same time, sometimes feeling a little uprooted everywhere. That accounts for the personal tone of my article and for my not being able to present a more collective picture of contemporary Protestant Italian women's spiritualities.

Images of God

The issue of the nature of God has always been at the very center of Christian theology, and that is obviously and intimately related to the way humans use analogical language to speak about God. The writings of several feminist theologians within the Jewish and Christian traditions made crystal clear that western male traditional theology spoke about a

God that is essentially "the ultimate macho". This God is omnipotent, has "dominion over" the world, is omniscient, all-controlling, self-sufficient, autonomous, impassible. Most important of all, since in this view God needs to be perfect, according to male standard God's perfection implies non-relationality, since relationship involves some form of mutuality or dependency. In this process, traditional male theology ultimately overlooked the meaning of its own concept of Trinity which shows instead that to be God is to be implicitly relational. These traditional images of God can be devastating to women's identity and faith, because they exclude from God anything related to femaleness, basically denying that women are created in the image of God.

We need new images of God and new theologies of God's power and God's work. In this process, we need to develop a new way of speaking about the power of God in relation to the world. This power is neither power over, or power of the weak, but power with, power in relationship and mutuality. It means that God makes a difference in the world, and that human beings and all creation can make a difference to God.

At the same time, the process of re-discovering and creating new images of God can be tremendously empowering to women because it can enable them to speak about God using a multitude of metaphors which finally come from women's experience, in particular embodiment, maternity and friendship. Furthermore, speaking about God as "She who is",[8] can restore in women the belief that they too are made in the image of God.

Thinking about God as She Who Is, I realized that her power needs human participation, and is inherently relational. As in all deep relationships, when we suffer, God suffers with us. When we don't nourish the relationship, God might seem far away, and we might doubt God was ever there. When we expect God to save the world without our participation and nothing seems to change, we might get frustrated and angry. When we perceive the pain and weakness of God, we panic and think death is going to have the last word. But I deeply believe that even if suffering and death exist, nothing can overcome the power of creation and love, and believing and joining in this power can only help to make it stronger. I see signs of the resurrective power of God in Jesus' story, and I keep recognising big and small fragments of resurrection all around me.

A wonderful moment in my spiritual journey has also been the embodiment of my experience of God not just through political and social action, but through my own body, a woman's body. Coming from a very dualistic culture and from a Calvinistic tradition which taught me to consider body and mind almost like two enemies engaged in an eternal fight, it has been wonderful to experience the power that comes from considering them as a whole. In my every day life, I learned how to look at my body as part of the reality of God. That taught me a new respect not only for myself, but for all other living creatures as well. One way of experiencing the erotic for me is to feel the vibrancy of the interconnectedness of all things among each other and with God. I feel the power of the erotic in all mutual and just relationships; in friendships with people or animals, in partnership with my life companion, in my doing theology or working for social change, in my worshipping or enjoying a work of art. To experience the erotic is to enjoy the beauty and goodness of life, constantly nurturing it, because life, like all beautiful things, is strong and fragile at the same time.

I also realized that the anger I felt when faced with all situations of abuse and oppression was also part of the anger of God, and that this anger was thus sacred because, as Beverly Harrison[9] powerfully expressed it, anger has an important place in the work of love.

The Bible

I realized in my own experience, that men and women cannot always find the Bible equally liberating in their common struggle. As Elsa Tamez[10] points out, there are major differences between reading the Bible from the point of view of the poor and reading it from a woman's perspective. This happens because the Bible is embedded in the patriarchal, oppressive values of the Judeo-Christian context that created it. When one reads the Bible without a deconstructive reading strategy or hermeneutics of suspicion, a conscious process of discernment of the contextual patriarchal values that shaped the Judeo-Christian understanding of faith, one could be led to claim that such values are the pure Word of God, thus legitimating women's inferiority and submission to men. This happened systematically in the history of Christianity. I would argue that this is a major issue for all Christians, but especially for Protestants, since women's critique greatly shakes their traditional principle of biblical authority. In the Waldensian context that means that if we have been able to read through the eyes of the poor and the needy - our social and political awareness - we still have a long journey to do in order to read the Bible from the eyes of women. And this might lead us to a painful contrast with the *Sola Scriptura* that has such a fundamental place in our faith. Personally, from a feminist approach I learned to see the Bible as bread for my faith journey,[11] refusing what I don't find consistent with God's overarching project of liberation, but also always being questioned by it. In my perspective, the Bible has a central role for the communities of faith, but its relevance is measured not by an internal canon, but from the contemporary struggles of women and men against the evils of patriarchy, racism, homophobia, poverty and colonization. In the words of Elisabeth Schüssler-Fiorenza[12], the Bible is not a mythical archetype but an historical prototype, it is bread and not stone.

However, my approach would probably scandalise many in my own church, who would accuse me of having my own personal canon within the canon. I could simply answer that everyone always does according to one's ideology. We can only pray that the Holy Spirit, the transforming energy of God, would continue to work through us, so that we might always mutually challenge our own assumptions.

Christology

The input of women's and indigenous people's theologies from all around the world also challenged me to have the courage to look with critical eyes at the very foundations of my faith and spirituality: my christology. Today I realise that, in my own Waldensian tradition, our *solus Christus* and *teologia crucis* were the only things that we never doubted until very recently, after the challenges of feminist theologians such as Letizia Tomassone and Daniela Di Carlo, both founder members of *Sophia* and active in *Cassiopea*.

One of the claims of the Protestant *solus Christus* is that it is possible to understand the Gospel outside one's culture. Furthermore, the pure Gospel was not supposed to have anything to do with culture, unless to radically criticise it. This claim generated several negative outcomes.

One of the worst outcomes is that it led to the attempt to universalise the good news, disregarding contextuality. As a consequence, what was supposed to be the core of the gospel according to a group of Western males, had to be the measure of theology and faithfulness for everyone else, quite a patriarchal and Eurocentric bias.

For instance, it never occurred to male Waldensian theologians that their christologies based on the necessity of Jesus' suffering and death for salvation, in many contexts and situations had become an instrument of oppression, as it justified and mystified the suffering of the victims of this world. This certainly happened in the case of women, African Americans and indigenous people.

Womanist theologians such as Delores Williams raised a strong voice against the validity of traditional doctrines of atonement, pointing out the role it had in the suffering and abuse of African American women. In my theology, I take Williams' criticism very seriously, as it gave new vital lymph to my faith. Today I strongly believe that Jesus came on this earth to live, to show us how to live, so that the reign of God could come on earth as it is in God's mind. At the same time, I still see the importance of the cross as a constant critical reminder: in a world where radical evil still exists, in its multifaceted structural expressions that oppress and crush people, I think it would be deceiving to believe that one can be Christian, and not have anything to do with it. According to me, the cross is not necessary for salvation, but as it happened to Jesus, in this world it would most likely happen to the ones that are most truly faithful to the Gospel. In a broken world, a church that does not experience brokenness in some forms, that does not take risks in its fighting for liberation is most likely to ultimately be on the side of the oppressors and the perpetuators of evil. In this sense, I agree with Latin American liberation theologians, when they see the cross as the symbol of God's solidarity with the poor and the oppressed. However, at the same time it is important never to think that suffering is redemptive *per se*. The cross must not be romanticised and justified as a means for salvation: it is an instrument of torture and death. If I see the importance of claiming that God was not absent but present on the cross, I see also the danger of romanticising God's death on the cross: the cross becomes a nice monument to the victims. The cross without a strong belief in resurrection can be a beautiful symbol of God's love for humanity, but can not redeem human suffering. Resurrection is what helps me to understand the cross and be empowered by it, as it means that love and life are more powerful than evil, and the forces of death do not have the last word. For me, resurrection, and not the cross, is at the core of Christian hope. As Jesus' resurrection had a strong impact on his friends and disciples, in the same way resurrection is something that transforms daily life, and is not just a hope for the future. Signs or fragments of resurrection are all situations were justice is made and wounds are healed. Because of these signs of resurrection, the difficult process of forgiveness is made possible.

Another shortcoming of the attempt to reach the true Christ beyond culture is the disembodiment of one's faith. As people are not able to meet Christ through their own cultures, they will not meet Christ in the others: the incarnation thus becomes disincarnated.

The alienation of one's faith from one's culture also generates an arid, disembodied spirituality, something I experienced first hand within my own church, where preaching the word and social action were the focus of one's faith. Rituals, traditions, forms of personal devotion were kept to the minimum, to avoid the "terrible" risk of syncretism, that Waldensians perceived as one of the worse sins perpetuated by the Roman Catholic church. Needless to say, this minimal choice of rituals and traditions was quite marked by a blatant androcentrism.

As I felt the poverty of this approach, I tried to re-imagine my own spirituality. This has been a process of liberation, as I allowed myself to experience God through my whole being, and not just through an intellectual reading of the Bible, typical of my tradition. In this process, the reading of feminist theologians such as Carter Heyward[13] or Audre Lorde[14] have been quite illuminating as they widened my understanding of the erotic and its relationship to God. But once again experience has been fundamental, as I witnessed and experienced that the Holy Spirit is not just present in words or in action but, as the power of God among us, touches us through relationships, through nature, through our own bodies, and we can be at unison with it in singing and dancing. When I started worshipping at Union Theological Seminary - an inclusive, challenging and embodied context - I finally felt rescued from years of alienation from traditional protestant forms of worship, so androcentric and lifeless.

During my theological re-discovery I also realized that the *solus Christus* so central in my tradition of faith was also problematic to many women, to Indigenous Christian people and to people of other faiths.

I also asked myself very seriously if the maleness of Jesus was an obstacle to my faith, taking into account the criticism of feminist theologians such as Mary Daly,[15] Rosemary Radford Ruether,[16] and Letizia Tomassone[17]. However, as I recognise patriarchal manipulations of christology, I see Jesus as an example of a new maleness, caring, sharing, dignifying and valuing women. Unfortunately, these elements are still overlooked and mystified by most traditional churches that use Jesus' ministry to justify male oppressive power. But rightly because of Jesus' liberating ministry to women, I think that all situations where women are violated and denied their full status of God's children are not simply unfair, they are blasphemous and contrary to the Gospel. This criticism certainly includes the theologies and the polities of all those ecclesiastical bodies, far too many, that deny women's ordination and downplay women's ministries.

My research work for the Gospel and Culture Study Process of the World Council of Churches has also been an important moment of my spiritual journey, as I realized more sharply than before that a Western exclusivistic understanding of the *solus Christus* has also been instrumental to old and modern attempts of colonization. With arrogance and hypocrisy, Western Christians often claimed their right to have the last say in deciding who is a true receiver of God's revelation. I had fine examples of this arrogance during the heated discussions on the "seeds of revelation" and on syncretism at the last World Council of Churches conference on Mission and Evangelism.[18] For instance, a paragraph of the document drafted by the section IV of the conference (*One Gospel-Diverse Expressions*) stated that Christians recognised the seeds of revelation present in other religious traditions. This affirmation stirred quite a bit of controversy, as the Indigenous people from all over the world affirmed indignantly that their religiosity was not a seed of revelation, but a full grown tree. The classical answer that was once again given by many reaffirmed the doctrine of the *logos spermatikos*, meaning that all cultures and religions might have glimpses of God, but that they never truly and fully meet God until they meet Jesus Christ. This has often been - and still is - the most enlightened position to be found even among liberal Christians. I myself come from a very exclusivistic background. But did Native Americans or Aboriginal people in Australia need Jesus Christ in order to fully meet God? Do Jewish people have a somehow incomplete faith? Do Muslims need to be evangelised by us? Couldn't God have revealed Godself to people in different cultures using different forms, leading to different systems of belief? A Maori woman told me this story. When the Christian missionaries came to her land, they said: "We come to you to bring you Jesus Christ". And the answer was "Yes, we already met him".

As I recognise the evils perpetuated in the name of a patriarchal and colonialistic understanding of the Gospel, I am challenged to constantly criticise, re-imagine and recycle my Christian heritage and faith. However, I hold on to this faith, because through it, in my context, I believe I truly met God, thus recognising that different people might fully meet God in different ways. But looking at the state of our world, feeling the pain and brokenness of the oppressed, I also claim that there can not be salvation outside love, justice and liberation.

The Reign of God and Eschatology

In this particular moment of my spiritual journey, I keep finding myself meditating, wondering, studying, speaking and preaching about the reality of God's reign, or God's household, a reality about which Jesus was also constantly talking.

In my reading of the New Testament, what Jesus did is to show us a radically different way to relate to God, to ourselves, and to others. In the midst of oppression and injustice, in his deeds and teaching he embodied the fact that a different way of living, according to God's project for creation, is indeed possible. He called this reality the reign of God. Around him, Jesus formed a community of faith that symbolised, embodied and contributed to spread the belief in this project. Among the most significant tracts of this project I see radical equalitaty and inclusivity, a preferential option for the poor and the oppressed, a mutual sharing of power, a sharp critique of the political and religious status quo, compassionate acts of healing, a deep commitment to justice. But the strongest belief of all is that if this way of living and loving can be shattered, denigrated, and abused, by God's grace and reconstructive power it is always going to be resurrected.

James Forbes'[19] definition of the Jesus' movement is illuminating (and I think it can apply to the church as well): it was " a peripatetic school of the kingdom of God". In fact, Jesus greatly resisted the temptation to create a model or a paradigm for the new community he was gathering. However, Jesus gave us many colorful and diverse images of what this community could be. In his parables and teachings, as in his actions, he embodied God's love and solidarity with the least of all societies, the poor, the oppressed, the outcast, the "unclean", many of whom were women. He also embodied a new attitude towards women, and demonstrated solidarity with them. In the same way, the church, having received the good news, should be able to experience and share the fruits of its new relationship with God, in particular in worship, solidarity and teaching. This means that to be people of God does not mean to be set apart from others, but to answer to a call for community, and that to be church means to have a new approach to relationships, where oppression and dependence are replaced by mutual responsibility, solidarity and justice.

The nature of the kingdom of the God Jesus is speaking about, and from which he is empowered, is best defined by the metaphors of open commensality and the seed of mustard. The kingdom is life as a process of radical justice and radical egalitarianism, it is a round table where all are invited and are guest of honor, and where there is abundance for all. It is a reality that everyone can experience in daily life, after being physically and metaphorically healed from the evils of abuse, oppression and injustice, to experience a new dimension of wholeness and mutuality. Like the seed of mustard, the kingdom first appears as a very small, contextual, even fragile experience, but, as the mustard plant, it has a great possibility for growth and is not easily extirpated by opposite forces.

During my theological studies, I came to an understanding of eschatology as an ultimate reality that, in a fragmented way, starts already in the present. In this process, I read Jesus parables' about the kingdom of God as an announcement about something that was already happening but will be completed at the end of times. However, a strong focus only on Jesus preaching and death, often undermined their intimate relationship with Jesus' lifestyle. Today I suspect that my Western Protestant background, focusing more on Jesus' teachings and death more than on his actions, ultimately mitigates the revolutionary significance of the Gospels.

For a long time, this kingdom of God in which I believed or that I joyfully announced, was mainly an eschatological reality, something that would be realised by God at the end of times. I also recognised that the reign was also something that was indeed happening in the present, but it wasn't happening to me. It was something I could observe in other people's realities - often far away from mine - but that I did not experience first hand.

Today, I dare to affirm that in its fragility and imperfection I experience this reality as a part of a community of faith and life at Jan Hus Presbyterian Church in NYC.

When I first walked in this church, I had a glimpse of what open commensality could mean: I sat among very diverse people, and some of this society's outcasts: gay and lesbians people, African American homeless, people struggling with AIDS, or substance abuse, mental illness, joblessness or immigration problems. I also recognized a Union Theological Seminary professor and a couple of Seminary students. The liturgy and the preaching spoke of love and social justice, and were obviously consistent with the broad spectrum of the community's social ministry. Passing the sign of peace, people seemed to be really intimate and loving with each other, and very welcoming and inclusive of newcomers. Women were celebrated and had obvious authority. During the service and fellowship hours, I could hardly figure out who the ministers and the leaders were.

At the same time, I remembered people defining this community "totally dysfunctional" and "crazy", to say the least. I was puzzled. Now, I have been a member of the Jan Hus community for the past two years. I still recognize my first experience of this community in its mission statement, that begins with the following affirmation:

> The purpose of the church is to celebrate the vision of God for the world. It is to live in hope, free from the power of death. It is to share life together in a community whose center is the Spirit. It is to act on the imagination of Jesus who sees enough bread to go around, enough courage to speak the truth, and enough love to overcome all things.
>
> The purpose of the church in society is to be the yeast that helps the whole loaf to rise. Because of resurrection, the church dares to give itself over to challenge and heal social structures in every age, breaking down barriers and creating community and wholeness.
>
> The purpose of the church is to be people who live in the real world and yet can still imagine a different reality. It is to

give thanks, to celebrate life, and to grow as individuals and together. It is to live in the faith that we and all creation are being formed into the risen body of love.

My ongoing experience at Jan Hus has been wonderfully empowering on a personal level, as it is empowering for the community as a whole. Worship itself is like an open table where everyone is invited and receives strength for his/her mission in the world. In our community life as in our ministry to the world, we try to live in today's consumerist society as if a different way to live were possible. It is embodied in our realities, and involves our whole bodyselves in praying, singing and dancing Our ministries to the city, to our sister churches in Haiti and Salvador and to ourselves try to reach the deep ends of human needs: homelessness, joblessness, hunger, physical and spiritual poverty, substance abuse, illness, solitude and alienation. In this process, we recognise that the root causes of those situations must be addressed and radically fought against: capitalism, colonization, sexism, racism, homophobia.

In our personal and communal struggle, we overcome powerlessness rejoicing in the fact that God works through the little ones.

At the same time, our community is very small, frail, sometimes disturbed, dysfunctional. We have very weak institutional ties, and very little money on our own. Yet, it seems to me as though through our programs we have an incredible influence on many people's lives, in the midst of this city, or in another part of the globe. In this community I have been clearly aware for the first time of the power of the Spirit at work. Often this community reminds me of my homechurch in Italy, and in fact they share a common historical heritage, as both descend from pre-reformation heretical movements, and a common vision, as they both see justice and peacemaking as the core of their faith. Many of my feminist friends were quite surprised to hear that I felt so comfortable in a mixed community. Honestly, I often feel more at ease at Jan Hus Church that in some of the feminist rituals I have been attending for the past ten years. One of the reasons is that at Jan Hus the language is down to earth, is a feminist and liberating language for everyone, not just for theologians. In fact, I like meeting in church the kind of people I would meet in the street of New York, as for me worship is more about life as it is than about a sheltered reality. Furthermore, as I enjoy and need all-women moments of sharing, I strive for communities of life and faith where women and men can work and worship together as equal partners: in the process of liberation no one can be left behind.

I recognize that my perspective on the reign of God could be taken as a classical example of a "realised" or "inaugurated eschatology".[20] However, my perspective has been shaped far more by practical experience than by theology, as in real life situations I realised that the Holy Spirit was at work and was giving me a foretaste of the reign of God.

Probably because of my "orthodox" Protestant background, I am very aware of the dangers of having a totally realised eschatology. If we believe that the reign of God is realised in the church, then we might believe that our narrow and contextual perspective of the church is the reign of God. We could end up justifying uncritically the validity and even supremacy of our own perspective, something that I have too often experienced first hand in dealing with Italian Roman Catholic church. Thinking that our church is simply God's reign realised on earth might ultimately lead us to worship ourselves, with catastrophic results for us and for others.

At the same time, I strongly suspect that focusing only on the reign of God as an ultimate reality that has nothing to do with the church and humanity ends up being quite instrumental to the forces and structures that benefit from the status quo. I also take into account the question raised by one of my young catechism students: "Why should God have gone through the trouble of creating this world, if anything beautiful and important has to happen in another one?"

My position does not want to be only a reasonable middle ground between two extremes.

In my life and theology, I want to take seriously the radicalness of Jesus' preaching and living, that created situations and realities of liberation and healing where the reign of God was partially realised. I also believe that through the power of the Holy Spirit we can continue to experience this reality in the present, and that we are called to spread it in the whole world. At the same time, I hold this belief in tension with the recognition that evil is radical and powerful, and that we easily fall into its alluring temptations, as when we think about liberating only ourselves, or when the victims of the past become today's victimizers. However, because of my belief in resurrection I do believe that love will overcome death and oppression, as in the midst of a world where slavery and Exodus coexist, I constantly hope for a reality where all of us will be fully liberated.

Conclusion

Today I still pray with my eyes open, as I consider all aspects of my life as part of my ongoing dialogue with the One who is life in its fulness, She Who Is. She is like the source of my river, as She gave me life. She is like the bed of my river, as She sustains, guides and challenges me, but also gives me the freedom to change my course and to make a difference to Her as well.

Thinking about myself as a river, I remember all the different countries that I have visited, and all the different peoples that I have met. I know that they too, for better and for worse, are part of what I am. I also daydream about my future course. As a child, I used to dream about changing the world. Today, I just dream about making a difference to it. However, I still have a vision, a vision of communities of simple people, women and men, that between life and death choose life. I dream of a day where all our rivers would join, and we will have the strength to gently move the mountains.

Notes

1 Phoebe Willetts, "Magnificat", in *Celebrating Women*, eds. Hannah Ward, Jennifer Wild and Janet Morley, London: WIT&MOW 1987, 14; Harrisburg: Morehouse, 1995, 37.

2 Jan Hus Presbyterian Church; Rev. Jan Orr-Harter, Senior Pastor.

3 This definition "prostituzione del sorriso" comes from Italian feminist pedagogue Elena Gianini Belotti, Dalla parte delle bambine. *L'influenza dei condizionamenti sociali nella formazione del ruolo femminile nei primi anni di vita*, Milan, Feltrinelli, 1973.

4 Lucia Chiavola Birnbaum, *Liberazione della donna: Feminism in Italy*, *Middletown*, CT: Wesleyan University Press, 1986, 119.

5 Walter Map," De nugis curialium", in Giovanni Gonnet, *Enchiridion Fontium Valdensium*, I, Torre Pellice: Claudiana, 1958, p. 123.

6 In fact, one of the disparaging comments made against the early Waldensians was that they even allowed women to preach. Unfortunately, not unlike what happened in the early Christian churches, under social pressure Waldensian women were progressively but drastically "put back at their places". It was not until centuries later, in 1962, that women ministers were ordained again in the Waldensian Church.

7 Bruna Peyrot, "L'identité des femmes chez les Vaudois du Piémont", in *Women Churches: Networking and Reflection in the European Context*, Angela Berlis, Julie Hopkins, Hedwig Meyer-Wilmes and Caroline Vander Stichele eds., Yearbook of the European Society of Women in Theological Research, Volume 3, Kampen, the Netherlands: Kok Pharos, 1995, 139.

8 See Elisabeth Johnson's *She Who Is: The Mystery of God in Feminist Theological Discourse*, New York, Crossroads, 1992.

9 Beverly Harrison, "The Power of Anger in the Work of Love: Christian Ethics for Women and Other Strangers", in *Making the Connections: Essays in Feminist Social Ethics*, Boston: Becon Press, 1985.

10 Elsa Tamez., "Women's Rereading of the Bible", In *With Passion and Compassion: Third World Women Doing Theology*, ed. V. Fabella and M. Oduyoye, 173-180. Maryknoll: Orbis, 1988.

11 One reading was particularly helpful in defining this new understanding of the Bible: Elisabeth Schüssler Fiorenza, *Bread Not Stone* (Boston: Beacon Press, 1995).

12 Elisabeth Schüssler Fiorenza, op. cit.

13 Carter Heyward, *Touching Our Strength: The Erotic as Power and the Work of God*, San Francisco: Harper and Row, 1989.

14 Audre Lorde, "Uses of the Erotic: The Erotic as Power", in *Sister Outsider: Essays and Speeches*, Trumansburg, NY: Crossing Press, 1984.

15 Mary Daly, *Beyond God the Father: Toward a Philosophy of Women's Liberation*, Boston: Beacon Press, 1973.

16 Rosemary Radford Ruether, *To Change the World: Christology and Cultural Criticism*, (New York: Crossroad, 1981).

17 Letizia Tomassone, "Cinque punti di lavoro teologico", *Gioventù Evangelica* 12, 1992.

18 Called To One Hope - The Gospel in Different Culture; Salvador, Bahia, December 1996.

19 I heard this definition in James Forbes' preaching at UTS, Chapel Service, September 30, 1996.

20 See Dulles, Avery. Modells of the Church, New York, Image Books, 1987, 109.

Lene Sjorup

In The Beginnng Was This Body

*The folowing article was written in a moment of inspiration but after
many deliberations. I had for some time been immersed in the history
of religion as this was told by different authors from a feminist point of
view. I also was engaged in the stages of psychical development, as
well as in how religious institutions tend to twist and distort religious
feelings, the religious experiences of women in particular. And yet
something, what ever this dimension could be called in order not to be
coopted, still existed, in spite of all distorsions, but this something in
reality could not be expessed. Thus, in my moment of inspiration I
knitted all these elements together: an individual development: from
childhood to death, of body, feeling, gender, soul, thought, and spirit; a
historical development: animism, the Great Mother, hieros gamos,
polytheism, God the Father, and energy; each with their "colours and
symbols", the personal and political distortion, corruption and
exploitation of this transsubjective reality; the insufficiency of the
image of the holy in the light of history; what carries through and
tentatively stands firm.*

*I do not assert that my vision is representative for others or
describes any correct line of religious development, but I hope it will
inspire others to follow their own intuitions and develop new
theological systems. When women, as I maintain in my book Oneness
(Kampen: Kok Pharos 1997), where this essay is included, begin
recounting their different religious experiences and theologizing about
them, traditional theological paradigms will change.*

1. Nature-Animism

In the beginning was the this body, a part of nature, of the ocean,
the trees, the wind, the earth, the breast. Going in and out of shadows
and light, it knows, without any doubt, of needs, abandonment and
fullness.

The child follows through to old age: tree, stone, river: a goodness,
a companionship. Yes, they speak without words, yes, we know
together. There is a fundamental love, streaming through it all, which
cannot be lost: When I was four years old. . . I saw a harebell growing. .
I worshipped it.

The relation to the earth body represents the fundamental: food; and abundance: that there is enough for everyone, that each patch of land will produce exactly what we need and more than that: fruit, grain, roots, flowers, for humans, birds, mammals, snakes, insect; that each species fits exactly into the entire pattern; that there is abundance in our lives, enough, enough - only to be asked for.

God is the entire blue organism we breathe into, and without us, it would not be perfect. God is there pulsating in the deep blue shadows of the mountain and in the eternal sea: this unforgettable night walk on the beach with the big boulders where you were united with me and the entire universe. This is the knowledge we try to recapture in theories: ecology, deep ecology, animal liberation, creation theologies.

And then enters fear, power and death: At a meeting in June 1989 at Georgetown University, where specialists from the North American Ministry of Foreign Affairs, the CIA, and several delegations were represented, the question was asked: What can we do, if the Soviet Union gives up armaments and produces as many cars, power stations, refrigerators and washing machines as we do? (*Der Spiegel* 29/89). In June 1989 at a UNEP (The UN environmental organization) meeting in Nairobi, one expert stated that North American standard of living may under no circumstances spread to the rest of the world. Why? The world's climate would deteriorate dramatically. According to the Brundtland Report (1987) by the year 2025 there will be 8. 22 billion humans on this earth. In 1985 there were 4. 84. If the global average use of energy per person stays at today's level - in other words if it does not rise to North American standards - the global temperature will increase by between 1. 5 and 4. 5 °C, at the polar extremes it will increase by two to three more. Melting ice will raise oceans by between 25 and 140 centimeters. Bangladesh will be one of the first countries to suffer from this.

Why do so many First World, white men feel so alienated from their roots that they cannot but contribute to and further a system that is ruining the entire planet? Do they not realize they are part of the whole, or do they fear being reabsorbed in nature? Why do women shy away from challenging this? Why lean back masochistically when so much is at risk?

The image of God as stone, tree, river changed when humans preferred the company of each other to that of sky, flower, grain, stone, started seeing the other, celebrating the other, fearing her absence, wanting her for myself. When humans formed larger communities, their relation to nature changed: a long, painful process, a triumph of knowing.

The process of forgetting and almost remembering is itself close to magic. On the shelf, on the windowsill lie stones, feathers, seashells and conches. God loves you, and you know it.

2. *Creation and Birth - the Great Mother*

Where one starts and the other ends, we do not know. She is there, and yet she is not. At one moment a gesture is met with food, dryness, air - and the next it is not. The light shifts, and there she is. The body tingles, all the fine small hairs stand on end: her skin is felt, it is sweet, soft and wet. She was pulled by the gesture of this tiny hand. Or was she? Is she the same as last time? And is she the one who spoke inside you?

The longing for this endless fulfillment, does it ever stop? It was there in the brief, almost remembered moments, and it continues.

The relation to her represents what you can know of me: the depth of feelings, the quiet talk by the fire, the laughter at good and nasty jokes, the love and confessions we can endure, the limits and dragons we fight. Where you end and I begin we do not know. Animals and trees with flowers and fruit, bread, and the good, red wine are part of this continuum, it comes from nowhere.

Yes, she has many and big breasts as she stands there, holding them. She is shaped in clay, cut in wood, she is in the green tree, which she is, or she is simply the cliff. The awe: that children and all good things stem from her body. she is the bountiful fish mother, the bird, laying the world egg. Under every tree she is worshipped (Hos. 4:12-13), caves are painted red as her blood, at the entrance are double spirals, in the churches she stands above the cross, dressed in silk and diamonds, holding her child. Lions and snakes lie at the foot of her throne, in her womb is the moon. How can we not love her?

God knows me. She knows me. She is the soft darkness into which I pray. If anyone is omnipotent it is she. Yet, without me, she would not be. There on her arm, I am her pride, her reason for being, just as I myself hold this child.

Thoughts and theories follow her path: movements for peace and right relations, psychological theories of working through loss and grief to right being, sharing, daring to trust and love so that we receive what we need.

4. 84 billion inhabitants on this earth in 1985, 8. 22 billion by 2025. Between 1/3 and 1/2 of poor families on this earth consist of mothers and children. How could poverty be feminized if wealth were not masculinized? "My mother walked 4 hours to collect enough firewood

to cook. I walk for 8 hours. My daughter probably will have to walk 10 hours. " A hierarchy of white and colored men cut the trees in the commons, and planted monoculture trees. Irrigating, draining, digging, moving, leaving the locals, the poor, the small people, the birds, the cattle, the insects and the endlessly not-known without food and space. Women need the children to lighten their increased workload and for security in old age; cash crops, pesticides, deforestation, and irrigation pushed about 29% of the earth's soil into various degrees of desertification (the Brundtland Report). The children move to big cities.

Realizing what we could do, the Great Goddess was not sufficient. Water could be dammed, although the beavers left, mills constructed, although the herons could no longer be found in their nearby night trees. Men could do it all, giving birth from the head, the thighs.

The Chipco women in India embraced their trees, protecting them from being cut, knowing them: vraksha, that which is cut, mahiruha, that which grows on the earth, sakhi, that which has branches, padapa, that which sucks water through roots, taru, that by which people get coolness, agama, that which cannot move, palasi, that which has leaves (Shiva, p. 58). "What does the forests bear?", the sing, "Soil, water and pure air. Soil, water and pure air. Sustain the earth and all she bears" (Shiva, p. 77).

The tree, you spoke to, your special tree. And the God who loves you.

3. Sexuality and Love - Hieros Gamos

The breath, heaving and falling. Faster and faster, between you and me. Where do you end, and where do I start? You caress part of a body, no longer knowing if it belongs to you or the other. Food, newspapers, wine, clothes are lying in a circle around the bed. The tenderness spreading, encompassing the universe. Did you know it was so big?

The relation to these forces represents sexuality in its many aspects, multiplication and separation. Being a gender, having a gender, enjoying it.

God never was separate from sexuality. Be fruitful, multiply, enjoy! This red desire to unite: women and men, men and men, women and women, hummingbirds, giraffes, a lust for living and continuing to live. There she is, the tree behind her, and in front of her, her own divine son, the erection showing. This is what he is for: plowing the field, sowing the seed. He knew, but tried to forget. This fearsome clinging to the female, to mother. And there he is, magnificently showing his horns, the bull over which she leaps. Under every tree they make love, satisfaction will not come. The trees and the bush are pulsating, the birds and the cattle make sounds.

There it is, the holy, in this red hot desire, pulsating, breathing, stroking, cuddling with us, a heaving embrace. The theories of sexual politics follow: gay, lesbian, feminist. To love with pride, to love with awareness, to love with love, recognizing it when it comes, magically.

And then taking by force what cannot be had with love. 7000 American soldiers from the Sixth Fleet, led by the aircraft carrier "Midway," are rewarded for their service in the Gulf war with a sex holiday in Thailand. The Thai prime minister says: "They are not welcome. They can go home and exploit their own women and children. " The fear that she will not give. Possessing, so that she might love: Buy land, build more, invest. Give her children, so she will stay. Spread the breast so broadly so at least she will fear: make the purses big. 100,000 Philippine girls work in Japan as dancers and prostitutes.

Transfer guilt, imply, gossip.

The image of the divine couple changed as agrarian societies became dominated by city states, so much going on in one place. One god, two gods would not do, a whole family of gods followed.

And the hot desire remains, holy. And the God who is love.

4. Family, Work, and History - Polytheism

This meal together, resting. Sitting down finally, sharing food, talking, teasing, telling stories, sharing memories. The extended family of relatives, friends, colleagues, children, lovers. The laughter and the good spirit, planning what to do next. It is repeated endlessly, now with one group and then with another, people spilling over, some from childhood others as newcomers, sharing their soul, their abilities and vocations, being special persons, the yellow me-ness, they are: the one with the wonderful mimics, the carpenter, the potter, the singer, the quiet person with the big heart, the old and wise woman. The entire group breathing as one organism, each playing her or his role with bravado and in harmony, each extending backwards in history to foremothers and forefathers, all meeting somewhere in the past, across continents. Extending upwards, sidewards, the group moves the globe's energies through its abilities, all the special people that we are.

The multiplicity, the richness of life in its plenum, the ability, the techne is God's own body. The blessing when the book completes itself in the light, when the skiing is perfect, the glasses are found, and the focus firm, when friendships are found, their history known.

Goddess of the hunt and of the moon, Goddess of the crossroads, cow-eyed Goddess, God of the artists and the craftsmen, Virgin Goddess, God of the thunder, Goddess of the fire, God of the thieves, Goddess of the prostitutes, the grain Goddess, Hera, Demeter, Athena, Artemis, Juno, Jupiter, Venus, Vesta, Freya, Frey, Odin, Thor, Ishtar, Astarte, Baal, El, Isis, Osiris, Re, Varuna, Mithras, Indra, Soma, Zeus, Dionysos, Cybele and the unknown God.

Yes, our vocation is holy, we have been given our place among the many, we are part of the network, laughing at it, shifting it, planning, with the right to work and love, knowing our history as our theories show: the socialist and communist visions of an egalitarian society, ecological, green - contributing what we are, taking what we need, giving what we can.

The fear that we will not be seen in the supermarket of life: the employer's associations, the unions, the military, the rich fighting for their rights. And their big success: that money and power means the right to decide over the lives of people, the nature they live off, and cosmos. The lonely banker, playing with computer screen investments one rainy morning in New York, Tokyo, London, his kids with their nanny, his wife teaching, decides the fate of far-away children in cash crop nations. 40,000 children die daily in this world of malnutrition and easily avoidable sicknesses. The capital flow from the poor southern hemisphere to the wealthy North is 240 billion dollars, the aid to Third world countries from the First World included.

When city states became empires, many gods did not suffice. There came one emperor, an exalted idol among the many god, and then, finally, one male God.

"Let me pass the exam", prays the child; "make my child well", prays the mother; "give me work," prays the adult to the Gods, knowing they will get all they need, because they are loved.

5. Authority and Politics - Monotheism

She speaks up. She knows what to say, is well-prepared. What she says, will change lives. The words could be no different, they are spoken with her life and with larger forces. She confronts others who do not want to change, although they must. She is charismatic, passionate and true. Trueness stands as a halo around her. She tells them stories they love and need. Yet, they try to ridicule her, to trivialize what she says, to keep information from her, to project guilt and shame onto her, to punish her doubly for being who she is while doing what she does (Ås, 1982).

175

Confronting evil power and sending the one word that was in the beginning is the responsibility of the good father, the good mother.

It is linked to the suffering God. The authority of the one truth cannot but be usurped, and yet it must be spoken. The one God and the many pregnant Christas, hanging on their crosses, are interrelated. Yes, we know: we ourselves crucified them, deafness and commodities being more convenient than knowing this unspeakable.

The fear, the projecting onto an enemy what I will not see in myself. Saddam Hussein is trying to take power and will not stop, until he has conquered the world: dominating, aggressive, unfeeling. He is creating a Muslim territory that oppresses women. The US spends 102 billion dollars to "help" Kuwait, "protecting" the state against Iraq, another 100 billion to reconstruct the state, leaving the oil fields for themselves and the Kuwaiti royal family to exploit. "The world could wait no longer," US President Bush said upon starting the war. Some months after its termination he admitted to the world press, summoned in his own church, that he cried when he pressed GO. Or was it GO. D?: patriarchs mirroring patriarchs, omnipotent, omnipresent, leaving the dead and the maimed behind. Shown on world copyright CNN news, the money they made from the war in the Gulf by far outdistanced the several million paid by US publishers to General Norman Schwarzkopf for his memories.

The monotheistic God the Father lives well in the White House, the Vatican, in very many churches, as well as in third world countries, where he is mixed with the Virgin, foremothers and forefathers, voodoo, spells, Snow white and the prince, ancient Gods and Goddesses. Every mountaintop, formerly dedicated to the local God and later to the Virgin or the cross, is now occupied by antennas. The authority of the monotheistic, male God is failing as rapidly as the marxist states in the Eastern World. As communication spreads, making the world one, it is changing the concept of the divine.

The good father, Our Father, his knowledge and his freedom: children wait for him endlessly, await his coming, his remembering. And he does come, seeing them into individuality with love.

6. Culture and Postmodernist Life - Energy

What can be seen are merely tendencies: in one corner a Greek column, in the other a six-pack, somewhere in between a grazing deer and the naked woman of Monad, painted in light-filled aquarelle, whitely. This vivid past is so well-known, yet somehow over, transcended. The ineffable new is just beyond reach, yet is a presence of the beyondness. Hesitatingly, you stand in front of the paper, waiting, almost not breathing, as this stream finally presses forth, and the figure is there, perfect. For this moment you studied, refining your knowledge and technique. Now you will elaborate on the form for months. You did not know it existed in you.

This energy of the holy, meeting you right here, how can it be named "God" after the prolonged collapse of all these mighty empires, their deeds so well-known? And still, you search for it, cannot live without it.

In the church, in the wood, in meditation, in sudden synchronicity, at a funeral there is a deep concentrated silence, an almost palpable presence, and wisdom: yes, you know now. This is how it is: hands sinking, the decision is almost made.

It is called power, energy, God, Goddess, it. It is seen through tarot, chakras, meditation, personal development, new consciousness, physics, holistic health, astrology, in the caves, in ancient cult centers, in mountains and on islands, in churches, mosques, and stupas. It is learned from myths, traditions, archaeological evidence, from primitive (original) religion and the main religions. And it is known first from women: grandmothers, old wives tales, wise women brought up sensing what is barely perceptible and from the men who have ears to hear.

Then the fear, trivialization, curiosity enter, and the endless rationalizations: spiritual advice for 100 dollars an hour, death and love predicted from the left and right hand, self-management courses taught with overhead projectors, group dynamics and headlines, books full of superficialities and fast conclusions. Meditation centers, rainbow centers, gurus, priests and authors all have to make a good living: the beautiful house by the sea is Calvinistic proof that god is with you. The book is rewritten to make it as tasty and sellable as hamburgers with ketchup and mustard, french fries and mayonnaise. It is the spiritual gluttony and consumerism The Cloud of Unknowing warned us against. The white wisdom is that God comes from the future under many guises and will not be stuck with this elected people this gender, this group, on this continent.

In nature, the body, the social and aesthetic, and quiet daily life, God is the energy of love in the universe, there for you. Yes, you live from this love as hummingbirds from flowers.

7. Sickness and Death - the Violent Goddess

The body will not heal, the eyes shine too brightly, food is lost, sheets are wet, sleep will not come. The child moves restlessly; in the end she loses strength even for that. Breath heaves and falls, sounds are heard, gaggling, whimpering. "Mummy," she mumbles. And the mother is there, as she has been for months, weeks, days, hours, comforting, holding, stroking. "See," the child suddenly exclaims. With this vision, she releases life, the mother still holding her hand.

She is the goddess of death, sickness, draught, famine and war. Catastrophes follow in her wake. Where she goes, pest and cholera fall like arrows. She wades in blood. Her father's gray hair is saturated with blood. "Pity," they cry. "I have paid heed to thee, my Lady; my attention has been turned to thee. . Subdue my haters and cause them to crouch down under me. Let my prayers and my supplications come to thee. . . let me glorify thy divinity" (Pritchard, 1950. 384f).

When humans in the bright city light denied death, God was also declared dead. The dying are stacked away in hospitals hidden from friends, children, the weak and the hysterical, becoming organ banks: hearts still beating, blood still pulsing, but brain-dead. The utmost Cartesian vision of the body.

"Let them drive carefully," she prays, "let them arrive safely, and I will start believing in you. Help me believe. "

And they will be safe. She has touched love with her prayer.

Annette Esser

Inspired by Women Mystics
Meditations in the Holy Week

Monday, April 1, 1996
Thoughts on my Spirituality

> *Today while beseeching our Lord to speak for me because*
> *I wasn't able to think anything to say nor did I know how to*
> *begin to carry out this obedience, there came to my mind*
> *what I now shall speak about, that which will provide us with*
> *a basis to begin with. It is that we consider our soul like a*
> *castle made entirely out of a diamond or of very clear*
> *crystal, in which there are many rooms, just as in heaven*
> *there are many dwelling places.[1]*
>
> Teresa of Avila

These words by Santa Teresa came to my mind, when I sat down in Lampman Chapel of Union Theological Seminary, New York, and looked at "her" stained window. I thought about what I could, and wanted, to say about prayer and meditation today. I searched for an insight. I have written and said so much about spirituality in my articles and in my teaching over the last years. But right now, I felt oddly empty. What about my real praying life today? I feel to have neglected it. I don't go to mass regularly as I used to; I do not pray or meditate each day; I don't like to pray often in a formal language; and all too often, my prayer without words - what Teresa called "Inner prayer" - has become more like a mixture of undirected reflection and thoughts in the middle of my days.

Looking back into my spiritual life, these words come to my mind that I wrote ten years ago, inspired by Teresa.[2]

> Spirituality - this is praying for me, still and always again.
> Praying - this is being in presence of the Divine Spirit,
> sometimes speaking to her, mostly in harmony with her.
> Since I know about this harmony with myself, with the
> Divine Spirit, I look more often for solitude, for stillness,
> and my stillness has become different, fuller.

179

Then it is mainly my heart that beats and my vision that sees, grasped by the unconditional and yet not manifest. It is the fire that burns and yet does not burn me. It is the knowledge about going my path and yet not its goal.

Spirituality is - to say it more theoretically than poetically - the opening of oneself for the Divine Spirit and the life in harmony with her. How this opening happens may be different for different people. That may depend on the psychic constitution, the life story and the socio-cultural background of human beings.

Teresa has said, and I believe it is so for Christians - or at least for myself - that prayer is the gateway to the interior, to the soul, to God. Prayer is a way of increasing spirituality. The dialogue between I and Thou becomes increasingly intensified in love and is transformed in the sphere of the unity of both. I and Thou, to grasp and to be grasped: this is an encounter, a dynamic attraction that draws the two together - God and human - and leads them to mystical unity.

This is what the human desires most and yet, from which s/he recoils most. This is the fire of God that can not be borne too early and what binds the human ego, her/his separate being irretrievable to her/his essential being, to God. This is what lets the ego become an instrument of the will of God.

Finally to say, "Your will shall be done. Let it be with me according to your word!", is the goal of mysticism and spirituality. The goal of a religious life is then to manifest this will in practical work, in the actions of everyday life.[3]

Today, my spirituality is still prayer, even when my prayer sometimes turns into a meditation, or my meditation turns into a prayer. And when I sometimes find no words and there is just silence, or when far too many words haunt me and my thoughts wander off to my everyday life as a teacher and to all kinds of feelings of vulnerability, pleasure, pain, love, guilt, annoyance, shame, disunity. . . , then I always find my way back to prayer. And my prayer consists of relating all my experience again to God - not only as the abstract ground of being but also as the loving partner. And again I experience that out of this relationship an answer arises that enlightens me, and that an inner knowledge grows that liberates me so that I can go on in my life with a glad heart and an easy walk.

My spirituality is female because I am a woman and feel with a female body, and because my religious language has - there where it is living - its source in bodily and psychic experiences. So, when I try to understand God's will and let it happen, then I feel this with body and soul as a woman. And, when I think about the new life that wants to be borne in me, I can not only think about spiritual and psychic processes, but as woman I am also aware of the biological and existential possibility to give birth to a child. And when I finally think about love to God, then my heart is inflamed in a love that cannot be separated from my human love to children, men, women and creation, to whom I open my heart.

My spirituality has become feminist where I became and become increasingly aware of the social, the physical and the psychological situation of women in patriarchy, and there where I express this consciousness together with other women. I have hardly heard any critique about patriarchy from the woman mystics, but only the talk of the "poor little female". It seems not unreasonable to suspect that here often the Christian virtue of humility towards God - the word "Thy will be done"- has been confused with humility towards men. After my personal dealing with Santa Teresa, I have learned from feminist theology to also discover my own strength and will as something positive and to take responsibility for my life and my tasks with self-consciousness. And I want to stress here, that I would not have developed this feminist consciousness without learning from and together with other women.

Tuesday, April 2, 1996
Images of Teresa of Avila, Francis of Assisi and Martin Luther
Today, I sat down in Lampman Chapel once more. I looked at the three stained windows and began to meditate. The figures seemed to disappear and come up again. Sometimes I just saw colours. What a delight red, blue, green and yellow, and even a bit of royal purple are for the eyes! There they appeared, these figures, these Catholic and Protestant Saints - Santa Teresa, Saint Francis and Martin Luther - all European - what a telling assembly in this Seminary-place in the New World.

Saint Francis sings his song about our brothers and sisters the sun, the earth, the wind, the water, the animals. . . God's creation is being exploited all over the world right now. Our brothers and sisters do suffer. We need to love and cherish them. Cosmological thinking is needed in Christian spirituality. This perspective connects us also with the other religions in the world.

Martin Luther seems to me a very different, all in all very 'male' person. He spoke to the Emperor in Worms: "Hier stehe ich und kann nicht anders!" - "Here I stand and can not do otherwise." These words teach me as a Catholic women the very Protestant principle. Beyond all dialectical relativity and everlasting assimilation it means not only having an opinion of one's own, but also to stand up for it. Still, as a woman, I do not know whether my faith can and should be *on principle* 'sola scriptura, 'sola gratia', 'solus Jesus Christus'.

I looked at the window of Santa Teresa. She and Martin Luther were contemporaries. They both struggled with the same patriarchal God. Luther gained - sola gratia - the insight into the "justification alone through faith", and thus enthroned the punishing God. Teresa found herself in the love to her Divine Bridegroom. In calling herself "Teresa de Jesus" she related herself definitely to God the Son whom she dared to communicate with on the equal level of mystical-erotic love. She also enthroned the patriarchal, punishing God, yet, in a very different way than Luther - in the image of spiritual, bodily, and active love.

Wednesday, April 3, 1996
Sacred Spaces - Inner Spaces

> *O God eternal, in your light I have seen*
> *how closely you have conformed your creature to yourself.*
> *I see that you have set us, as we are, in a circle,*
> *so that wherever we may go we are still within this circle.*[4]

> *Catherine of Siena*

In the beginning, I quoted Teresa's image of the "interior castle". Today, when thinking about spirituality, I want to take up with Catherine of Siena's image of the circle. What does she mean by saying that we are always in a circle, wherever we may go!? Is this circle the same image for the soul that Teresa uses in the "Interior castle"? Why do both women mystics use a spatial image instead of the image of "the path" or "the stages" - preferably used by male mystics who describe the development of "via purgativa, via illuminativa, via unitativa"!? Thinking about female spirituality, I simply want to look at it less as a time-journey than a spatial experience. So let's talk about rooms!

As most women in history, Catherine of Siena (1347-1380) had not got a room to herself. Yet, from her childhood on, she desired to be alone in order to dedicate herself entirely to God. Her parents -

opposing her "strange behavior" in order to interest her in worldly matters during her adolescence - deprived her of a room to herself. Thus, she built in her mind a secret "interior cell". It was in this place that she managed to rest completely in God, regardless of how outwardly busy she had to be.

What about outside and inside rooms in women's lives today. Do we now have "a room of one's own", as Virginia Woolf demanded it, -a room in which we can withdraw and sit and work and listen to music and draw and sleep. . . alone? Or, are we able to build up an "inner room" in which we are not dominated by responsibilities for children, everyday tasks, and by "male" thinking?

When I was sitting in Chapel today, I thought that I indeed need such a sacred space to withdraw and to immerse into from time to time. I enjoyed the smell of the incense and felt elevated by the spirit of a room in which many others (how much more women than men!?) have been praying before me. Somehow this knowledge of connectedness with women who went "to pray" in churches through times and spaces gave my own meditation another quality. I also thought about my wish to escape "reality" from time to time, my wish to not see and not talk and not smile in order to be with myself alone. I reflected about my wish not to go out for three days, after I arrive in another country. My soul wishes to arrive in this space as well. And then, I thought about Santa Teresa again. She went in a carriage through the endless roads of 16 century Spain, and wanted to close the curtain to not see anybody in order not to be distracted from her inner space.

What is this inner space? Following Teresas "Interior castle", it is the soul and it is ourselves. We may truly enter ourselves through the "gate of prayer". All the inner rooms are already there, even if we cannot see them, and God is residing in the center waiting for us, even if we ignore "Him". Following Catherine's image of the "interior cell" and the "circle" it is the place in that God has set us - maybe like in the Garden of Eden. This circle is surrounding us so that we find space in it and may breath all our life. Thus, I think spirituality is about both this *space* that we find *in ourselves* and this space *in which we find ourselves*. It is *like* our womanly womb that may bring forth life, and it is *like* the garden of Mother Earth that brought us to life. It is about all that what really nourishes us!

Maundy Thursday, April 4, 1996

The Body of Christ - Loving, powerful and courageous women

> *Another time, I was once standing in prayer and meditating sorrowfully on the passion of the Son of God incarnate. Then, through God's will, the passion was shown to me, that is, he himself granted me to see more of his passion than I have ever spoken of. For Christ had foreseen all the hearts impiously hardened against him, everyone contriving to destroy his name, and how they constantly kept in mind their purpose to destroy him. . . On still another occasion, I was shown the acute pain which was in Christ's soul. I was not surprised that it was a great pain, for that soul was most noble, and did nor deserve any punishment, but Christ suffered what he did out of his immense love for humanity.*
>
> *The soul of Christ suffered still other pains from all the torments and afflictions his body endured - all of these converged in his soul. This acute pain, so intense that the tongue cannot express it nor is the heart great enough to imagine it, was all part of the divine plan. I saw such deep pain in the soul of the Son of the Blessed Virgin Mary that my own soul was deeply afflicted and transformed in such pain as I had never known before; all my joy was gone.*

Angela of Foligno

Today, I missed the Maundy Thursday service. Instead of this, I went to a lecture on the *"Image as Source in the Study of Some Late Italian Female Mystics"*. It was talked about Angela Foligno, Chiara or Claire of Assisi, Agnes of Montepulciano, Margarete of Cortona, and Catherine of Siena. I could not follow the lecture well, but I emerged in some of the images that were shown. The lecturer was an Art Historian, a woman, who tried to systematize the imagery of the female mystics and set them into an historical framework. Listening not-listening to her, I was more engaged in what she did not say rather in what she said in her academic style. For example, in her "scientific" perspective the image of a devotional woman, a nun kneeling down in front of the altar to pray to the crucifix on top of it, was looked upon as a merely medieval - and that equalizes dead - form of spirituality. Finally also a judgment was made by the lecturer that Italian female mystics are not as "intense" as Germans. I spoke to her afterwards, and said that maybe the Italian mystics were more bodily or physical in their mysticism. And the lecturer replied that the German mystics are not as "down to earth" as the Italian ones. Opposing this, I mentioned that for instance Hildegard von Bingens gynecological medicine was very much down to earth.- What about these judgments? They appear to be "objective". Yet, they only distance us from the women figures we are looking at. Identification is not possible and/or seems to be a pretty weird or spiritual desire that draws us into the sphere of no more being academics, but emotional or romantic women. There was no intention in this "academic" lecture to ask for a deeper understanding of these women, or for a living tradition and relationship to the spirituality of women today. The woman figure were looked at as an "object" of research. Knowing this, I would never have stood up and said:

"Yes, I want to identify with these woman, I also want to deepen my faith by understanding the mystery of the body and blood of Christ, and I try to relate it to the mystery of the body and blood of women today!"

Christian meditation can lead to identification with Christ and the figures of the Saints. Guiding to a participation in their lives is also the original purpose of the images painted onto the walls of churches. Picking up this tradition, I try to see them, these young woman, beautiful to look at in their religious garments. I see those young brides who suffer with the suffering body of Christ, who desire to unify with their Divine bridegroom, for whom the body and blood of Christ is a reality to take into their own body, to internalize within the holy sacrament of the Eucharist, and to care about in actions to the sick and poor - men, women, children and creation. I imagine this act in which "subject" and "object" get unified in a holy-healing communion, in which "male" and "female" bodily emerge into each other in the "holy marriage" on Mount Calvary.

I saw that while the Son of God was hanging on the cross,
the image of the aforesaid woman (Ecclesia) came
hastening down from the ancient counsel like a splendor.
By divine power she was led to him, and suffused with the
blood that flowed from the side, she rose up and was joined
to him by the heavenly Father's will in happy betrothal, with
the noble dowry of his flesh and blood. And I heard a voice
from heaven saying to him, "Let her be a bride to you, Son,
for the restoration of my people whose mother she will be,
regenerating souls through the saving mystery of water and
the Spirit. [5]
Hildegard of Bingen

I can see her, this female figure, "regenerating souls through the mystery of water and the Spirit", Ecclesia, the "body of Christ". But, as a theologian, and as spiritual woman today, I have also to ask whether this images is still strong enough today, or what new kind of images we might need. I have to ask for the real presence of the holy-whole body of Christ that we are longing for and that we need to internalize. I have to ask how we can really participate in the suffering of the world in order to contribute to its healing. I ask the question what images of loving and courageous woman do catch me and may catch us today, if it is not the images of medieval Italian female mystics!?

And there I try to see them, the women who can be intellectual as well as spiritual; the woman who bring birth to a child and do not give up themselves; the women who do suffer and have mercy with other human beings and yet do not get lost in their suffering; the women who are spiritual and political at once, who find a way of going into action; the women who can see the body of Christ in children, men, women, and creation. And I try to envision the body and blood of Christ today.

Good Friday, April 5, 1996

The Impact of Our European Tradition on the Suffering and/or Healing of Women All Over the World

> *O God, you have searched us and known us,*
> *and all what we are is open to you.*
> *We confess that we have sinned:*
> *We have used our power to dominate*
> *and our weakens to manipulate;*
> *We have evaded responsibility*
> *and failed to confront evil;*
> *We have denied dignity*
> *to ourselves and to our sisters (each other),*
> *and fallen into despair.*
>
> *We turn to you, O God;*
> *we renounce evil;*
> *we claim your love;*
> *we choose to be made whole.*

Janet Morley[6]

There is a guilt that lies not in our activity but in our passivity. True mysticism shows its fruits in political and social action. Contemplation and action belong together like Martha and Mary. Contemplation that looks only into oneself might never lead to activity into this world! So, Teresa may also be criticized for not looking out of her window, while traveling trough the landscape of Spain. Her contemplation might have lacked an appreciation of nature, God's creation. When I just pass by the homeless people in the streets and do not dare to look into their faces, I might be criticized for having missed the chance to look into the image of God in any single one of them. A life of prayer can only be healing if it is dedicated to others!

Our Western Christian Religion has caused much suffering to women all over the world. European women are connected to European men who went (and still go!) out to "discover" the world, where they have "taken other women" - women of color, poor women, women who have needed to prostitute themselves in Africa, Asia, America, and also in Europe.

When Teresa was about twelve, she escaped home together with her brother to discover the land of the Moors and to bring them the "Christian mission". Both of them had to return home by then. Later, Teresa got more and more immersed into a spiritual life of contemplative prayer, while several of her own brothers went out to discover the New World. There, white men did not only exploit nature, but also abused native women as merely another form of "nature" to be conquered. As they perceived the "otherness" of these women not only in their gender, but also in their color, abusing "the other" as a sexual "object" appeared a self-evident right to them. European women did not stop European men and hardly ever confessed their own guilt. One might justify European women by arguing that they had no long-reaching power over their men, husbands and brothers.

European men went out into the world - European women stayed at home! European men were active - European women were passive! European men did harm - European women were harmless?

This sounds somehow like the well-known story of the woman whose husbands becomes unfaithful, "*er geht fremd*". Then, the one who is deeply blamed by her is "the other woman", much more than "her" husband, or even herself. - The position of European women towards women of color reminds me to that story. What has to be looked upon is the structure and the impact of triangle relationships, psychologically: married women - husband - other woman as sex-object; and historically: white woman - white man - woman of color / native woman. And we white woman have to look at our role, and our specific contribution.

In the time of Teresa the Catholic Church discussed whether "the Indians" were at all human beings, worth of mission. And, European women looked at themselves as "daughters of Eve". The dominating understanding of the "original sin" as mainly a sexual act, blinded woman for centuries to see their "guilt" in other than sexual actions, namely in their own non-acting. Our ignorance today lacks mercy and the ability to see the "other" women as "made in the image of God". We have played with our weakness and lacked actions of solidarity. We have still not understood that passivity, ignorance and non-participation might be our original sin. How can we contribute to the healing of women all over the world and how can our religion have a positive impact in this process? It seems to be clear that no more traditional "Christian mission" is needed, and I think that it is also not financial help which is demanded of us in the first place. Rather important seems to me awareness and understanding of each other. For being open to the difference of the "other", we may discover the difference in ourselves; and we might be able to admit and confess our ignorance and even our guilt towards other cultures and religions.

Let us now go into a true ecumenical and inter-religious dialogue in which we are willing to learn and to face ourselves. Let us be in active solidarity with "other women" and let us learn to confront "our men", so that there will be healing and becoming whole in this world.

Easter Vigil, 6. April, 1996
Oh Truly Necessary Sin of Eve!?

> *O mira circa nos tuae pietatis dignatio!*
> *O inaestimábilis diléctio caritátis:*
> *ut servum redímeres, Filium tradidisti!*
> *O certe necessárium Adae peccatum,*
> *quod Christi morte delétum est.*
> *O felix culpa, quae talem ac tantum meruit habere*
> *Redemptórem!*
>
> *O how wonderful is thy goodness towards us!*
> *O how inestimable is thy love!*
> *Thou hast delivered up thy son*
> *to redeem a slave.*
> *O truly necessary sin of Adam,*
> *which the death of Christ has blotted out!*
> *O happy fault, that merited so great*
> *a Redeemer![7]*

Missale Romanum

Tonight I went to the Easter Vigil in Corpus Christi Church. The introductory words in this old liturgy of the "Roman Mass" include a whole theology. The words in the Easter Vigil are the only place where the "necessary sin of Adam" is not dammed but praised. Understanding

Adam as the prototype of "mankind", women had to think that they were included here as well.

But why then does the liturgical text not talk about the "truly necessary sin of Eve"!? Was it not her "fault", mainly understood as sexual misbehavior, that otherwise has been damned so many times!? As "daughters of Eve", women had to suffer so long in history for "Eve's sin". In this Christian tradition, there is no escape: even being virgins, women can never reach the status of the virgin Mary who was mother and virgin at once. As daughters of Eve, women always have to share in her "original sin". But even if male theology will not do it, shall not women finally begin to praise the "happy fault" of Eve - the fault that led her grab for Divine wisdom, the fault of acting as the first one, before man dared to do so, the fault "that merited so great a redeemer"!?

In a service that I conducted in the "Frauenfriedenskirche" in Frankfurt, we celebrated "wisdom". As "daughters of Eve" we ate from the "fruit of wisdom". We reminded ourselves that Eve ate from the tree of knowledge, and that since then we all participate in this knowledge:

> So we may follow her and also eat from the fruit of that tree. Come do not only think about this symbol, but taste the apple fruit! And share it with another person. But before we bite into it, let us say the Benediction.

In this way we shared consciously a bowl of apples in our midst. We gave ourselves to eat from these apples. This act of eating suddenly appeared to be a strange, nearly forbidden act. Even after having blessed the apples, it took us some kind of courage to bite into them. It is hard to overcome the thought of "sin" as something to be avoided and to understand the idea of "sin" as something that might be necessary, the necessary sin of action. How can we transform our understanding of this? How can we become more courageous and gain strength? Can we change the words in our liturgy?

> O truly necessary sin of Eve,
> which the birth of Christ has blotted out!
> O happy fault, that merited so great a Redeemer!

The idea that our faults can merit something may lead us to a new understanding of spirituality. It is not about avoiding "sins", but rather about risking ourselves in actions of love in order to gain knowledge and to find new life. I think, it takes courage to admit this space of experience to ourselves and others.

Easter Sunday, April 7, 1996

Songs of Wisdom

Easter is about the new life after death. It is about the resurrection or the rebirth of Christ. The Son of God is reborn in his body; the old body that was born by a women and that has derived form Eve, the first mother, has been transformed. In Christ every body is elevated and worth of resurrection. In Christ, new life and old wisdom, has come back to us.

Wisdom has been praised in many songs. This Easter, I heard about her behind the lines of the Hymn of Christ in Phillipians:

> *Christ Jesus . . . humbled himself*
> *and became obedient to the point of death -*
> *even death on the cross.*
> *Therefore God also highly exalted him*
> *and gave him the name*
> *that is above every name*
> *so that in the name of Jesus*
> *every knee should bend,*
> *in heaven and on earth and under the earth.*
> (Phil 2:5-11)

This Hymn of Christ praises Christ's humility and exaltation. There is also a strange passage about "knees" who are in "heaven and on earth and under the earth"; these may represent not just human beings but spirits who are to be found "on high", "in heaven" - traditional (Christian) places of the "male" God and his angels -, yet also "on earth" and "under the earth", imagined places of "spirits of the death" and "demons". All these sprits bend their knees, and thus subordinates to Christ. How does this happen?

Hildegard of Bingen describes a similar movement of Divine Wisdom in all these dimensions.

> *O power of Wisdom!*
> *You encompassed the cosmos,*
> *encircling and embracing all*
> *in one living orbit*
> *with your three wings:*
> *one soars on high,*
> *one distills the earth's essence,*
> *and the third hovers everywhere.*
> *Praise to you, Wisdom, fitting praise!*

Hildegard von Bingen

Hildegard's figure of Wisdom is no unmoved mover, ordering the universe from on high. She creates the cosmos by existing within it. Her ubiquity is expressed through the image of ceaseless, circular motion. What is moving "are the three "wings" of wisdom: one soars on high *(quarum una in altum volat),* one distills the earth's essence *(et altera de terra sudat),* and the third hovers everywhere *(et tercia unidque volat).* The image of the wing derives from birds and is symbolically associated with angels, thus with spiritual beings.

What is interesting in Hildegard' image is that she sees the fluid of the earth, distilled through the wing of wisdom. What is this fluid? The water of the earth might be imagined like womanly blood or milk; to me it seems that likewise the destined essence of the earth must be something wise and healing. Hildegard imagined the third wing of wisdom everywhere. I think that in giving us this image of utter immanence of wisdom, Hildegard "transcends" traditional male and female locations of the Divine. Only Wisdom recognizes the obedience of the humble one not as a form of hierarchical subordination but as an expression of uttermost love. Love that goes beyond death becomes exalted. The deepest wisdom of all three dimensions shows Christ - the love that goes beyond death - the gratitude and respect that it deserves.

Postscript

Easter was a rainy day, but I was happy to have undergone this writing-process. It was not always easy. In the beginning, I felt, that I did not have to say anything, and then in the process of writing the thoughts developed themselves. Sometimes it felt hard to have to write them down. I did not always manage to write everyday, yet, I was always thinking about what I could write. Thereby I combined "our" questionnaire with the topic of the Holy Week. Sometimes it appeared to me that I was almost picking up my topics "just by chance". Then, it got more and more interesting for me to reinterpret the Christian tradition in every single aspect from a female-feminist perspective. Thus I included liturgical and other holy texts and also looked at Christ whose figure is so much in the center of attention in this Holy Week of passion. Otherwise the topics I came up with were mainly dealing with the mystical women's tradition with which I am familiar. In my meditation, I put myself into this tradition not as a dead but as a living one; I did not stop in the Middle Ages; I did not stop with Eve's Fall.

I dared to reformulate the old wisdom and visions of women in my own words. If I have talked about "mother Earth" and the "female" naively, not taking into consideration feminist literary and social criticism, this is partly due to my rather psychological and spiritual orientation. I would wish to understand and to learn more about this criticism, yet, I also want to make a clear statement and tell in my own narrative style, where I am: Putting myself in the tradition of the female mystics rather than the feminist critics.

Notes

1 The Interior Castle, Chapter One

2 Before, I had written my Thesis on Teresa: "Die Mystik Teresa von Avilas als Weg der Selbsterfahrung und der Gotteserfahrung", Münster, 1985 (unpublished)

3 This text was published twice in the German original version: (1) Peter Lengsfeld, Zum tieferen Sinn von Religion. Religionsgespräche in Asien und anderswo, Vianova, Petersberg, 1993, p. 30. (2) Annette Esser, Meine Spiritualität ist weiblich, in: "Die christliche Frau", Vol 1, 1994, p.7. In the English version, I have now chosen to speak of the Spirit inclusively as "she".

4 Prayer of Catherine taken from a leaf-let in Chapel that Day

5 Scivias II.6

6 Janet Morley, All Desires Known, London: MOW, 1988, p.33

7 Missale Romanum, Vigilia Paschalis

Lise Tostrup Setek

When Good Friday Seems No Good...
Still Rays of the Easter Sun Break the Fog of Suffering.

The Nordic spring

In Norway, Easter is celebrated in the midst of the Nordic spring. Nordic spring is the time when the rays of the sun no longer give a pale winter twilight, but melt the snow by the sun's warmth and sparkle. The streets of Oslo are dusty from sand that should prevent people from falling on iced pavements; the little snow that is left is all dirty; the inhabitants gaze at the sun, feeling spring in their veins. Alas! It is time once more to experience the snow in the land of eternal snow.

A large segment of the population travel to the mountains at Eastertime. It is the last possibility for skiing, the national winter sport of Norway. Most people associate Easter with a week's stay in a cottage in the mountains, ski-tracks, and, hopefully, sunny days in the highlands. The church's chaplains celebrate Easter services at chapels and holiday resorts in the highlands. People who don't travel to the mountain-plateau for skiing find the cities quiet for a whole week. Snowlillies and crocuses begin to spring forth in gardens and thus the miracle of new life becomes manifest.

In 1996 the time shift to summer time began on Palm Sunday. Everyone wants to get as much daylight as possible after the long and dark winter. Some, however, have a tendency to get into a gloomy mood in spring. The sale of pills to cure depression rises considerably during April.

Hilde and Solveig

This was the case for Hilde. She is a social worker, 45 years of age, living in a suburb of Oslo, taking care of her two teen-age sons after being divorced from her husband. Her husband was not Norwegian and as a foreigner he was never fully integrated into the Norwegian culture and way of life. He was discriminated against when he applied for jobs, lived by welfare money for extended periods of time, and was constantly confused by the freedom and power Norwegian women exibit in their life-style and way of bringing up children. Hilde had met him at the University. He was exotic and charming; but the marriage turned into a disaster when they raised children together. Towards society she managed to keep a stiff upper lip, but at home she was bossed around by her husband in such a manner and to such degree that her self-esteem became very low. Drained by conflicts at home, financial worries and a hard job, she realized that the only way out was to file for divorce. Alone with two children, she worked extra overtime, since her parents were willing to help her by baby-sitting. She used to have an active social-life, but suddenly she felt overpowered by fatigue and lacked her usual initiative. Too long she had tried to make up for the shortcomings of her husband. She always felt that the responsibility for the well-being of her little family was hers alone, since she was in her home country.

The fog of depression

During winter 1996 she went skiing and injured her right arm. She barely managed to drive her old, bumpy car home. The family doctor gave her six weeks sick-leave. At home she could hardly dress herself alone, she could not write or do any housework. Her teenage boys were rather unwilling to assist her at home, and she became more and more depressed. Her house became increasingly untidy, so she did not feel like receiving visitors. Most of the time she stared apathetically at the TV screen. Getting up in the morning became less and less meaningful. Some of her friends would give her a ring, but she answered barely 'yes' and 'no' on the phone and could spend all day long in bed, under her eiderdown blanket.

To behave like a donkey on Palm Sunday

Hilde had a few good friends. One of them, Solveig, served as chaplain in a congregation not too far away from where Hilde lived. Popping in without notice beforehand, Solveig was immediately aware of how deeply depressed Hilde seemed to be. They agreed that it was necessary for Solveig to keep in close touch with her during the Holy Week. Solveig picked up the phone by Hilde's bed and let Hilde herself speak to the family doctor.

On her way home from Hilde, Solveig could not help thinking:

She was thinking of the donkey Jesus was riding on Palm Sunday. The donkey, an animal used for transportation of goods and humans - hardworking, but stubborn. When overloaded, it may stand still, completely unwilling to move an inch. When beaten it may neigh in a manner that reminds us humans of the sound of a laughter of mockery.

Hilde, my beloved donkey, she sighed. Solveig felt a bit ashamed that such an image of a donkey came to her mind. Hilde, her very best friend. At the same time she could not help smiling.

Am I really depressed?

In agreement with the family doctor, Hilde started taking pills against the depression. At the beginning Hilde felt she was a failure and resented the pills. However, with her brain she realized that the medication was necessary. Before she herself realized it, it was thoroughly confirmed by herself how deeply depressed she actually was! She looked at random in her bookshelves and found among her old study-books a test schema that social workers could use as a guide-line to test whether their client was depressed or not. With a pencil she marked a small cross among six alternative answers to every question. Gloomy in the morning, want to sleep longer, no joy on waking up. No wish to even brush her teeth or comb her hair. To dress felt like a big job. She was existing, not living, in an emotional landscape of grey, longing for a land that does not exist. She was breathing in an atmosphere of dull routines, whatever she was thinking of or trying to do, it was all drained of meaning. The sap of life was drained from her. Less appetite for food, no wish to leave the house, nauseated. Her existence was beyond words, beyond description. One question in the schema:" Do you consider putting an end to your life ?" Automatically she crossed in the "Yes, very often" option. She was shocked at the very moment the pencil was put on that very spot of the paper. Well,I am in fact depressed, I have to face it with my brain at least, she mumbled to herself.

The hiding of real feelings

She had always been the strong social worker, helping others. She had never exposed her inner feelings to anyone, except Solveig. Hilde was afraid of her own feelings. Deep down she was aware of rage and hatred in herself, as well as love and tenderness which made her extremely vulnerable. With a pale smile and forced laughter she shook off comments that really hurt her deeply inside. She had the gift of knowing by pure intuition. As a child she had always conformed to the wishes of her mother. She was regarded as an obedient girl, easy to handle. Hilde showed great care for the well-being of people around her. Her choice of profession was quite in line with her image of herself as a pleasant and caring person. But those dark corners of her personality where sparks of anger and rage glowed—those were the feelings that she could not handle or show to anyone.

When aggression pops out

Surprising even herself, she had been aggressive to Solveig when she came popping in on Palm Sunday. Hilde was wondering in her mind:

Palm Sunday, what the hell is that name good for? She could wish to lie underneath a palm at a beach in the sun, but she did not ever have money for such a holiday. Now, she did not even feel like it. To pack a suitcase, to buy a plane ticket, to fasten the seatbelt and feel scared when the plane took off ... No, it was not even worth dreaming of it.

"Why is it Palm Sunday, what the he.., eh, is that name good for?" She was almost snarling at Solveig, but she had avoided the swear word she knew her friend could not stand. Solveig did not answer her back, but said she would come back on Maundy Thursday after she had celebrated the communion service at the old people's home. Solveig had spoken of Christ riding into Jerusalem. "Was Jesus glad or sad when he sat on the back of the donkey? What do you think, Hilde? The crowd cheered as he rode past, but he himself knew that he was going to suffer and die on the cross a few days after." Solveig had spoken with a voice mellow like velvet.

Why did she nearly always speak like a counselor and pastor? Were they not just friends anymore? Hilde had to admit that Solveig's voice was beautiful. From the pulpit the voice of Solveig could flow over the churchgoers as a cello played by sordine. But if Solveig, for some reason got nervous, the pitch of her voice would rise into the squeak of a swallow. Hilde was reminded of the time Solveig had begged her on the phone to come to a service where Solveig was supposed to preach. The Dean of Oslo would be present, and some professors of Theology, Solveig's own teachers from the Free Faculty of Theology. Solveig had sounded scared, and Hilde should have given emotional support by being present. But Hilde had caught a flu, coughed all night before and did not dare to turn up. When Hilde had tried to notify Solveig that she could not come to the service, she had no luck getting hold of her. Solveig was very busy and hard to contact. Later on, Hilde had understood that Solveig had thought she had forgotten about it, and felt let down. Her voice had taken on the disastrous swallow-quality during her sermon, but the mellow velvet quality of her mezzo-soprano had saved her liturgical singing. Solveig was always well-prepared when she celebrated service. The content of her sermon had been just right for the occasion, and the language poetic. The stumbling in pronunciation and the high pitch of her voice had nearly spoiled it for her. Hilde felt sorry for Solveig, and sorry for herself. Bad luck, bad luck and failure; that is what life is all about. Hilde was mad at herself.

The silent week

Hilde's two boys left Monday morning. They had been invited by classmates to a cottage at the Geilo ski resort. Hilde was quite exhausted after packing their back-packs with clean, warm clothes. Her right arm ached and her feelings of helplessness and loneliness grew even stronger when the boys slammed the door in a hurry to reach the train, not giving her the usual hug.

Hilde went back to her bed in her pyjamas. She lay on her back and started to count the nails in the ceiling. With no aim. She fell asleep. Woke up and sighed. Stared at the ceiling. Counted more nails. Slept. Woke up. Went to the toilet. Knew she needed food, but felt no appetite. Went into the living-room. Switched on the TV. No programme on any of the 12 channels caught her interest. The sky outside was clear and blue. She ought to go for a walk. But she did not feel like it. With pain in the arm, she managed after a while to make a cup of tea, but she left the cup in the kitchen after the first sip. She had a snooze on the sofa in the living-room. When she woke up she realized that the sun was about to set, and it was too late for a walk in the park nearby.

Do girls want to have fun?

Suddenly the phone rang. Her sister Ruth's voice on the receiver. Ruth would arrive next day from the Western coast of Norway and stay in Oslo with a friend of hers. She invited Hilde to the cinema. Ruth was eager to see the movie "The Other Side of Sunday" and did not want to go alone. Ruth was living in a small, isolated place with no cinema. Ruth loved the cinema. Hilde sighed. She did not feel like going anywhere. She knew the film was a serious one. She knew she needed some program for tomorrow otherwise she would probably not get out of bed at all. She had not seen her sister for a long time. She knew Ruth would be hurt if she said no. So Hilde sighed and said: "Yes, why not?" Ruth seemed relieved. They agreed on meeting downtown half an hour before the show started.

The movie was a serious one, indeed. A strict and heartless country chaplain, with two teenage-children who were not permitted anything fun at all. "Girls want to have fun!!" The daughter on the screen insisted to her father.

"Fun." In Hilde's ears the word "fun" sounded as something she had never experienced. She felt sad. She had always complied with the wishes of her mother, being helpful at home rather than going out with boys as a teenager. Always doing her homework diligently. She was a bright child, and her marks at school were not at all bad. She was keeping her room in order most of the time. The daughter in the film reminded her of time she herself was a teen-ager. And she suddenly wondered whether her own boys had fun or not in the mountains, staying in a small cottage without TV. The weather man on the telly yesterday had spoken of fog. Then the boys would stay inside. She was sure of that. Fog in the mountains was no fun. Every sensible Norwegian would stay inside. Mostly tourists from Denmark, or further south in Europe, get lost and had to be searched for by the Red Cross rescue teams.

The only way out?

The plot in the film became more dramatic. The wife of the chaplain became sick and was put in the hospital. While she was there, the chaplain became initimate with the woman who cleaned the church. The daughter intuitively understood the erotic mood of her father and felt helpless. The cleaning woman, who was as beautiful as the chaplain was good looking, felt abused by the chaplain. When the wife returned from the hospital, the cleaning woman saw no other way out than taking her own life. She drowned herself in the river. When she was standing on the shore gazing at the waves, Hilde felt how she would like to be dead. Just drown into wet, pleasant waves or simply sleep and never wake up again.

Her own boys, when they returned from the mountains sunburnt and happy, would find her dead in her bed. Dead from an overdose of pills. Her youngest son's pale face filled with despair appeared before her inner eye. No, she had no right to make them unhappy for the rest of their lives. They would feel guilty; they had not even taken time to hug her when they left Monday morning. Tears came to Hilde's eyes.

Ruth noticed and wondered. Hilde composed herself. She felt even more depressed than ever. She could not share her inner feelings with Ruth.

Look at the birds!

On the way home she hardly spoke. Ruth wanted to deliver some flowers at the local hospital to a friend of hers who would be operated during Easter. Hilde did not feel like walking to the hospital. Her legs felt like if they were made of lead. She avoided that visit by sitting on a bench in the park nearby. She told Ruth she said that her feet were aching. A few sparrows walked by her feet. Hilde had no breadcrumbs to feed them.

As a child, it had been one of her favorite activities, to walk in the park with Grandma. Grandma used to save old, hard bread for breadcrumbs for the birds. Feeding the ducks and swans in the pond was the best of the trip, sparrows and pigeons were of lower rank. If Grandma was too busy baking bread, she would send Hilde and her sister alone to the park. Ruth used to carry the brown paperbag with crumbs as she was the oldest one. Hilde would get hungry on the way to the park. "Please, Suuth," she would stutter, not being able to prononce "r" distinctly. "Let me taste a few breadcrumbs! Ple-a-s-e!" Ruth hesitated. Hilde bothered her sister until Ruth opened the brown paperbag. "Only three pieces," said Ruth in a strict manner. Hilde picked four clandestinely and chewed only a few times before she swallowed her mouthful. Ruth could not know for sure how many pieces Hilde had taken. Ruth felt like tasting the crumbs, too. She picked three; and they were good, not very hard and dry. Ruth picked one more, and gave Hilde too. Without thinking the girls ate the food for the ducks and when they arrived at the pond in the park, the paperbag was nearly empty. They felt suddenly both ashamed that they had eaten the bird-food. They were humans, they would get freshly baked bread when they returned from the park to Grandma's house. Their mouths watered. The poor ducks looked hungry and the sparrows and pigeons, too. When they turned the paperbag inside out, some small crumbs fell on the ground. An instant competition and fight broke loose among the birds by their feet. Humans are not in harmony with the nature and the other animals. That is a real pity, Hilde thought. We humans are as greedy as the biggest pigeons and as scared as the smallest sparrow. Are we really worth much more than many sparrows?

Finally Ruth came back. Hilde was cold. The sky was rather cloudy and the sun rays did not warm through the clouds. Ruth made a cup of tea for her sister when they reached home. Hilde sat in the sofa. Ruth gave her a blanket. Hilde sat on the sofa also when Ruth bade her good-bye and left her flat. Some long hours later Hilde realized that she had been sitting and sleeping in the same spot of her sofa. She glanced at her watch and it was in the middle of the night.

A Maundy Thursday without bread and wine

In a few hours time it will be Maundy Thursday. All shops are closed until Tuesday after Easter Monday. No milk in the refrigerator. No wine either. Not even a beer. She might have to walk to a gas station nearby to buy bread and milk. Shell or Statoil? Rather Statoil, the staff there are more pleasant. Kind of kind. The boss uses theological students as staff in the holidays. They do not steal the goods as so many other employees do. Maybe she should rent a video. Something to laugh with, not any more dreadful suicides. The movies will be closed, too.

Until Tuesday. Most restaurants, too. The city will be dead. Everybody will be out of town except sick and old people. And the poor, who cannot afford to ski in the mountains. No fun. Oh well, she does not want to have fun anyway.

Does Christ's passion cause pain or bliss?

Solveig phoned: "Are you alright, Hilde?" Hilde put herself together and replied "yes" as best as she could. Solveig was preparing a sermon for tomorrow, Good Friday. A lesson from the Old Testament and reading of the Epistle are replaced on Good Friday with reading of the passion story from the Gospel according to John (Joh.18,1 -19,30). Solveig will speak about a female mystic from Medieval England, Julian of Norwich. She got sick and nearly died when she got visions of Christ as he died on the Cross. Solveig is quoting from her *Showings*:

> "Christ showed me part of his Passion, close to his death. I saw his sweet face as it were dry and bloodless, with the pallor of dying, then more dead, pale and languishing, then the pallor turning blue and then more blue, as death took more hold upon his flesh. For all the pains which Christ suffered in his body appeared to me in his blessed face. In all this time that Christ was present to me, I felt no pain except for Christ's pain... And here I saw a great unity between Christ and us; for when he was in pain we were in pain, and all creatures able to suffer pain suffered with him. And for those that did not know him, their pain was that all creation, sun and moon, ceased to serve men, and so they were all abandoned in sorrow at that time. So those who loved him suffered pain for their love, and those who did not love him suffered pain because the comfort of all creation failed them. At this time I wanted to look to the side of the cross, but I did not dare, for I knew well that whilst I looked at the cross I was secure and safe. Therefore I would not agree to put my soul in danger, for apart from the cross there was no safety, but only the horrors of devils... Thus I chose Jesus for my heaven, whom I saw only in pain at the time. And suddenly, as I looked to the same cross, he was changed to an appearance of joy. The change in his appearance changed mine, and I was as glad and joyful as I could possibly be. And then cheerfully our Lord suggested to my mind: Where is there any instant of your pain or of your grief? And I was very joyful.

Then our Lord put a question to me: Are you well satisfied that I suffered for you? Yes, good Lord, I said; all my thanks to you, good Lord, blessed may you be! If you are satisfied, our Lord said, I am satisfied. It is a joy and a bliss and an endless delight to me that ever I suffered my Passion for you, for if I could suffer more, I would. In my response to this, my understanding was lifted up into heaven, . . ."

Hilde sighs: "my understanding is very much down to earth, I don't take all this talk of suffering as bliss. How awful!" Hilde still feels angry and she cannot control it. Solveig is at a loss. *Showings* is a favourite book of hers. It is a book of deep Christian wisdom and comfort. But Hilde is not in a mood to listen to anything at all. Solveig sighs, too. Then she wonders whether the very last words of Jesus: "It is finished!" could form a suitable theme for her short meditation. These words of Jesus do comfort us today, Hilde, don't they?"

Calm or desperate?

Solveig's voice sounded like velvet. How could she be so calm? Hilde felt like if the words of Jesus on the cross were uttered in despair: It is finished! This is the bitter end, the very, very bitter end. Hilde does not manage to follow Solveig's pious thoughts. She replies "mm", "yes", "no" and says "good luck! bye!" Hilde feels the despair, the bitterness, the rage, the grit. No grace. Hilde wants only to sleep and rest in peace. It was night.

When Good Friday seems no good.

The church bells wake her up at five to eleven. Maybe 'Seven - Eleven' is open, so she could take the tram and might get some fresh bread. But the tram goes only twice an hour on Sundays and she is dreadfully hungry. She makes herself a cup of instant coffee at the kitchen sink. Dirty plates and cups have been piling up since last week. The boys left Monday morning and their plates from Sunday dinner are stale with grease. Her right arm is aching so she cannot cut bread. She butters a couple of sandwiches and puts a layer of sliced goat-cheese on top. She takes a bite and chews slowly. This was her favorite food in childhood, just like she got for breakfast at school together with a slice of cod-roe-pate. The brown color of the goat-cheese suddenly reminds her of shit, and she rushes to the toilet. She throws up and is feeling lousy. A little drink of cold water takes away the luscious taste in her mouth. The water in Oslo tastes good. She crawls to bed. Stomach cramps are to her discomfort. She remembers that there is still a bottle of Coke in the fridge and fetches it. When the Coke alleviates the pain in the stomach she begins to wonder what Coke is made of. She reads from the label of the bottle: water, sugar, acid, E 150, E 338 ... What wishywashy stuff! The Coca-Cola trademark is designed like a wave of white and grey colour on a red background. The same trademark everywhere, all over the world. Now even in China and Tibet. No ethnic, local design, only different signs and letters. The world is going to pot! It is Good Friday, but it seems no good. The day feels as long as hell. Christ dies for our sins. That is supposedly for our good. Our sins. The church makes us feel small, and weak. With no self-esteem at all. Sinners, filled with guilt towards God and fellow men. Guilty in front of a punishing God. How can Solveig believe in this? She is preaching God's love and care for us in Jesus Christ, whatever may befall us in life. She means well. In time of hardships Solveig has shown in many practical ways that she cares. Really cares. Hilde wishes that Solveig would come and visit her just to-night. But Solveig is certainly tired after the service and she has to prepare for Easter Sunday. It is no use giving her a ring and asking her to come. It is no use to cherish the friendship, because at last we are all and everyone alone with death. Even Christ who was Son of God felt lonesome and lost on the cross. "Eli, Eli lema... My God, my God, why did you abandon me?" The day grows dusk and Hilde does not switch on the electric light. The Nordic dark night is just outside her window and she feels as if the darkness fills her soul, too. Through her brain runs an image of her own death. Again and again, like a nightmare that never ends. She sees herself walking to the garage and fetching a rope from the boot of her old car. She makes the rope into a noose by the stairs of the living room and puts the loop around her own neck. She screams in horror! The sound of her own horrified scream makes her realize that it is only a nightmare. She needs not die, she is maybe going mad, but she is still alive. Oh God! The pale face of her youngest son appears in her mind. His blue eyes are so sad, she feels like crying. No,it is not possible to die. But she feels that she cannot go on living with her depression. To be or not to be, that is the question. She does not manage to clear her mind. She does not manage to think. Nor feel. Nor sleep. Nor be awake. She bows her head. The grey fog of meaninglessness fills her soul. It is a long Friday. Of no good. And again, it was night.

Saturday

Hilde is crawling out of bed. In the bathroom, she forces herself to take a shower. While dressing, she realizes that it is of vital importance to keep herself spic and span while she is depressed, as she usually does when she is healthy and working. When she opens her dressing-closet she notices the scent of the mixture of myrrh and aloes. Her aunt in London had sent her a mini-jar to put in her dressing-closet for her birthday March 25th. It is not even a fortnight ago and she finds the unusual smell a bit unpleasant. Myrrh reminds her of Christmas and the wise men from the East bringing the child Jesus gold, frankincense and myrrh. But at Easter, did myrrh have any connection to Easter? -- she wonders while looking for a suitable jumper. She puts on a jumper with a warm, orange colour even though she feels inside grey and dull.

Strength from hell

The door bell rings. Solveig is standing on the doormat in a mist of tears. Hilde spontaneously gives her a warm hug and pulls her inside. "Solveig, what is the matter with you?" Solveig takes off her overcoat, which is wet from the morning showers, and pulls off her rubber boots. She had slipped and fallen on the miry road. Her knees are wet and dirty, with stains of blood. Her hands are full of grazes. Hilde helps her off with the jeans and fetches a tube of antiseptic ointment and plaster. While she nurses Solveig's wounds, she realizes that Solveig's sobbing is not primarily caused by her physical pain. She is sobbing her heart out. Hilde brushes gently the tears from Solveig's eyes and let her hand slide through Solveig's long, blond hair.

Solveig's father is seriously ill. He was put in hospital after a car accident yesterday. He is an old man of 76, but, was very healthy and bright, fit and full of plans and hope for the future. He was immediately operated and is now still asleep, under an anaesthetic. Whether he will wake up or not is very uncertain. "Last Friday when I talked to him, we disagreed and I was quite irritated by him," Solveig sobs. "Still you love your father!" Hilde replies, "it is normal to get irritated, Solveig. A pastor is also a human. You need not be afraid of your negative feelings. We have them, all of us. Your father, too! Angels are in Heaven, on earth are hardly any." Hilde notices that she who is so depressed is actually comforting Solveig. The sacrifices of God are a broken spirit: a broken and contrite heart. Hilde is giving her friend comfort. It feels good to do so. Their rôles are turned around. Christ is dead and in the grave this Saturday, but the love and care for a friend is very much alive. Yesterday, I was descending into hell, like Christ, when the image of the rope tortured my mind. What strength did Christ get in hell? Today I am out of bed, showered and dressed, comforting Solveig. How is it possible? What kind of strength did I acquire when I was at zero and below ? Love is stronger than anything else on earth. Even stronger than death.

When they are sitting together at the kitchen table with a cup of tea, Solveig notices how Hilde's orange jumper blends well with her red hair. The walls of her kitchen are blue, the curtains white with yellow flowers. The room is full of colours, of warmth, of friendship. Still, outside the kitchen window the sky is cloudy. The pine trees nearby have silverthaw.

The Nordic winter is lingering on; and it is getting cold and dark. Again, it was night.

The rays of the Easter sun

Early on Sunday morning, while it still was dark, Hilde went out. She wanted to see the sunrise.

She had memories of how she had been skiing in the mountains in Telemark, Easter two years ago, together with a few Christian friends. They had all wanted to see the Easter sun rising from the very highest mountain top in the area, Gaustadtoppen (1883 meters above sea level). They got up while it was dark, and they had been climbing upwards and upwards one after the other on an icy ski-track. The wind was rather rough. She had rubbed her face with sunscreen-creme when she got up. Still she felt how her skin prickled from the severe wind. In the skitrack she had to pull hood of her anorak up over her ski-cap. The hood was lined with wolf fur and she tightened the draw-strings of the hood around her face. She could hardly catch a glimpse of the skiier in front of her. She was dead tired when she reached the top, and one of the guys had carried her back-pack the last kilometers when the climbing became really steep. What a panorama they gazed at from the top! What a wonderous sunrise. The wind was still strong, but the sky was clear and they could see mountain chains on the horizon. White snowcapped mountains, white, with eternal snow. They had sung together "Thine is the glory, Risen, conquering Son; Endless is the victory Thou o'er death has won." She had a unique feeling of oneness with the surrounding nature. The white snow, the orange and red rays of the Easter sun breaking forth in the very far East, the blue sky, a pale moon and a few morning stars, - the scenery was really beyond description. The mountain peaks on the horizon seemed not that far, it was as if she could touched them in her open mindedness. As if she was breathing in a cosmic unity. The air was crisp and she felt as if she were breathing Christ's endless victory over death into her own lungs while she was singing. "...Lovingly he greets thee, scatters fear and gloom" she was singing. Tears came to her eyes. Her soul became filled, filled with something indispensable, something quite inconprehensible. A peak-experience. It was a distinct sensation, not only a vague feeling. She could recall it later, when she was relaxed and at ease.

She tried to recall it now when she was walking down the street towards the park. It was not that easy. She felt she needed to be in nature to find herself in the right mood. A pigeon flew over her head. It held a leaf in its beak. A leaf, from where Hilde wondered, looking around at the bare trees and bushes in the park. Maybe from a balcony with evergreen bushes nearby. A pigeon with a leaf, a sign of hope. The sky was beginning to become orange in the horizon. She hurried into the park and went up the hilltop overlooking the city. The rays from the Easter sun spread the smog over the city. The distinct sensation rose in her heart. Christ is risen. Easter has come.

Easter Monday, Christ's springtime

"When the Easter holiday has come to an end and we return to our every-day lives, Jesus Christ is still risen and wants to walk by our side," Solveig proclaims from the pulpit,"for the love of God is stronger than death." Her voice shivers slightly. She is preaching to herself. She is in need of courage now when her father is so sick.

After the service, Solveig hurries to Hilde's flat.

Her father woke up on Easter morning. She was sitting by his bedside praying and suddenly his blue eyes opened for a few minutes and his pale, dry lips curved into a smile when he saw his daughter. "Father forgive me," she sobbed. "Hush, Hush, do not cry, my Solveig, I forgive you," he whispered. He was weak. "My time has come," he said, "greet Mum and say good-bye from me. May you always stick together and ..." He had no more strength, and closed his eyes. He slept further. Solveig had phoned Mother and wept when she was referring to his words.

Solveig felt exhausted, but relieved. Now she needs to assure herself that Hilde is alright. At the same time she feels that she herself needs the comfort and understanding that Hilde had offered her on Saturday. It was as the golden-red color of Hilde's hair and the orange of her jumper that had put her in the mood of Easter morning. The stained glass window with the Risen Christ in the apse of her church has just that golden, shiny, almost orange colour. As if the Risen Christ's gown emanates hope and victory. She had seen the very same colour in the illuminations in "Scivias" by Hildegard of Bingen. A golden, warm orange, the contrast of sky-blue. As in the illuminations "The choirs of angels", "The Redeemer" and "The trinity in the unity". Orange and blue, a combination so strong that she feels as if it infuses her with life-energy.

She has put the German edition of "Scivias" in her bag. The German edition has the most beautiful colour illuminations. She wants to show Hilde the pictures.

Hilde is dressed in her orange jumper when she opens for Solveig: "Happy Easter!" They hug. They smile at each other.

The flow of friendship and care circulates between them.

Eva Vörös

"And She Laughs at the Time to Come..." (Proverbs 31:25)

Survival in the Time of Manna-Withdrawal.

My own spiritual context - my own spiritual image

I remember the day, the deepest time of my depression, when I could not do anything but cry, and the reading in the Bible was about the praise of heroic and worthy women (Proverbs 31:1). In my life, I have never felt that God's command could be so difficult: to laugh at the time to come. I had good reason to fear:

In a time of existential crisis: I am unemployed and I cannot find a job, because I was told that, first of all I am a feminist, and only secondly a Christian. I blamed myself for leaving my secure job. I used to be a director of a home for the elderly run by the Church. That provided a kind of concrete existence for me. I also lived there for more than six years. For me, this job was not an intellectual challenge because I had the feeling that I was hiding my talent in the ground. I realized also that I became dependent on my workplace. I had this strange feeling that if I was not there, the staff would not be able to manage without me. If someone among the residents was close to dying, I was not able to sleep any more, and I waited to be told. I had all the characteristics of being burnt out. So I left that job, not knowing what kind of wilderness and uncertainty I was going to face.

In a time of financial crisis: Since 1989 the country has had a 30% inflation rate, and because of the high national debt we have lost hope for a better future. The common joke on New Year's Eve was that 1996 would be a good year, anyway, better than 1997.

Living alone in a town in Eastern Hungary, having bought a nice little two room apartment, I could not enjoy it because I had borrowed money to buy it, and how could I pay it back when I cannot even earn my living expenses?

In a time of mid-life crisis: I am over forty. Will I ever get married, and what about not having children? Whose fault is it? Is this my mother's fault because of her frustrated marriage? The more you study psychology the more angry you become with your mother! But who wrote the psychology books which are taught? Do I have hope for any change? When I was working in the home for the elderly I felt like I was running a household of 50 people, and at that time I was longing for the privacy and solitude of an uninhabited island. When I moved out of the institute I did not even have a telephone. If you lose your job you tend to lose your daily relationships as well. I felt like someone who was going through withdrawal from being a human being.

In a time of a spiritual crisis: I felt that God was punishing me for running away: that is why I could not find any other job. I blamed myself also for not taking care of myself and allowing myself to be burnt out. My faith was not working. I could not believe in God, the father anymore, but I could not contact anybody else in Heaven either. Also, people blamed me by telling me that I should give up feminist theology because I would lose all my faith.

Was this not like the manna-withdrawal that comes before eating of the fruit of the promised land? (Jos 5:12) Will I ever find it? Does it exist at all? Is not my life experience a kind of paradigm of the whole Eastern European region concerning manna-withdrawal in terms of economy, social-politics, and spirituality? You really need to be a fool to be able to hope against hopelessness, to be able to laugh at the time to come! On the other hand, to find reason to laugh means survival (by knowing that Hungarians are the most pessimistic people on the face of the earth.)

Thoughts on meditation and prayer

The walk to Emmaus (Luke 24) is more a kind of end product of a long conversation, of sharing and staying together. No matter how many years Jesus spent with the disciples (the life he was to sacrifice for them), they still did not have any idea who he was. He allowed them to take quite a journey until they recognized him. What patience!

Why do I expect that open eyes are something to start with? Why do I want to know, to recognize things immediately? To understand involves taking a long spiritual road. Open eyes are the result of long conversations, of sharing and staying together, or maybe allowing others to tell my story from quite a different perspective. Am I ready to listen, not to interrupt, not to correct them? The divine patience is eye-opening!

Meditation means working through false images, story telling, articulating expectations and hopes for the stranger who seems to be so ignorant.

Thoughts on spirituality

Women's spirituality in Eastern Europe: I went to a wedding in the Ukraine in the Subcarpathian region where my relatives, ethnic Hungarians, live. I have never experienced anything like that in my life: to see an organic community at work! The love that surrounded me, the care of the people for each other, the beauty of their entertainment in spite of the fact that the music hall did not have any heat on a cold February weekend. My biggest surprise was the way women and men acted! Everything I have read about in western feminist theology about women's integrity, I saw at work there! Since then I have been confused, not knowing what is ahead anymore and what is behind. As far as their standard of living is concerned they live 100 years behind, but the women there certainly had a lot to offer to the spirituality of western women! Perhaps not the learning, but the re-learning is what needs to be done!

The impact of our religion on the suffering and healing of women all over the world

As far as the manna-issue is concerned, there are two difficulties to deal with:

To accept a way of living where your basic needs are dependent on God's providence. To learn to trust in daily provided manna.

Not to be addicted to manna, but to be able to recognize when the time comes for sowing.

I remember the women who were chased out to the wilderness, instead of being led into it. They died hungry, without experiencing the manna-providing God.

I remember those who spend their lives in slavery and never dare to move out of it.

I remember the women who are addicted to 'heaven' - Church, men, professionalism etc. - for providing spiritual food for them. They don't recognize when the time comes for them to take responsibility themselves and work for their spiritual meal. They never grow up. They are attached to a dependency which is the main obstacle to their liberation.

I am mourning because for me this never-prepared spiritual food means the unwritten Eastern European women's theology!

Images of loving, courageous, powerful women

Powerful woman to me has a name: Zsófia Juhász. She lived out her theology, which was called diakonia-theology. Men misused the

Biblical idea of service for compromising the communist State. The only way for the Church to survive in a hostile regime was - they thought -to serve, however unjust the circumstances were. That is why the Church runs various diakonia homes, mainly for the elderly and for mentally handicapped people. These are places where one cannot be done any ideological harm.

Zsófia accepted the margins as a place to be called, and started a country-wide spiritual movement. She challenged the pietistic, dualistic theology with her holistic approach: like abolishing the division between manual and spiritual work, care for the body and the soul, holy and profane, sick and healthy, teacher and learner. She used to say after giving bath alone to twenty handicapped children on Saturday - having no other staff available - I am sure, this kind of preparation for my Sunday sermon is just as highly appreciated by the angels, then to study commentaries. She went to preach with mentally handicapped children and let them contribute to her sermon. In a theology of corruption she created a unique contextual theology, which died with her death.

Wisdom

Wisdom means richness - royal privilege. The Queen of Sheba (I Kings 10) was interested in wealth, not just in materialistic but also in spiritual wealth, and she was willing to take the risk to experience it. She was a receiver, but also a giver of it.

Strength

Women's power was very much abused in the socialist ideology, when they were forced to drive tractors on the fields and work hard. To liberate women's strength may mean to allow for the desire to be weak, to be looked after, to be cared for: to find our own strength, which is different from men.

What came to my mind that last day - Easter 1996

Resurrection means a Bibliodrama, when we play the Lazarus story. I am the fool of the village, a child who is free even from the Bible and has the privilege of the unwritten text. At the end of the performance before the curtain is dropped, the little fool runs to Jesus asking him to do the same with him when the time comes. Resurrection is the trust: I know Someone who can do it, and can repeat it even with me when I need.

Letter from Nagykereki, Hungary, Christmas 1996

Dear Friends,

It is now after Christmas as I start to write and I thank you for your Christmas greetings. My life has changed. In September I moved to a small village at the Rumanian border and became the minister there. It is 50 km from Debrecen - the real wild East of Hungary!

After the collapse of the socialist politics of culture, there is hardly any social life in the villages: no movies; the previous 'house of culture' is closed, it is only open for the sale of second hand clothes. There are no shops, only one food store. The only public places are the pub and the church. The museum used to be the mansion of the Transylvanian landlord Bocskay from the 16th century. It was very richly furnished, but nowadays it is empty, and the public library is about to close. Fortunately, the railway is still at work: this is the end station - you feel like you are arriving at the end of the world.

At the beginning of this century Nagykereki was a very flourishing part of the country. The Church here has its origin in the 15th century, and the golden cups I am using for the Lord's Supper are from the 17th century. Due to the cruelty of history, this culture was not able to survive because the village became the site of the country's border in 1920. From the cemetery you can see the other villages of the county, one of them is Bihar that belongs to Rumania. Some ethnic Hungarian families moved to Nagykereki from Rumania; but mainly Roma people have been coming.

Many elderly families live here. Hopelessness, unemployment, crime, apathy, and alcoholism are the main features of the community of 1,200 people. History and the newly introduced capitalist system sentenced to death this community, but I believe God had another plan.

I was brought up in the capital and never thought that at one time I would be happy in such a very isolated small place. But after a long journey through the wilderness of unemployment, sickness, loneliness, financial needs, silence and emptiness, I learned to believe that the margins are very important places in God's eyes. Jesus was not born in the capital, but in Bethlehem. I experienced many miracles here: one of them is that I am able to communicate God's love in an effective way here. The small congregation is growing. Young people appear from nowhere, and little children have learned to greet me, shouting in the streets: "Blessing and peace, woman minister!" 'Blessing' which became an unknown word in our world today amongst so much cursing and frustration.

Liberation theology gives me a lot of strength. I can see all the themes at work in my ministry: like overcoming the dualism and the division between intellectual and peasant, man and woman, nature and society, young and old, rich and poor, blood relationship and soul relatedness, Roma and Hungarian. I cannot communicate theology at an intellectual level, so I try to preach in another way. It is a big challenge and also a very interesting experience for me: to feel what has to be said. It is not hard work, not dead-serious, more like an enjoyment, a lot of wonder, gratefulness, and power.

Once a week I go to Debrecen and work on some post-graduate studies at the university. It is good to have contact with my previous world, and it is also very useful. I study psychology, sociology, social politics, and I learn psychodrama. It always gives me a new vision of how to help and how to see all the problems of my village. I am just not sure how I can pass my seven exams in February. . .

Actually, I was hoping to have a silent life in my new place. But right now, I am facing one of the biggest challenges of our new history. The law enables the churches to reclaim their confiscated property which was taken away by the Communist regime.

The elementary school was build by the Church. Because of the nationalization of the last decades, parents who wanted a religious education for their children suffered a lot of humiliation, lived in fear, and soul terror under the Communists. Those people who controlled the believers and terrorized so many of us who, in spite of the threat, dared to go to Church and wanted the confirmation for their children - are still among us.

It seems that God is using these Communists, because nowadays they are the ones who think that the Church could run the schools better than they. Still, the decision about taking the school back to the Church has not been made yet.

Actually, I am the most educated person living in the village, one who speaks a bit of languages. I feel responsible for the whole community. On the other hand, the elders of my congregation are mainly elderly people, quite divided and without any vision for the future. For them, the most important thing is to have a minister who can bury people nicely. The most attended sermons are always the funerals ones. I can reach the villagers only through these open air sermons, next to the open graves - what a symbol!

The school is a cross-cultural institute because of the many Roma children. It is not a place to educate the elite, but it is a place for those who are struggling to survive. If not the minister, who can believe that God loves and hopes even for them? Struggling with these issues this advent, I went through all the spiritual pains of Mary after receiving the unusual proposition, feeling like being asked "to do something that seemed impossible", beyond my capabilities, something that would "alienate others. . .".[1]

When I was younger, I really wanted to be a missionary. I just never thought I would be one in my own country. Though I believe missionaries were always interested in schools and also in hospitals. . .

I would like to find sister and brother Churches across the border. Why not make a center out of the end of the world? These people who are about to leave this place and long to be somewhere else are badly in need of encouragement. They need to know that God moves this place and cares for them!

. . . It is a hard winter, minus 20 degrees Celsius, and the trains cannot run because of the freeze, so we are a bit cut off from the world. . . I end here because it is late on Saturday, and I need to prepare my sermon for tomorrow. So, all my love to you and God's blessings.

Eva

Notes

[1] Jan L. Dickardson, Sacred Journeys: A Woman's Book of Daily Prayer. Upper Room Books: Nashville, 1995.

Authors

Annette Esser, M.Ed., S.T.M., was born in 1957 in Cologne, Germany. Studies in Catholic theology, art and geography at Cologne and Münster Universities (1976-1985), and at Union Theological Seminary, New York (1994-1995); tutor at the Catholic-Ecumenical Institute of Münster University (1983-1987); training in art therapy, Bibliodrama and psychodrama from 1986; training and work as a secondary school teacher and lecturer (1987-1996). Translation and publication-work; co-editing the first volume of the ESWTR-Yearbook (Annette Esser / Luise Schottroff, *Feminist Theology in a European Context. Yearbook of the European Society of Women in Theological Research*. Mainz: Grünewald / Kampen: KOK Pharos, 1993), and German contact person and board member of the ESWTR. In 1996 she began the PhD.-program in "Psychiatry and Religion" at Union Theological Seminary, New York.

Maaike de Haardt, Ph.D., was born in 1954 in Nijmegen, Netherlands. Studies in vocational counseling and systematic theology (PhD.) She lectures in Women Studies in Theology at the Tilburg Faculty of Theology and is co-director of the national research program in women studies in theology, 'Corporeality, Religion and Gender', at the University of Groningen. She has published '*Dichter bij de dood. Feministisch-theologische aanzetten tot een theologie van de dood*' and several articles on God, embodiment in theology and on feminist christology.

Anne Hunt Overzee, M.A. (Cantab) Ph.D., was born in 1952 in England. She read Theology and Religious Studies (a joint degree) at Girton College, Cambridge (1972-1975); researched "The Mandala. . . as a Religious Symbol" and Indian Christology at the United Theological College, Bangalore (1975-1977); and her doctoral research (Lancaster University, 1980-1986) was published in 1992 as *The Body Divine: The Symbol of the Body in the Works of Teilhard de Chardin and Râmânuja* (Cambridge University Press). She has lectured in Buddhism (Lancaster University, 1988-1989) and in Indian Religion and Philosophy, and The Goddess in Hinduism (Edinburgh University, 1990). She has also been an Academic Tutor for the Open Learning B.Th. Course at Westminster College, Oxford (1993) and lectured in Religious Studies at S. Martin's College of Higher Education, Lancaster (1986-1987). She is currently working as a psychotherapist in Edinburgh and the Scottish Borders. She is a staff member and trainer for Karuna Institute, Devon, and is involved in the development of the Association of Accredited Psychospiritual Psychotherapists (AAPP), which is a member body of the United Kingdom Council for Psychotherapy.

Annie Imbens-Fransen was born in 1937 in Eindhoven, Netherlands. She is originally trained in secretarial skills and as a social worker. She gave birth to two sons and a daughter, organised and co-ordinated different environment and peace organisations as well as activities to reform liturgy in the Roman Catholic Church. She started studying theology in 1979 at the *Theologisch Catechetisch Instituut*, Tilburg, and Women's Studies in Theology at the Universities of Tilburg, Utrecht and Nijmegen, The Netherlands. In 1986, she established the *Foundation of Pastoral Care for Women* (*Stichting Vrouw en Pastoraat*) to provide pastoral care for psychologically, physically, and sexually abused women. She has counseled hundreds of women; publishes extensively, and gives lectures and courses different organisations and professionals. Since 1987, she has given presentations and workshops at women's symposia and World Health Organisation symposia in Europe, and she has participated in exchange programmes with China, South Africa and India. In 1996, she was Coolidge Fellow at the Coolidge Research Colloquium at Yale University. Since 1997, she participated in the *United Religions Initiative* (URI) to prepare the establishing of the organization *United Religions in the Year 2000*.

Eleni Kasselouri was born in 1968 in Thessaloniki, Greece. She studied Orthodox Theology at the Theological Faculty of Thessaloniki (1986-1990). She did post-graduate Biblical Studies in the Theological Faculty of Thessaloniki, as well as N.T. studies and ecumemical studies (Prof. Konrad Raiser) at the Faculty of Protestant Theology of the Ruhr-Universität Bochum, Germany (1990-1992). In 1993, she became a Ph.D. Canditate; her dissertation-theme is: *"The Anointing of Jesus (Matth. 26: 6-13par). A Feminist Approach"* . Since 1991, she is assistant at the Department of Biblical Studies of the Theological Faculty of Thessaloniki. She is member of the Society of Ecumenical Studies and Inter-Orthodox Relations, as well as a member of the European Society of Women in Theological Research. She is married and mother of a son.

Marianna Kiraly was born in 1967 in Debrecen, Hungary. She studied theology at Debrecen Theological Seminary and graduated there in 1992. She worked as a pastor in Tiszaszentimre and Tiszaderzs, Hungary for one year. She received a scholarship and attained her Master of Theology at the Princeton Theological Seminary, USA. in 1994. She served as a pastor of the First Hungarian Reformed Church of New York City and is since 1995 the pastor of the Hungarian Reformed Church of Passaic, New Jersey as well as a student in Christian education at Princeton Seminary.

Gabriella Lettini was born in 1968 in Turin, Italy. She is a graduate of the Waldensian Theological Seminary in Rome and an ordained minister of the Waldensian Church in Italy. She also studied at Union Theological Seminary in New York, U.S.A., where she is currently in the Ph.D. program in the field of Systematic Theology. She is the author of "Jesus on the Screen: The film world as a Setting for Theological Discussion" (to be published). She worked for Church World Service and Witness (CWSW) - National Council of the Churches in the USA as a researcher and writer on the Gospel and Culture Study Project of the WCC. Gabriella has been Assistant minister at the First Waldensian Church in New York City, and Interim Minister for the Waldensian Church in Vasto - S. Salvo, Italy. She is currently serving as the Ecumenical Associate at Jan Hus Presbyterian Church in New York City.

Caroline Mackenzie was born in Reading, UK in 1952, and is an artist. After graduating from St. Martin's School of Art in 1976, she traveled to India where she lived for twelve years. For six years, she studied with Jyoti Sahi, who is well-known both as an artist and theologian, at INSCAPE Art Ashram. From 1983-88, she lived in Melkote, a Hindu temple town. There, she studied Sanskrit and Indian Philosophy. Since 1988, she has lived in Wales. She has held numerous exhibitions of her work both in India and Europe, the most important being: *Sita as a Woman Artist*, British Council, Madras, 1987; *The Calming of the Storm*, Crypt Gallery, London, 1990; *Votre Foi Eveille La Mienne*, Cathedral St. Michael and St. Gudula, Brussels, 1996. She has also undertaken commissions for the Church both in India and Europe. The most important ones include: *Ananda Matha Ashram* (Cistercian Sisters), Kerala, S. India: designs for 19 windows, altar, tabernacle altar etc.; *St Anne's Catholic Church*, Newport, S. Wales: 3 stained glass windows.

Mercedes Navarro Puerto, Ph.D., was born in 1952 in Cadiz, Spain. She has a doctorate in psychology from the "Universidad Pontificia" (U.P.), Salamanca, and a theological doctorate from the "Pontificia Gregoriana", Rome, as well as a licentiate in Biblical studies by the "Pontificio Instituto Biblico", Rome. She is professor of Psychology of Religion in the U.P. Salamanca and teaches Old Testament in the theological faculty of U.P. and in the "Centro de estudios claretianos", Madrid. She also teaches ethics and gender in the "Instituto Superior de Ciencias Morales", Madrid. She is a founding member of the "Asociation de Teólogas Españolas (ATE), and a member of the International Association of Physicians and Psychologists of Religions (AIEMPR). Amongst her publications are *Psicología y Mística. Las Moradas de Santa Teresa*, ed. S.Pio X, Madrid 1992; *Barro y aliento. Exégesis* *narrativa y anthropología de Gn 2-3*, ed. San Pablo, Madrid 1993; (ed.) *10 Mujeres escriben teología*, EVD, Estella (Navarra) 1993; *I libri di Giosue Giudici e Rut*, Città Nuova editrice, Roma 1994 (Barcelona 1995), (ed.) *Para comprender el Cuerpo de la mujer*, EVD, Estella (Navarra) 1996.

Susan Roll, Ph.D. was born in Clarence Center, New York State, in 1952. She completed her doctoral studies in the Faculty of Theology, Catholic University of Louvain (Leuven, Belgium), where she also taught liturgy and pastoral theology. She is presently assistant professor of liturgy and systematic theology at Christ the King Seminary, Buffalo, New York, U.S.A. She is the author of *Toward the Origins of Christmas*, Kampen, 1995.

Ursula Rudnick, Ph.D., was born in 1963 in Hannover, Germany. She studied Protestant theology in Göttingen, Tübingen, and Berlin, and Judaism in Jerusalem and at the Jewish Theological Seminary in New York, where she received her PhD for her research on the image of God in the Lyrics of Nelly Sachs. She was working for the *Frauenwerk* of the *Evangelisch-Lutherische Landeskirche Hannover* and is now teaching at Hannover University.

Lene Sjørup, born in Denmark in 1946. She holds a Ph.D. in theology from the University of Copenhagen. Her dissertation *"Oneness. A Theology of Women's Religious Experiences"* is based upon qualitative interviews with women from the US, Denmark and England on women's religious experiences in the North. It shows a strong tendency toward mysticism. She was a Fullbright scholar at the GTU Berkeley, 1980/81. After this she taught feminist theology and held a research fellowship at the University of Copenhagen. Her book *Du er Gudinden* (You are the Goddess) was published in 1983. In 1987 she was ordained as a Lutheran pastor. In 1992 her book *Enhed med Altet* (Oneness) which is now forthcoming in English (Kok Pharos, 1997), was published in Danish. In 1990 she obtained a research grant which permitted her to do research in Chile. Since 1991 she has been a research fellow at the Centre for Development Research in Copenhagen. She just finished the manuscript of a new book on the nationalist theology of Pinochet and the theological repertoires of resistance of women living in poverty in the shanty towns of Santiago de Chile. Lene Sjørup is the Vice President of the European Society of Women in Theological Research.

Lise Tostrup Setek was born in 1949 in Oslo, Norway. She is a Church of Norway Chaplain in the Diocese of Oslo. She holds a BA Degree from the University of Melbourne, Australia (1974), and was a Candidate in Theology at the Fee Faculty of Theology in Oslo from 1975. She had a scholarship in 1976 and completed her practical theological training in 1977. She was ordained to the ministry on "The International Day of Women's Rights", March 8th, 1978. She was awarded "The Olavstipend" in 1993 to study the theologies of Hildegard of Bingen and Julian of Norwich in comparison with the spirituality of modern women in Norway. She has contributed articles to anthologies and journals, and was co-editor of a book in Norwegian which concerns theological issues when counseling battered women in 1984. She gives courses in women's spirituality.

Eva Vörös was born in 1955 in Budapest, Hungary. In 1980, after finishing 5 years of theological study, she was among the first women to be ordained in the Reformed Church of Hungary. In 1984, she studied in Great Britain. In 1985, at the first ESWTR-Conference in Boldern, Switzerland, she was introduced to feminist theology and since the has been instrumental in introducing it in Hungary. In order to find an alternative model for ministry, she worked as a chaplain in a home for elderly people. In 1989 she was made Director of the Retired Women's home in Debrecen. In 1992, she studied in Chicago and took classes with Rosemary Ruether. Since 1996 she has been a pastor in Nagykereki, Hungary.

Ulrike Wiethaus, Ph.D., was born in 1957 in Unna, Germany. She studied Theology at the 'Kirchliche Hochschule', Berlin (Colloquium) and Religious Studies, at Temple University, Philadelphia, USA (Ph.D.) She taught in Minnesota and Michigan. Currently she is Associate Professor of Humanities at Wake Forest University, Winston-Salem, North Carolina. Her main interests are in medieval mysticism, women and spirituality, and feminist studies. She is editor of *Maps of Flesh and Light: The Religious Experiences of Medieval Women* (Syracuse University Press 1993); coeditor of *Dear Sister. Medieval Women and the Epistolary Genre* (V of Penn Press, 1993); and author of *Ecstatic Transformation. Transpersonal Psychology in the Work of Mechthild of Magdeburg* (Syracuse 1996).